ROT

ALSO BY PADRAIC X. SCANLAN

Slave Empire: How Slavery Built Modern Britain

*Freedom's Debtors: British Antislavery in
Sierra Leone in the Age of Revolution*

ROT

A HISTORY
OF THE IRISH
FAMINE

PADRAIC X.
SCANLAN

ROBINSON

ROBINSON

First published in the US in 2025 by Basic Books,
an imprint of Hachette Book Group

First published in Great Britain in 2025 by Robinson

1 3 5 7 9 10 8 6 4 2

Copyright © Padraic X. Scanlan, 2025

The moral right of the author has been asserted.

Excerpt from 'Bogland' from *Door into the Dark* by Seamus
Heaney. Reprinted by permission of Faber and Faber Ltd.

Print book interior design by Amy Quinn

A CIP catalogue record for this book
is available from the British Library.

ISBN: 978-1-47214-687-8 (hardback)
ISBN: 978-1-47214-688-5 (trade paperback)

Printed and bound in Great Britain by Clays Ltd, Elcograf S.p.A.

Papers used by Robinson are from well-managed forests and other responsible sources.

Robinson
An imprint of
Little, Brown Book Group
Carmelite House
50 Victoria Embankment
London EC4Y 0DZ

The authorised representative
in the EEA is
Hachette Ireland
8 Castlecourt Centre, Dublin 15,
D15 XTP3, Ireland
(email: info@hbgi.ie)

An Hachette UK Company
www.hachette.co.uk

www.littlebrown.co.uk

For Rafe and Moira Jane

CONTENTS

Butter sunk under
More than a hundred years
Was recovered salty and white.
. . . .
They'll never dig coal here,
Only the waterlogged trunks
Of great firs, soft as pulp.
Our pioneers keep striking
Inwards and downwards,
Every layer they strip
Seems camped on before.
The bogholes might be Atlantic seepage.
The wet centre is bottomless.

         —Seamus Heaney, "Bogland," 1969

The tempest rag'd with ceaseless din—
A wilder tempest rag'd within
The bosom of that wretched man;
(Upon whose visage pale and wan,
The hues of death were quickly stealing,
The fever, famine's work, revealing;—)
For he had done a fearful thing,
In presence of the famishing.

         —C. A. Rawlins, "The Famine in Ireland:
           A Poem," 1847

Introduction

IRISH QUESTIONS

RICHARD WEBB WAS RECTOR OF CAHERAGH, A VILLAGE IN County Cork. In February 1847 he asked two men he trusted to visit the homes of the poorest families in his parish. It was the second year of famine in Ireland. The potato crop had failed in 1845, and again in 1846. Authorities in Dublin and London, however, believed that the Irish rural poor might be feigning destitution. As Webb's men made their rounds, farmers told them to avoid a knot of houses at the edge of a certain field. They were typical Irish cottages: drafty and damp, without windows or chimneys, little more than dirt-floor rooms with slimy stone walls and thatched roofs. Those houses are cursed, the farmers warned.

The men Webb had sent heeded the warning. There was enough misery in the village and the surrounding countryside to prove that the Irish poor were not dissembling, that many were starving to death. But Webb was curious. He prevailed on another member of his congregation to go back to the "cursed" cottages and make a report. In a cabbage garden near the cottages, the man

1

found the corpses of a woman named Kate Barry and two of her children half buried in loose soil. Dogs had dug up Barry's head and legs, ripped the flesh off the skull, and gnawed and cracked the long bones. Barry's scalp, with her hair attached, was close by. The man at first mistook it for a horse's tail. In the two small cottages about thirty yards farther from the garden were four more bodies—those of two adults, Norry Regan and Tom Barry, and two children, Nelly Barry and Charles McCarthy. Their corpses had been decomposing for two weeks. Another man, Tim Donovan, had died a few days earlier. His wife and sister, ill with typhus, did not have the strength to move the body or the money to bury it. "I need make no comment on this," Webb wrote, "but ask, *are we living in a portion of the United Kingdom?*"[1]

IN 1844 OR 1845, *PHYTOPHTHORA INFESTANS* CROSSED THE Atlantic. A fungus-like water mould that attacks potato and tomato plants, the pathogen probably arrived in Europe in a shipment of seed potatoes unloaded in Belgium. The disease it causes, now often called late blight because it strikes late in the growing season, spread quickly and virulently. From Sweden to northern Spain the mould killed potatoes in the ground and turned potatoes in storage to stinking pulp. Death rates rose across the continent. And yet nowhere in Europe—or the world—did the poor depend as completely on potatoes as in Ireland. Millions of Irish labourers ate little else. In 1801, after centuries under English control, Ireland had become a partner with Great Britain in a new country, the United Kingdom. By 1845, nearly one-third of the population of the UK lived in Ireland. Union, however, did not reduce Irish dependence on potatoes.

The potato blight caused crisis everywhere it appeared in Europe; in Ireland, it caused an apocalypse. Between 1845 and

1851, at least 1 million people died of famine-related causes. At least 1.5 million more left Ireland as emigrants to Britain, North America, Australia, and elsewhere. The 1841 UK census counted about 8.2 million people in Ireland; ten years later, as the famine was coming to an end, there were about 6.5 million. Ireland's population would continue to decline for nearly a hundred years.

The blight eventually appeared in all of Ireland's provinces—Connaught in the northwest, Munster in the southwest, Leinster in the southeast, and Ulster in the northeast—and all its thirty-two counties (further divided into smaller baronies and parishes). Deaths related to famine happened everywhere but were most concentrated in western Connaught, Munster, and the southernmost parts of Ulster. Although the labouring poor ate potatoes throughout northern and western Europe, only Ireland experienced demographic collapse during and after the blight pandemic. In 1845–1846, for example, excess mortality (that is, a rate of death greater than the expected statistical average) in the Netherlands was roughly 2 percent of population, and in Belgium 1.1 percent. And yet in these two countries, which after Ireland were likely the most vulnerable to potato failure, overall population increased by about 200,000 between 1846 and 1856 in Belgium, and by about 130,000 in the Netherlands between 1845 and 1851.[2]

The consequences of the potato famine were reckoned in more than death and emigration. Years of starvation and disease dissolved bonds of community and family in the hardest-hit parts of Ireland. As two scholars of international law who focus on the use of starvation as a weapon of war explain, with clinical restraint, "the process of destitution degrades not only physical assets but also social bonds." When a person starves, their body consumes its own muscle and fat, digesting itself to supply energy to vital organs. Parts of a person's being that seemed permanent and sacrosanct give way to animal need. Starving people can oscillate between apathy and enervation. They can become willing to do things to survive that would be unimaginable and shameful with a full belly.[3]

This book answers Richard Webb's plaintive question: Did the Irish poor "live in a portion of the United Kingdom"? By the time the blight pandemic spread to Irish fields, Ireland had been politically, legally, and economically integrated into the United Kingdom for decades. Before the Union, Ireland had been a subordinate sister kingdom to Britain, with its own parliament. Ireland was never a British colony, but "colonialism" is not exclusive to formal colonies. Before and after the Union, and before and after the Great Famine, Ireland was imagined, governed, and exploited in strikingly colonial ways. The blight was a consequence of a novel pathogen spreading among fields of vulnerable plants. But the *famine*—a complex ecological, economic, logistical, and political disaster—was a consequence of colonialism.

The potato embodied the ambiguities of Ireland's place in the United Kingdom. Some Victorian Britons speculated that the Irish had an irrational racial affinity with the potato, but the hyperdependence of so many of the Irish poor on the crop was an adaptation to English and British conquest, and to the subsequent growth of the British Empire and imperial capitalism. In the seventeenth century—during the wars of religion that followed the Protestant Reformation and redrew the map of Europe—Ireland, already long under English dominion, was definitively and brutally conquered. English forces seized almost all Irish land remaining in Catholic hands and redistributed it to Protestant loyalists. The English Parliament passed the Penal Laws, which legalised the persecution and dispossession of Catholics and strictly limited Ireland's political and economic independence.

As the conquest of Ireland proceeded, the potato arrived in Europe among the spoils of the Iberian conquest of Central and South America. Brought to Spain by returning conquistadores, the potato may have been introduced to Ireland by Basque ships stopping for water and provisions before crossing the Atlantic to the cod fisheries off Newfoundland. Potatoes were a welcome backstop against pillaging armies and crop failure, especially of oats and other staple grains. Potatoes cannot be siloed and are difficult to store, but they are nutritious, hardy, adaptable, and can produce generous and reliable yields, even in indifferent soil. Potato cultivation spread quickly and widely in Ireland and across western Europe.[4]

From the eighteenth century through the early years of the Union, the pressure exerted on the Irish economy by the growth of the British Empire shifted the potato from a fail-safe to a staple. Potatoes could feed more workers on less land, allowing landlords to raise more livestock and grain for export, primarily to colonial markets. When grain was valuable, landlords called for tillage. When speculators were bullish on beef or wool, fields of wheat and oats were flattened to graze cattle and sheep. The shifting market created unstable and insecure employment for many Irish labourers, but potatoes were usually abundant enough for subsistence. Potatoes allowed landlords to hire cheap and plentiful labour to work larger, export-oriented farms while also collecting rent from subdivided and subleased farms and potato grounds. Ironically, although the potato abetted these new forms of exploitation, it also became a symbol for many British commentators of an intractable, essential, and ancient Irish poverty. Irish potato-eaters were condemned, as though they had planted the crop purposely to indulge in unwholesome superstitions, whiskey, and blarney.[5]

At the end of the eighteenth century, revolutions in North America and France rearranged Ireland's constitutional relationship to Britain once again. In 1783 the Irish Parliament was restored to a limited independence, in part out of fear of an Irish rebellion in the image of the American Revolution. In 1798, while Britain was at war with revolutionary France, a group known as the United Irishmen, inspired by France and led by Protestant intellectuals, rose in rebellion against the Crown. In 1801, the United Kingdom was created, in part to cut off the possibility of a French invasion of Britain from Ireland. Enthusiasts argued that in addition to security, the Union would give Ireland a greater share in British prosperity. British capital would flow to Ireland; Irish grain, dairy, and meat would flow to Britain. The new United Kingdom was a single market, with a single currency. There were no internal borders, tariffs, or obstacles to trade. From 1829, the last of the Penal Laws were repealed and Irish Catholics were restored to most civil rights. But the Union faltered. The joke that Ireland and Britain had not consummated their marriage was cliché on both sides of the Irish Sea.

The growth of the British Empire and the uneven economy of the United Kingdom increased pressure on Irish land but afforded opportunities for Irish labourers willing to leave Ireland. In the seventeenth century, anti-Catholicism had been a dominant ideology in the English Parliament and in England's colonies. But a growing empire needed workers, and many Britons were able to overcome their scruples. Irish Protestant elites became senior figures in UK and imperial politics; Arthur Wellesley, the Duke of Wellington—a war hero and two-time prime minister—is the most prominent example from the era before the Great Famine. As the Irish political and professional classes integrated into the Union, humbler Catholic and Presbyterian Irish soldiers, sailors, settlers, and merchants also served the empire. Irish and British identities intertwined. Irish labourers were subject to British colonialism in Ireland but could serve as its agents abroad.[6]

After the Union, the Irish upper classes grew closer to their peers in Britain, and Irish farms exported more meat, dairy, and grain. Year on year, the pressure on Irish land increased. Poverty is relative; the Irish poor, by the standards of European peasants in the nineteenth century, were not exceptionally deprived—economic historians have, for example, found that many Irish labourers were able to afford imported goods like tobacco. But the Irish poor were exceptionally vulnerable. The Irish economy, structured by colonialism, was precarious. Demand for Irish exports within the Union built a new façade over rotten boards. Moreover, even within the Union, Ireland remained partially militarised. Ireland was governed by both Parliament and the Crown (like the rest of the Union), but also by an appointed executive, the lord lieutenant, whose position carried over from the era of conquest. Ireland was regularly subject to Coercion Acts, laws that gave the lord lieutenant the power to declare Irish districts "disturbed," suspend civil liberties and due process, and impose martial law. In the cabinet, the chief secretary of Ireland also had expansive direct power over Irish affairs.[7]

THE POTATO WAS A MODERN CROP, NATIVE TO THE AMERICAS AND introduced to Ireland. Potato culture became a pillar of Irish life in the eighteenth century, when landlords found potatoes convenient for exploitation and Irish labourers found potatoes useful for survival as Britain consolidated its conquest. And yet, influential British commentators considered potatoes an ancient feature of Irish culture. And since cyclical potato failures were common in Ireland long before 1845, hunger also became "natural" in Ireland, a feature of an Irish landscape and rural economy that was portrayed as archaic, unchanging, and stubbornly resistant to modernity and reform. As one writer commented in 1812, "Everyone who knows Ireland, is convinced that years of scarcity in that country are very frequent." To colonial eyes, potato shortages threw into relief a primitive, monomaniacal appetite for potatoes among the Irish, as well as fecklessness and disregard for the future. Colonialism is not only material exploitation, or applicable only to distant colonies. In the British Empire, differences between coloniser and colonised became, for many Britons, evidence of British superiority—and a justification for conquest after the fact. A writer in a London periodical speculated, "If the people of England were for only one day to be reduced to the condition in which the population of Ireland have existed for centuries, every institution connected with the preservation of private property in this country would be annihilated within four-and-twenty hours." The comparisons were clear: Britain was energetic, Ireland was listless; Britain was combative, Ireland was apathetic; Britain was modern, Ireland was backward; Britain was industrious, Ireland was lazy. Britain was made to rule; Ireland was made to be ruled.[8]

The Union was supposed to both cut off a pathway to a French invasion of Great Britain and to bring prosperity to Ireland. When it didn't, Irish poverty became a chronic political problem for the United Kingdom. "Once at least in every generation," John Stuart Mill wrote, "the question, 'What is to be done with Ireland?' rises again." Between 1801 and 1845, Parliament convened many royal commissions and select committees, and sent many fact-finding missions to Ireland to answer this "Irish question." These parliamentary reports are an enormous archive, rich and full of surprises. They are an important primary source for this book, but many in the nineteenth century were frustrated that all the government seemed to be able to do to mitigate Irish poverty was strike a committee and publish its evidence. "The

Government seems to feel it *must* issue a Commission," one pamphleteer complained.[9]

Ireland's relationship to Britain—a restless partner in an unequal union; a frontier of empire, subject to military rule at the pleasure of Parliament; a poor and mostly agrarian hinterland of the world's industrial centre—preoccupied the UK government throughout the nineteenth century. The political economist and public servant Nassau William Senior wrote in 1843, "When Irish questions, or rather the *Irish Question* (for there is but one), has been forced on our attention, we have felt, like a dreamer in a nightmare, oppressed by the consciousness that some great evil was rapidly advancing." In 1844, Benjamin Disraeli complained in the House of Commons that the "Irish question" was quicksilver. One critic might say "it was a physical question; another, a spiritual. Now, it was the absence of the aristocracy; then the absence of railroads. It was the Pope one day; potatoes the next."[10]

THIS BOOK IS ALSO A HISTORY OF THESE *OTHER* IRISH QUESTIONS. Long before Irish potatoes rotted, many Britons were certain that something was rotten in Ireland. Although many Irish observers agreed, as the movement to repeal the Acts of Union gained ground in the years before the blight, some rejected British criticism on principle. *Punch* even satirised this contrarianism in a "report" from "Ballymuckandfilth," an encomium to obvious rural poverty (after noting the piles of human and animal waste near Irish cottages: "How very different are the dung-heaps in Ireland! They positively steam with sweetest odours"). Irish poverty was bleak and unsustainable, and all the more so within the context of the United Kingdom, the era's most sophisticated and powerful economy. What was incorrect was the usual British explanation of the cause of the rot. Successive governments, officials, and reformers concluded that Ireland was poor not because it was overexposed to the modern British market, but rather that Ireland was not yet modern *enough*. Many concluded that Ireland, and especially the Irish poor, seemed trapped in the past. To improve Ireland, the world of the Irish poor needed to be renovated and disinfected through the discipline and values of capitalism. Ireland, many Britons agreed, needed civilisation.[11]

In the rhetoric of British imperialism and colonialism, civilisation was a powerful but inchoate concept that was often a synonym for idealised British institutions and habits, especially in economic life. Civilised people earned wages and kept working even after they had earned enough for subsistence. They embraced markets. They were alert to the risks of unemployment and planned for the future. They bought things to meet their needs and wants, and then found new needs and wants to continue the cycle. As the commissioners who revised the English Poor Laws in the 1830s argued, paraphrasing Jeremy Bentham, poverty was "the state of one who, in order to obtain a mere subsistence, is forced to have recourse to labour." A civilised person did not need to be forced to work, and anyone in a civilised society who did not work steadily was likely an invalid or a deviant. To be civilised meant to live within the social order made by British capitalism, to survive its challenges, and to embrace its virtues.[12]

In the late eighteenth and early nineteenth centuries, the new discipline of economics—"political economy"—enjoyed exceptional prestige and even glamour in British political circles. The deep conviction of many British imperial officials in crude conceptions of human motivation in response to market forces seemed at the time to have a solid foundation. It is difficult from the present to fully grasp the subversive appeal of markets in the first half of the nineteenth century: free markets seemed modern and modernising, a clean break from absolute monarchy and feudalism. Through the eighteenth century, British power and wealth expanded dramatically as the British Empire came to dominate the northern Atlantic and to expand in Asia, Oceania, and the Indian subcontinent. During the same era, Enlightenment, a cosmopolitan flowering of scientific, ethnographic, and philosophical research, transformed how Europeans saw themselves and Europe's relationship to the rest of the world. Scientists discovered regular and predictable rules and systems in the physical world and the human body.[13]

By the 1840s, for many influential Britons, faith in the market had become so profound as to be nearly invisible—an atmosphere to breathe, not a belief to examine. This deep confidence reflected how "the purpose of political dominion" for the British Empire transformed during the eighteenth and early nineteenth centuries. Colonies that had been principally considered as sources of tribute became instead sources of raw materials for British factories and new markets for British goods. The beginning of the crisis in Ireland coincided with the decision, taken in late autumn 1845 by the prime minister, Robert Peel, to open a free trade in grain to the United Kingdom. Although some in Parliament were skeptical, many liberal officials and merchants were ecstatic—"the millennium had arrived," a critic scoffed.[14]

In this context, the idea that markets also had discoverable, inalterable rules that could be used to predict and refine the progress of society seemed self-evident. What if there were laws of economic life as fixed as the laws of gravity described by Sir Isaac Newton? Political economists posited that the market was as miraculously self-organising as the natural world. Political economy, an Irish nobleman wrote, was "the only safe guide." It was as certain, he believed, as "the Newtonian Philosophy," and rejected, like physics, only by "the profoundly ignorant." Early Victorian ideas of natural law and divine Providence added moral authority to these economic principles. The laws of physics seemed to prove the existence of a lawmaker. As Edmund Burke wrote, the God-fearing ought to recognise that God would not look kindly on "breaking the laws of commerce, which are the laws of nature, and, consequently the laws of God." If the free market had natural laws, markets were also a part of the divine clockwork. Britain's empire, in 1845, was a prosperous, dominant, and dominating empire of commerce and free labour, of colonies of settlement founded by independent emigrants and commercial colonies founded by swashbuckling entrepreneurs. Couldn't British power be explained, at least in part, by the empire's affinity with what seemed like natural laws?[15]

By the 1830s, theorists like Nassau William Senior (also a caustic critic of the Irish) were refining their definitions of poverty, emphasising work ethic as the primary determinant of prosperity. Poverty, they argued, was the condition of the unemployed, idle, and "indolent," a favourite pejorative. The true poor of the United Kingdom were the "paupers" who depended on either the government or charity for subsistence. The "working class," on the other hand, embraced risk, earned wages in the market, and prospered. The Irish seemed like natural paupers. "Belief and trust in luck," the reformer and folklorist Mary Leadbeater wrote, "never quits the Irish." The idea that the future was a matter of fortune rather than a product of effort, she maintained, eroded the Irish work ethic. The Irish were far from uniquely interested in luck—eighteenth-century Britons were mad for gambling on cards and horses, and Great Britain pioneered both the stock market and the state lottery. Reformers, however, saw the fatalism of many Irish tenants caught in the rent economy as evidence of a superstitious lack of civilisation, an obliviousness to the "real" power of markets to improve.[16]

Markets were idealised by political economists. The abstract market was rational, a place where buyers and sellers found equilibrium, in the form of a sale price, between desire and inventory. The abstract market was populated by autonomous and civilised individuals who responded in predictable ways to stimuli. Within this framework, governing a civilised society was a matter of creating the right incentives and stepping back to allow natural law to do its work. The abstract market left everyone happier. But markets were also real places, peopled and messy, shaped by deep asymmetries of power, wealth, and information and entangled in webs of debt and custom. The relative wealth and power of people entering the market always mattered, although by a formidable and deeply consequential sleight of hand, modern capitalism championed the illusion that markets were equal, as well as morally and economically uplifting.[17]

To political economists, the potato complicated the question of Ireland's relative civilisation—and of its poverty. Ireland seemed to be in a kind of civilisational twilight zone, between the noxious darkness of the precapitalist past and the disinfecting light of the industrial future. On the one hand, the potato made it possible for Ireland to produce exports and rent for the British market without much capital. On the other hand, the security potatoes afforded seemed to have made millions of Irish workers into paupers, unwilling to work steadily for wages. Ironically, some political economists argued that since the Irish might *never* be at risk of starvation while potatoes flourished, the crop would have to be uprooted to fully civilise Ireland. Potatoes seemed to insulate the Irish from the bracing risks of an open market.

Moreover, civilised people ate bread. Because it required sowing, reaping, threshing, grinding, and baking, and since many people did not grow their own wheat or bake their own loaves, bread demanded steady work and a complex division of labour. Bread, it followed to political economists, was civilised as well as civilising. Potatoes, however, came out of the ground virtually ready to eat.

Charles Trevelyan, a senior bureaucrat at the Treasury who over-saw famine-relief programs, wrote that the potato was "the deep and inveterate root of social evil." Irish workers needed to be moti-vated to work and save, and to give up the security of potatoes for the greater risks and rewards of an economy based only on wages. If each individual worker strived for their own betterment, the col-lective effort would reform all of Irish society.[18]

The potato became a symbol of Irish backwardness. This idea, that Ireland and its potato-eaters were trapped in the past and needed to be brought by the Union into the modern world, made it impossible for officials to see essential features of the Irish economy. Britons imagined Ireland as a place that existed outside of, or prior to, the world of imperial capitalism. The opposite was true. Within the Union, Ireland was poorer than Britain, and many blamed this inequality on Irish backwardness and the earthy insulation of the potato diet. The idea that the market was *always* the best mechanism for addressing social problems made it impossible to imagine a solution to Irish poverty that was any-thing other than more of the same: a series of gestures to support and honour the "savage god" of the British Empire, "the Invisible Hand."[19]

In reality, the Irish poor needed relief *from* the market, not relief *through* the market. The structures of land ownership and labour built in the seventeenth and eighteenth centuries, and an export economy and system of rent collection accelerated by the Union, weighed heavily on the Irish countryside. In Ireland, as in the rest of the United Kingdom, the population grew quickly in the early nineteenth century. The rental market for potato land became even more competitive. Even the poorest farmer made complex calculations on how to pay rent, whether in labour, potatoes, or cash, depending on the price of export crops and the relative avail-ability of potatoes in local markets. However, even at the peak of the famine, British officials kept the faith—market competition was always considered better than direct aid from the government or other institutions. Laissez-faire economic policies were a lot of work. Government officials were anxious to create conditions within Irish rural society that would lead the Irish to behave "naturally," as political economy predicted.[20]

THE AXIOMS OF POLITICAL ECONOMY ALSO SHAPED HOW BRITISH officials perceived the Irish. The Irish, many Britons believed, exaggerated their poverty, making what was called in Ireland a "poor mouth," "because they hope to get some of England's bounty, and to escape paying their rent." Grandiose, hyperbolic accounts of suffering, death, misfortune, and poverty *are* a feature of Irish literary culture; the modernist writer Flann O'Brien's 1941 novella *An Béal Bocht* (*The Poor Mouth*) is a parody of the genre. However, Britons construed these flourishes of Irish storytelling as an insidious plot to steal from the empire, lies told from "the extreme of impudence or the extreme of wretchedness."[21]

The seeds of these assumptions about the capacities and motivations of Irish labourers in the 1840s had germinated in the eighteenth century, in the plantation colonies of the British Caribbean. When political economists imagined the least civilised possible labourer, they often imagined an enslaved worker. An enslaved worker had no reason to work without violent compulsion; a civilised wage worker in contrast *welcomed* having to work for wages to survive. "It is obvious that a man can be subjected to the hopelessness and the irresponsibility of a slave," Nassau William Senior wrote, "without incurring the vices of slavery." To justify mass enslavement, colonial officials argued that people of African descent were too uncivilised to work without coercion, and that coercion and enslavement, in a limited sense, could themselves be civilising forces.[22]

Consequently, what it meant to be "free" in the nineteenth-century British Empire was often indistinguishable from what it meant to be "civilised." To be free, a British colonial subject would have to work for wages and participate in the market—and a civilised subject would accept that working for wages was both necessary and moral. The Irish were higher up this imaginary ladder of work ethic and civilisation than formerly enslaved people, but not by much. This view was shared by both passionate abolitionists and vulgar racists, albeit for very different reasons. Frederick Douglass, on a visit to a village near Dublin in 1846, described the cold, filthy housing occupied by so many of the Irish poor. Remembering open cesspits bubbling as human and animal waste decomposed, Douglass wrote that he would be ashamed "to lift up my voice against American slavery, but that I know the cause of humanity is one the world over." To Douglass, the Irish poor and the enslaved and free Black workers in the United States were united by a common struggle to survive in different, but pitiless, conditions. Thomas Carlyle, who advocated for the reimposition of slavery in the British Caribbean, wrote that Black labourers in that region "are emancipated, and it appears refuse to work: Irish Whites have long been entirely emancipated; and nobody asks them to work." Carlyle feared that Britain had created in the Caribbean "a *Black Ireland*, 'free' indeed, but an Ireland, and *Black*." To Carlyle, the whiteness of the Irish poor was a thin but indelible proof of superiority over Black people in the Caribbean. Otherwise, in Carlyle's view, both required a firm hand—or a switch—to be made to labour usefully.[23]

From these principles, it followed in Ireland that austerity in poor relief—and, eventually, in famine relief—was both necessary and moral, and that generosity posed a moral hazard to the semicivilised Irish work ethic. Even in the deepest years of

famine, many officials believed that anything given for free, without conditions—what was known as eleemosynary assistance—
would threaten all wage labour in Ireland after the crisis passed.
In the twenty-first century, the word "eleemosynary" is archaic.
It was also archaic in the nineteenth century, only in currency
among practitioners of the law of corporations, for whom it
meant a lay (rather than a religious) corporation dedicated to "the
perpetual distribution of the free alms, or bounty, of the founder
of them to such persons as he has directed." When reformers
used it to discuss poor relief, the word was meant to evoke the
antiquity and perhaps the sulphurous popery of giving charity
without expecting labour in return. There was no eleemosynary
famine relief in Ireland. In 1845 and 1846, Robert Peel's government focused on intervening in the Irish grain market to keep
prices steady. From the summer of 1846, John Russell's government initially focused on regulating the Irish labour market by
sponsoring public works before experimenting with nationally
organised soup kitchens. The kitchens offered the closest thing
to free relief in famine-era Ireland but were still expected to test
the means of the hungry, to make sure that those seeking food
had no other means of growing or buying it. Finally, the Russell
ministry made Ireland's workhouses, organised under the 1838
Irish Poor Law, responsible for famine relief.[24]

The laws of political economy could never fail; they could only
be failed. As the famine continued, and one policy after another
did little to resolve the disorder and desolation, many in the government became nihilistic, arguing that it would be better to do
nothing to slow the famine or palliate the suffering of the Irish
poor—to "let the evil work itself out like a consuming fire," as
a politician wrote in his diary. Charles Trevelyan considered the
possibility that the blight was "some great intervention of Providence to bring back the potato to its original use and intention

as an adjunct, and not as a principal article of national food." For most British officials, the object of famine relief was to ride out the crisis, reduce dependence on potatoes among the Irish poor, and allow the influence of the market to restore balance to an otherwise sound economic system. The crisis, however, *was* the system.[25]

HISTORIANS HAVE FOUND IN THE IRISH GREAT FAMINE MORALity plays and sagas of exile and national becoming. Some treat the famine as an opportunity to lay charges of genocide, or at least of genocidal intent, at the feet of British officials. Others search for villains and heroes—sifting gimlet-eyed administrators from fearless rebels. Still others emphasise the role of the famine for the origins of the Irish nation, or for the dispersion of the international Irish diaspora. These questions about the famine—of why it happened, of whom to blame, and of what meaning and purpose we can find in a catastrophe—were being asked even before the blight had receded.

Charles Trevelyan's sleek official history of famine relief, *The Irish Crisis*, appeared in 1848, when the famine was far from over but after Lord Russell's government had devolved responsibility for famine relief onto local authorities in Ireland. Trevelyan, a fine and forceful writer, blamed the famine on Ireland's dependence on potatoes. The blight, he concluded, was a "sharp but effectual remedy," a "direct stroke of an all-wise and all-merciful Providence." Other early histories, written by survivors, emigrants, and exiles, argued that the blight invited the English to attempt to exterminate the Irish. Ireland, "an ancient Nation," an exiled revolutionary wrote, was "stricken down by a war more ruthless and sanguinary than any seven years' war, or thirty years' war." To many in Ireland and in the Irish diaspora, the famine was a proof of British cruelty. It is no accident that hunger strikes would become powerful symbolic weapons for future Irish revolutionaries. In the later nineteenth century, partly in reaction to a more confident and belligerent Irish nationalism, leading historians revised their analyses, downplaying the unique trauma of the crisis. More recent histories, especially economic histories, are more evenhanded, but the question of whom to blame for the famine continues to structure many historical debates.[26]

Among the most contentious questions for historians has been whether the United Kingdom, or the British Empire, can be blamed for the famine. Mass starvation, scholars of international law have argued, can be a tool of extermination, control, conquest, punishment, or exploitation. It might be satisfying retrospectively to arraign the British Empire on similar charges of "starvation crime." And indeed, at least some prominent British officials, especially in the first year of potato blight, argued that the threat of famine would encourage mass emigration from Ireland, reducing pressure on land and dependence on potatoes. But in international law, starvation crime requires *intent*. A government or military committing the crime must act either to destroy the means of producing or obtaining food, or to forcibly displace people to cause starvation. Despite the morbid hopes of some political economists for a bracing food shortage to reform Ireland, the UK government—including its hundred Irish members of Parliament (MPs) and its many Anglo-Irish officials—did not intend Ireland to starve. There was no plan to destroy the potato crop, and successive Conservative and Whig governments spent millions of pounds on famine relief.[27]

Writing about rural County Donegal in the 1980s, an anthropologist noted that "death seems to enjoy an almost casual pre-eminence." The Great Famine did not create these cultural preoccupations with death; if anything, the famine conditions were all the more horrific when wakes and funerals stopped as the living became too weak to mourn the dead. Accounts of the dead and dying in Ireland moved the British public to give to charity when the blight was at its most widespread and the famine at its most deadly, in the winter of 1846–1847. At the same time, emptying Ireland of people seemed like a crude but ultimately useful solution to Ireland's poverty and "surplus population."[28]

And so, blame matters. The suffering of so many people, subjects of what was certainly the most powerful country on earth at the time, calls out for moral judgement. Although the UK did not commit the crime of starvation in Ireland, it was not innocent. *Rot* is not a history of individual culpability for the Great Famine. The blight broke in a wave over structures in Ireland that were already in decay. No individual caused the Great Famine; no individual could have prevented it. However, Ireland relied on potatoes because of its position within the British Empire. The Irish poor suffered during the Great Famine as legacies of conquest and colonialism collided with a deep imperial faith in markets, commerce, and capitalism as the only remedies for social problems, even amid catastrophic ecological and economic collapse.

Some histories of the Great Famine imagine alternative possibilities for Ireland in the 1840s—if only the right voices had been heard and the right policies implemented, mass death might have been prevented. Closing Irish ports, seizing and redistributing Irish crops, nationalising Irish land, and forcing or paying farmers to plant oats instead of potatoes for subsistence—these policies might have worked. However, these proposals—though we might yearn for them in retrospect—were so far beyond the political horizons of the United Kingdom in the 1840s as to be fantasies. Colonialism and capitalism made the British Empire; colonialism and capitalism made Irish poverty advantageous to Britain; colonialism and capitalism created conditions that turned blight into famine. Although structure does not excuse individual viciousness, the moral crimes that led to the Great Famine were committed over centuries. Ireland's poverty and vulnerability, made by colonial dispossession and exploitation, shaped its relationship to Great Britain, its ostensible partner in the United Kingdom. Rotten potatoes, markets, poverty, and hunger give a tangible shape and meaning to British colonialism, its ambitions, limitations, structures, oversights, and catastrophes.

The scale of the Irish famine, and its central place in the history of nineteenth-century Ireland, can camouflage the reality that the Irish crisis was less singular than it seemed; it was the most destructive example of a European pandemic of potato disease, food shortages, and unrest. The United Kingdom was not swept up in the waves of revolutions in Europe that broke in the 1830s. However, Ireland was Britain's "local volcano," prone to explosion in times of general crisis. The potato failure of the 1840s accelerated and deepened an economic crisis across all of Europe from 1846 to 1848, as a downswing in the business cycle put industrial labourers out of work while poor harvests—not only of potatoes— drove up food prices. In 1848, the "Young Ireland" movement attempted to bring to Ireland the energy of the revolutions sweeping continental Europe. Like the potato failure, the revolutions of 1848 spread quickly across Europe, toppling governments in Hungary, Italy, France, Denmark, Poland, and elsewhere. The potato failure, like the revolutions, was a European crisis, "nationalized in retrospect." Mass emigration was also not a uniquely Irish phenomenon, nor was Ireland the first primarily agricultural European country to send emigrants in large numbers overseas.[29]

Moreover, the Irish Great Famine was neither the first nor the last cataclysmic food shortage in the Victorian British Empire. Unstable climatic conditions caused by the El Niño oscillation in ocean temperatures in the southern Pacific caused droughts and famines in 1876–1879, 1889–1891, and 1896–1902 that killed tens of millions of people in British India. Crop failure was

triggered by natural phenomena—drought, heavy rains, population explosions of pests—but famine in the empire followed
crop failure when imperial administrators placed their faith in
the market to solve food shortages. There was almost always
enough food; the obstacle was a stubborn insistence that private
merchants deliver food to the hungry, and that the hungry pay
for it with money or labour. As in Ireland, the faith of the British
Empire in the power of the market made it impossible to imagine alternative solutions to famine in India.[30]

If any factors set Britain apart from continental Europe in
the era of the famine, they were the breadth of its empire and the
depth of the faith of the British political class in free trade, free
labour, and the power of capital. Ireland was a part of the British
Empire, a conquered island that conquest had brought close, geographically, economically, and culturally, to the imperial centre.
Consequently, the "Irish question" was a constant, and discom-
fiting, reminder of the limits of British power, "a critical abyss"
that refused to obey the laws of civilisation and political economy that constituted and justified imperial power. Ireland proved
the hollowness of a theory that was supposed to both structure
the empire and give it moral purpose. Proximity to Britain and
British capitalism was not civilising for the colonial empire—it
was humiliating, and often immiserating. As John Pitt Kennedy
wrote in 1835, "reckless indifference" to Ireland was profitable for
the British ruling class, the "selfish English oligarchy, who found
that every successive act of exasperation exercised against Ireland,
added to their own wealth."[31]

THE BLIGHT EPIDEMIC WAS A SUBSISTENCE CRISIS, BUT IT WAS
also an ecological crisis—not an "act of God" but an unintended
consequence of the exploitation of Irish land and labour within

a shrinking and accelerating world. In this, the famine was also disconcertingly modern. Although Ireland's potato fields looked rustic, they were intensive monocrops, often of a single variety of potato, cloned and cloned again when farmers planted potato cuttings instead of seeds. *Phytophthora infestans*, geneticists believe, originated in the valleys, carved by ancient lava flows, outside Mexico City, where potatoes are a native species. Wild potatoes usually have the genetic diversity to resist *P. infestans*, and the drier climate is less conducive to the rapid spread of the mould. In Ireland, though, *P. infestans* found an agricultural ecosystem and climate that could not have been better designed for a population explosion of the microorganism. A landscape shaped by the demands of the British Empire met a pathogen brought to Europe by capitalism's steamships and global trading networks.

The Great Famine is a troubling preamble to a twentieth- and twenty-first-century world where capitalism, for all its power to create and satisfy human desires, can find few answers to the threats to human life posed by introduced species, novel pathogens, and climate catastrophes. The arrival of an organism like the blight mould was a predictable biological accident made possible by the transformation of human beings' relationship to the natural world. Many scientists consider the human era to be the Anthropocene, a new period distinct from the earlier Holocene. It has been an era of human-made changes to climate, land use, the nitrogen cycle, ocean acidity, and so much else. The evolving conditions of the Anthropocene—the surprises and disasters of a new chapter in the turbulent history of the planet—present new threats to food security. The global homogenisation of crops and agricultural techniques threatens the biodiversity and resilience of the many plants and animals that human beings have domesticated. Intensive monoculture

made Irish potatoes vulnerable to blight. The solutions proposed to mitigate famine were themselves the product of a
kind of intellectual and political monoculture. Solutions were
unimaginable outside the market that fueled the crisis to begin
with.[32]

There are many people on earth in a similar position to that of
Irish labourers in 1845: growing staples for subsistence and producing agricultural commodities for global markets. In 2023, at
least two billion people subsisted on food grown by smallholding
farmers. And just as in Ireland in 1845, many present-day small
and subsistence farmers are also wage workers or commodity
producers. When there is no escape from the market, it eats the
weakest first. The Irish who survived on potatoes were agricultural
labourers estranged from their land, eating only a single introduced crop so that a small class of landlords and larger tenant
farmers would have the freedom to flip their fields from oats to
grazing land to meet favourable markets in Britain. The Irish way
of life looked ancient—but it was heartbreakingly, almost quintes-
sentially, modern.[33]

The famine seemed like an act of God or a natural disaster, but
many of its features were man-made. Potato crops died by a natural
process, but the brittle structures of the Irish economy were built
by centuries of contact—conquest, resistance, exploitation, and,
finally, unequal and ambiguous partnership—between Ireland,
Britain, and the British Empire. The "laws" of political economy,
in contrast, were considered to be natural. Likewise, during the
Great Famine, while British laissez-faire policies proved to be anything but self-sustaining—ostensibly self-directed market forces
needed to be fussed over and carefully calibrated—the actual
Irish, who were actually starving, were left to their own devices
and to "natural" market forces.

THIS BOOK TRACES THE HISTORY OF THE STRUCTURES THAT MADE the Great Famine, and the history of the crabbed and market-bound efforts during the famine to feed the starving. I describe and analyse Ireland's place in the British Empire and the Union, as well as the structures of the market for food and rent in Ireland and the astonishing centrality of the potato there, essential both to exploitation and to small pleasures of everyday life in Ireland's countryside and cities. From the arrival of *P. infestans* in 1845, *Rot* follows the efforts of successive British governments to turn the principles of the market and its civilising power into schemes for providing food to the hungry without stepping on the toes of private traders or giving away too much without requiring something in return.

In 1845–1846, the Conservative government, led by Robert Peel, implemented plans to purchase maize, virtually unknown in Ireland, and introduce the grain into Irish markets wherever prices surged. In autumn 1846, however, the blight returned, obliterating an already historically small potato crop. In "Black '47"—the winter of 1846–1847—Ireland collapsed into desolation, death, and panic. A new prime minister, John Russell, and his Whig government funded public works and eventually soup kitchens to try to bring a disastrous situation under control. Epidemic blight reappeared in Irish fields with varying severity every year until the early 1850s, as hundreds of thousands emigrated in panic. However, by summer 1847, Russell's government—faced with a financial crisis and the failure of previous relief programs—declared that the famine was no longer a crisis for the United Kingdom as a whole. From late 1847, Ireland's Poor Law unions administered famine relief, operating on the principle that "Irish property pay for Irish poverty." In the face of failure after failure, both major British political parties rarely wavered from a commitment to the idea that with the right market incentives, the famine could end and Ireland could be civilised.

To British officials—and to many historians reading British records—the Great Famine appeared distorted, its shape and cause deformed by temporal and optical illusions. Irish farms looked primitive. The Irish poor, especially in the countryside, seemed to resist the modern rhythms of the market and empire, to cleave stubbornly to ancient, unchanged, and backward ideas, customs, and patterns of work. Ireland before the famine, however, more closely resembled capitalism's future than its past. Irish labourers were paid some of the lowest wages in the British Empire, and they relied on the abundance of the potato to survive. The staggering inequality, pervasive debt, outrageous rent-gouging, precarious employment, and vulnerability to changes in commodity prices that torment so many in the twenty-first century were rehearsed in the Irish countryside before the potatoes failed.

1

A HUNGRY ISLAND

IN KANDY, IN THE HIGHLANDS OF CEYLON (NOW SRI LANKA),
Irish officers in the British Army celebrated Saint Patrick's Day in
1823. The garrison fired a salute, and a regimental band struck up
"St. Patrick's Day in the Morning." The mess hall was decorated
with paper transparencies, Irish themes interpreted in a Sinhalese
decorative style by the officers' servants. One depicted a crown and
harp in the foreground, with a distant skyline of a "commercial
port and city" in the background, the other an elaborate Star of
the Order of Saint Patrick. At their evening banquet the crowd
toasted the saint, the Crown, and Ireland.[1]

Kandy, once the capital of an independent kingdom and the
site of a temple complex that held the Buddha's tooth, fell to British forces in 1815. Britain first claimed Ceylon as a Crown colony
in 1796, after seizing the island from the Dutch, and the fall of
Kandy consolidated the conquest. In 1823, before railways made
the journey easy, soldiers would march from Colombo, the colonial capital, along a carriage road that passed by a column raised

to remember the British Army engineers who had blasted through the rock. The soldiers hunted for game in the jungle at the edges of the road and contended with land leeches and diarrhea, while visitors rhapsodised about the green, rugged landscape. In the town, the former royal palace and seraglio were renovated and repurposed as offices and a military hospital. The barracks were new and airy. A mountain lake reflected picturesque, broad streets. The fields around the city promised riches for the British Empire. "Precious stones and rich veins of metals," a visitor wrote, "may be concealed within its bosom." Nearby hills looked perfect for growing coffee; after 1867, the region would be a centre of tea production. Imperial officials were certain that if the Sinhalese could be made to understand the value and potential of the land Britain had taken from them, they would see the justice of British rule. The rewards of the global market, imperial officials argued, would transform the "natives" and persuade them to work, save, and spend like Britons. "Should new wants excite the industry of the Kandians to supply them," a visitor wrote in 1818, "the many valuable natural productions of the country will amply furnish the means."[2]

In Ceylon in 1823, the Irish officers who drank the King's health and the Irish private soldiers who plucked fat leeches from their groins and armpits served the British Empire. Ireland, like Kandy, had been conquered by Britain. But Ireland had shared a monarch with England from the time of Henry VIII and had a parliament of its own. Ireland was subject to colonialism—to extraction, to exploitation, to violence—but it was neither a colony nor an independent kingdom. "Ireland," the British statesman Charles Greville wrote to the Duke of Rutland in 1784, "is too great to be unconnected with us, and too near to us to be dependent on a foreign state, and too little to be independent." Many described the islands as a family too interdependent to ever fully be estranged. Ireland, an eighteenth-century critic reflected, was like a parasitic conjoined twin to Britain, disfiguring and resented, but also nourished and cherished, joined in life and in death.[3]

The creation of the United Kingdom in 1801 did not dismantle the political and economic structures built during centuries of conquest in Ireland. In fact, the transformation of Ireland from a puppet kingdom to a junior partner in the UK only deepened the fissures in Irish political economy. Restrictions on Irish trade and political life were abolished, but the crash in commodity prices that followed the Napoleonic Wars pulled Ireland into a spiral of debt and unemployment. The island became what "Sicily was to the Romans," an impoverished and exploited agricultural district. Ireland supplied its partners in the United Kingdom with growing quantities of grain, dairy, and meat, but slid deeper into poverty. As Ireland grew more economically vulnerable to changes in British demand, more and more Irish families came to depend on access to land for potatoes for survival. Long before the arrival of the potato blight in Ireland, Britain's quasi-colonial relationship to Ireland had pushed millions to live or die based on the health of the potato crop.[4]

IN THE EIGHTEENTH CENTURY, IRELAND WAS ROUGHLY 80 PERcent Catholic, but only 5 percent of Irish land was owned by Catholic landlords. Dispossession, reinforced by laws forbidding Catholic participation in political and economic life, were key features of British colonialism in Ireland. Colonisation had a long history. In the twelfth century, Norman soldiers invaded Ireland, extending the Norman Conquest of England across the Irish Sea. After the invasion, the new Anglo-Norman nobility was all but independent until King Henry VII reimposed English government and limited the Irish Parliament's authority after his victory in the Wars of the Roses (1455–1487). In 1541, after a failed rebellion led by the Earl of Kildare against the Crown, Henry VIII declared himself king of Ireland as well as England.[5]

From the 1540s on, the Crown experimented with the colonisation of Ireland by English, Welsh, and Scottish settlers. These "plantations"—meant in the sense of a grove of trees planted to birth a forest—were supposed to pacify Ireland through gradual Anglicisation. The first plantations in Munster crumbled. But in the early seventeenth century, with the support of King James I, six counties in the northern province of Ulster—Donegal, Tyrone, Fermanagh, Cavan, Armagh, and Londonderry—were cleared of many Catholics by force and resettled by English and Scottish Protestants. A seventh county, Antrim, was settled "privately" by independent Protestant settlers with the Crown's tacit endorsement. Throughout the eighteenth and nineteenth centuries, the majority-Protestant "Ulster Plantation" (six counties of which now compose Northern Ireland) was often a relatively more prosperous exception to the poverty of the other provinces. On the eve of the English Civil Wars of the 1640s, there were one hundred thousand Protestant settlers in Ireland—some thirty thousand Scots and seventy thousand Welsh and English. Although outnumbered fifteen to one by Catholics, Protestants already owned more than 40 percent of Irish land.[6]

In 1641, during the Civil Wars, the Irish Catholic nobility rebelled and won de facto independence. But from 1649 to 1651, after the defeat of the Royalists and the execution of King Charles I, Oliver Cromwell—the leading figure in the army raised by Parliament and Lord Protector of England from 1653—launched a ruthless reconquest of Ireland. Historians question the degree to which Cromwell personally intended to exterminate Catholics, although some of his followers considered the invasion of Ireland a holy war. Reports of massacres of Protestants fuelled the fire. Irish Catholics, one pamphlet declared, "are the very offal of men, dregs of mankind, reproach of Christendom. . . . Cursed be he that maketh not his sword stark drunk with Irish blood."[7]

In 1652, many Catholics were formally stripped of their land by act of Parliament and driven from their homes to the western province of Connaught, designated as the new home of the "native" Irish. Catholic priests were executed. Many Irish soldiers fled the island to join the French and Spanish armies; thousands who were captured were sent as indentured labourers to England's Caribbean colonies. The humiliation and trauma of the invasion made Cromwell a figure of mythic evil in Irish folk memory. In one story, Cromwell punished a soldier who stole milk by stabbing the thief in the stomach, "out of which spurted the milk . . . a warning that none of his soldiers could do anything without his permission."[8]

After Oliver Cromwell's death, the Commonwealth collapsed, and in 1660 Charles II was restored to the throne (Cromwell's corpse was exhumed, put on trial, and convicted of treason). Two years later, select Irish Catholic landowners who had remained loyal to the Crown were restored to their lands. In 1685, Charles died. His brother, James, was Catholic. However, James was in his fifties, and his heir, Mary, firmly Protestant, was married to William of Orange, stadtholder of the Netherlands and a stalwart of the Dutch armed struggle against Spain, one of Europe's great Catholic monarchies. James was crowned James II with the grudging consent of Parliament. All but the hottest Puritans conceded that the accession of an older Catholic king with a Protestant heir was better than renewed war.

In power, James edged toward restoring all Catholic land in Ireland. In 1687, the Catholic Earl of Tyrconnell was appointed lord lieutenant and persuaded James II to annul the laws prohibiting the partial return of land to "innocent" Catholics. Anticipating that the Cromwellian settlement would be overturned, Protestant landowners fled. Paramilitaries in Ulster armed themselves. In 1688, James's wife, Mary of Modena, gave birth to a son whose claim to the throne would trump that of his Protestant half sister. A Catholic king was tolerable; a Catholic dynasty was not. A group of leading MPs secretly invited James's son-in-law, William of Orange, to take the English throne. In November 1688, William landed in England at the head of an army. James II fled, and William was crowned William III in 1689, ruling as co-monarch with the deposed king's daughter, now Mary II.

In England, the 1688 invasion was a "Glorious Revolution." In Ireland, it began a new war of conquest. When William's army drove James II from England, he fled first to Ireland, where many Catholic aristocrats rallied around his cause. William invaded Ireland, personally leading his troops against an army led by James, at the Battle of the Boyne in 1690—one of the last European battles in which two monarchs faced each other on the battlefield.

England tightened its grip on Ireland, and the persecution of Irish Catholics continued. In 1707, England and Wales merged with Scotland, formerly a separate kingdom (although under a single Crown), to form Great Britain. The new British Parliament, following on laws passed under Cromwell, passed a series of acts, known as the Penal Laws, to persecute Irish (and British) Catholics. Catholics had been barred from all public offices in Ireland since 1607, and in 1707 the ban was extended to Presbyterians. Catholics were forbidden to marry Protestants, and they could not sit in either the English or the Irish Parliament or vote in elections. Catholics were barred from many professions. Catholicism assumed a "catacomb existence." Although Catholics were the majority even in Ulster, by the nineteenth century there were only 2,015 Catholic churches serving Ireland's 6.5 million Catholics.

Priests would travel, sometimes in secret, on "stations," going out twice a year to hear confession and say Mass in private homes.[9]

The Penal Laws against Catholic rites were often indifferently enforced in Ireland, but the laws that disinherited and dispossessed Catholic landlords were scrupulously followed. The heirs of Catholics could inherit land only if they converted to the Anglican church, and no Catholic could inherit land owned by a Protestant. Any landlord who converted to Catholicism forfeited his property to the Crown and faced an indefinite prison term. Some two thousand landowners, many descendants of Cromwell's and William's soldiers and allies, owned virtually all of Ireland's arable land, some in estates larger than fifty thousand acres. Protestant landlords, however, depended on the despised Catholic majority for rent and labour.

As the new state of Great Britain consolidated, the British Empire grew. Ireland was largely shut out of trade to Britain, so Irish merchants sent most of their goods across the Atlantic, with 85 percent bound for the Caribbean colonies. A cargo of Irish linen, for example, might go to Barbados to be sold for sugar, with the sugar taken to England to be sold for cash. The risks of this attenuated trading network raised the cost of borrowing for Irish merchants, who both paid more for credit and earned less on exports. Meanwhile, Irish landlords collected rent on estates that some rarely, if ever, visited. William Petty, the English polymath who served Cromwell, Charles II, and James II, noted that as early as 1664, at least 25 percent of Irish landlords lived in England, where "all that belongs to them goes out, but returns not."[10]

As the gap between the British and Irish economies grew, the idea of the Irish as insinuating papists at best and ungovernable barbarians at worst solidified in British popular culture. Jonathan Swift's famous satire, "A Modest Proposal," published in 1729, skewered both the poverty of the Irish countryside and an already well-defined contempt for the Irish in Britain. In the essay, Swift proposed the slaughter of Irish children, "plump, and fat" as a solution to Irish poverty. "A child will make two dishes at an entertainment for friends, and when the family dines alone, the fore or hind quarter will make a reasonable dish," Swift wrote. "I grant this food," he continued, "will be somewhat dear, and therefore very proper for landlords, who, as they have already devoured most of the parents, seem to have the best title to the children." Swift was revolted both by Irish poverty and by the willingness of Britons to think of the Irish as not only poor but feral, cannibal, subhuman.[11]

Poverty bred crimes of opportunity, and oppression bred armed resistance. The eighteenth-century Irish countryside often erupted into what the British government called "outrages"—spasms of extortion, assassination, arson, threats, and robbery against landlords and their representatives by armed, often disguised, bands. Although it might be tempting to place rural outrages into a coherent history, or even prehistory, of national resistance, we should be sceptical. When a farmer burned his landlord's barn on a cloudy night, did he think that he was striking a blow for Ireland? It was all but impossible to prosecute outrages, unless the perpetrators were strangers. As Rev. Thomas Harman, of Wexford, explained, people who set fires or threatened murder to prevent an eviction were "supported by general opinion, and those who commit them are defended publicly both at the chapel and the forge." Outrages were especially likely when landlords threatened to evict their tenants, threatened to convert tilled land to pasture, or refused to pay rates of wages that communities considered to be set by long-standing custom.[12]

The febrile, hyperlocal politics of eighteenth-century Ireland and the durable stereotype of the Irish—and especially of impoverished Irish Catholics—as poorer, stranger, and less civilised than Britons, put even more symbolic distance between Britain and Ireland. Ireland had been conquered and colonised, but it was not a colony. The consequence was neither an independent Ireland nor a fully fleshed-out colonial legal order. Instead, Ireland was governed through a hodgepodge system of overlapping English and Celtic institutions. The island was divided into more than sixty-two thousand "townlands," divisions of an average of three hundred acres, each home to about fifteen to thirty households. The townland as Britain understood it was based on an interpretation of the "ballybetagh" (*baile biataigh*), a unit of land from Celtic Ireland, standardised as roughly one-thirtieth of a barony. From a British perspective, the townlands seemed useful for local taxation. However, in practice, townlands often overlapped, and their borders were often disputed. Moreover, "rundale," another holdover from before conquest (from the Irish *roinn*, a division of a part of something shared, and *dáil*, an assembly) rotated productive grazing and tillage land among and within families. An Irish family might hold claims, official or unofficial, to the leases of land scattered across townlands and rundale commons. Family stakes in rundale land were governed by the rules of "gavelkind," another remnant of Celtic law. Gavelkind divided a man's property equally among his children, at either his death or his "retirement" as the head of a family. Sons received their land immediately; daughters received it as a dowry.[13]

Ireland's landlords and the British officials appointed to oversee Irish affairs were content to suppress the Catholic aristocracy and extract exports and rent from the countryside. The consequence was a set of ambiguous and sometimes self-contradictory rules that added to the idea of Ireland as especially uncivilised. For example, the Irish unit of land known as the "gneeve" was roughly ten English acres—but the acres were estimated, and often divided imprecisely into "large" and "small" acres. Even after the Union, Ireland still measured acreage in two different

units, the Cunningham (or Irish) acre, and the plantation (or statute) acre. Twelve of the thirty-two counties were formed in 1210
under King John, and more were added in the Elizabethan era
and under James I. The last county to be formed was Wicklow,
separated from Dublin in 1605. Ireland's counties often had their
own measures of land, which created a patchwork. In Antrim, for
example, townlands were regularised at one hundred acres each; in
Longford, land was divided into cartons of about sixty acres, with
four cartons to a ploughland.[14]

As the pressure exerted by Britain and its empire on Irish
land increased, Irish labourers adopted the potato, once a backstop against crop failure, as their nearly universal staple. A potato
ground could provide subsistence regardless of the availability of
paid work. Potato cultivation allowed slightly richer Irish tenant
farmers to afford land with little capital. In 1742, for example,
Catholics, who were generally barred by the Penal Laws from
owning land for tillage, were permitted to claim peatland, as long
they paid to have the bogs drained. Many paid their workers in
land, allowing subsistence potatoes to make up the shortfall. From
as early as 1735, guides to British and Irish plants mention the
"vast number of natives . . . almost entirely supported" by potatoes. Dependence on potatoes made Irish labourers vulnerable
to famine at least a century before the late-blight pandemic. In
1740–1741, bad weather ruined the harvest of both grain and
potatoes. At least three hundred thousand people died of hunger
and disease—by proportion of population, a greater death toll
than the Great Famine.[15]

By the end of the eighteenth century, with the confusing
palimpsest of Celtic and English influence and the dynamic, often
reckless, transformation of agricultural land to earn profit and
subsistence in the imperial economy, it would have been hard to
imagine what Ireland had looked like before English conquest and

British capitalism. In the Irish peatlands the acidic bogs preserved old pine cones, many of Scotch fir and stone pine, as well as whole trees, including ancient yews and oaks. Ireland, the Enlightenment agronomist Arthur Young wrote, had been governed by Britain according to "the narrow spirit of a counting house." Resources and energy flowed out of Ireland, depleting the rural economy. When food was scarce, Irish labourers would sometimes sneak into cattle paddocks to bleed the animals. The bleeding was rarely fatal, though it left the cows anemic. Ireland was much the same, routinely bled alive, a little weaker each time.[16]

THE GROWTH OF THE EMPIRE INCREASED THE VULNERABILITY OF Irish labourers to famine and consolidated British influence over Irish politics. However, for some Irish soldiers, settlers, and sailors, the empire offered opportunities to find work along the paths and in the settlements carved by British naval power and colonial trade. In the eighteenth century, many of those paths led west, following Irish trade to the Caribbean. By about 1750, sugar surpassed grain as the most valuable commodity in world trade. And most of that sugar (about 80 percent by 1787) came from British and French colonies in the Caribbean, worked by millions of enslaved Africans.[17] Eventually, revolutions in France and British North America would force Britain to redefine its relationship to Ireland.

A casual (or unscrupulous) reader of eighteenth- and nineteenth-century sources might conclude that the Irish were also enslaved on the sugar islands—some nineteenth-century histories refer to Irish rebels sent "to toil as slaves on the plantations." In the wake of the Cromwellian conquest, thousands of Irish soldiers *were* sent to Caribbean sugar and tobacco plantations—so many that it was well known that the English were "very apt to barbadoes an unruly man." But those labourers were never enslaved—they were indentured, bound to work without wages for a fixed period of time. Their suffering was hideous. The passage was squalid; on the plantations, many died of disease or injury. But indentures ended, and former "servants," as indentured labourers were often called, became wage labourers, tenants, even landowners. Comparisons to slavery were not literal, but instead conveyed an Irish sense of how Britain saw Ireland: as a source of labour and cash subject to careless and violent exploitation, as a means to enrich the empire.[18]

Many Irish indentured labourers were exploited in the Caribbean, but far more Irish emigrants left for the Atlantic colonies of their own volition. About 30,000 English settlers left England for the American colonies in the eighteenth century, compared with 75,000 Scots and 250,000 Irish, primarily Presbyterians from Ulster. By 1793, the US census estimated that at least 17 percent of white Americans either had been born in Ireland or claimed Irish heritage. The practical need for manpower in the empire, and the need to govern an increasingly large and diverse world of British subjects, chipped away at anti-Catholic policies, if not at hostility to Catholics. In 1774, for example, the Quebec Act restored property rights and religious toleration to French Catholics in the conquered province of Quebec. Toleration of Catholicism in the empire, and perhaps even in Ireland, was a pragmatic adjustment to a changing British world. "An aristocracy of five hundred thousand Protestants," Arthur Young wrote, "crushing the industry of two millions of poor Catholicks, can never advance the public interest."[19]

This phenomenon was especially visible in the armed forces. After 1688, all Irish soldiers—Catholic, Anglo-Irish, and Presbyterian—had been expelled from the rank and file of the English Army and forbidden to reenlist (only Irish Protestant officers were allowed to keep their commissions). However, Irish soldiers, Presbyterian and Catholic, quietly rejoined British ranks during the Seven Years' War (1756–1763), and by 1830 more than 40 percent of British soldiers were Irish-born. The proportion was even greater in the armed forces of the East India Company. The humble Irish, an Irish writer boasted, provided "the sinewy arms, that chiefly man the British fleet and armies." During the famine, Irish military service would be used to shame the UK government, as the British Army had "never stood upon a battle-field that Irish courage did not advance her colours."[20]

As the British Empire in the Atlantic grew, and as Irish labourers and settlers found work in the colonies, Ireland's main exports—more than 50 percent of all direct Irish exports to Britain's colonies—were agricultural commodities produced by Irish graziers, especially butter, salt pork, and salt beef. Where Britain's American colonies had absorbed most of Ireland's exports at midcentury, by 1774 about 74 percent of Irish goods went to England, along with at least £3 million in rent. While the Irish economy remained agricultural, and reoriented toward Britain, the British economy diversified. The share of Britain's total gross domestic product from trade grew from about 4 percent in 1700 to 40 percent in 1770, fuelled by a complex Atlantic circuit of slave-produced commodities, colonial raw materials, and British manufactured goods.[21] In 1776, to prevent Ireland from supplying the Continental Army, Dublin Castle placed an embargo on Irish exports to the colonies. Two years later, when France joined the American side, more than sixty thousand Irishmen, mostly Presbyterians from Ulster, formed the Volunteers, a home-defence militia. Worried that the Volunteers might pivot from self-defence to self-determination, the British government loosened its grip on Irish trade. From November 1779 on, Ireland was permitted equal access to colonial markets, and the Irish Parliament assumed the power to set rules to regularise trade with Britain.

The prospect of the Volunteers rising, like the Americans, in the name of "British" liberty and free trade prompted further concessions to the Irish Parliament. In 1782, after the defeat at Yorktown, Henry Grattan in the Irish Parliament moved for the restoration of legislative independence. The new lord lieutenant, the Duke of Portland, and the new chief secretary, Richard Fitzpatrick, made no comment, and the motion passed easily. The Irish Parliament could now set its own agenda for legislation, Irish judges sat on the same terms as English judges, and the Irish House of Lords became the final court of appeal for Ireland. From 1793, Catholics in possession of property worth two pounds or more in rental income, either as owners or—far more often—as tenants, had their right to vote restored in what was called the "forty-shilling freehold." Grain prices were high in Britain, and the new "Grattan Parliament" encouraged landlords to convert their pasture to tillage. In 1783, Ireland exported some 210,000 barrels of grain to Britain; by 1789, nearly 650,000. The grain boom was profitable but brief—a "short age of gold."[22]

Ireland's new independence was brief as well. In 1798, during the French Revolution, the "United Irish" rose in rebellion. Although the group had many supporters among Catholics, its leaders were Protestant. The rebellion was swiftly and brutally suppressed. William Pitt's government concluded that the best course of action was to propose union between Britain and Ireland, to integrate Anglo-Irish Protestants and Presbyterians, and to begin to restore civil rights to Catholics. "The British Islands," an Irish supporter wrote, "constitute *one* Empire. . . . The Crowns (if I may so express it) are constitutionally blended." Others dismissed the proposal as a ruse to roll back the concessions of the 1780s. Why, a critic asked, should Ireland concede to Britain? Ireland, even within a United Kingdom, would still be a subject, not a partner, within the British Empire: "Empire," that "single sacrilegious word, which for six hundred years of our existence stood between us and our rights."[23]

Lord Cornwallis, William Pitt's trusted advisor on colonial affairs, was charged with finessing the Union through the Irish and British Parliaments. Many Irish Protestants were eager to create a "Union for Empire" and secure a share of imperial spoils. In 1707, Scotland's integration into the new Great Britain had proved to be a boon for ambitious Scots. Pitt explained to the House of Commons that although union was necessary, it would also be mutually beneficial, not only to London as the center of the system but also to Dublin. Ireland was a weak link in British defences, but union would also "communicate to Ireland, all the commercial advantages which Great Britain possesses . . . increase the resources, and consequently the strength, of the whole empire."[24]

The United Kingdom came into existence under the Acts of Union, passed in 1800 and coming into force on New Year's Day, 1801. The Irish Parliament was dissolved and integrated into the new parliament of the United Kingdom. Twenty-eight Irish peers and four Irish bishops took seats in the House of Lords, and one hundred new Irish constituencies were created to elect members of Parliament to serve in the House of Commons. The Church of Ireland was united with the Church of England. The Union Jack was embellished with a red saltire, overlaid on Scotland's white saltire and England's red Saint George's Cross.[25]

In the course of the eighteenth century, a common Protestantism and a common Catholic enemy—the formidable French empire—had helped to form a new British identity among Scots, English, and Welsh subjects. This posed a dilemma. Catholicism had been vilified for so long, and was so closely associated with France, that a vote for restoring political rights to Irish and British Catholics seemed to many MPs like a vote for the world turned upside down. In 1805, only 27 percent of MPs favoured granting Irish Catholics relief. But realists recognised that the Union could never be complete without what many called Catholic Emancipation.

The parliamentary majority preserving the Penal Laws dwindled, especially after Napoleon's final defeat and exile in 1815. Some made a pragmatic case for Catholic civil rights; sectarian distinctions, Thomas Malthus argued, rather than "the mere pressure of poverty alone" were the cause of unrest in Ireland, "a weapon of mighty and increasing force in the hands of the political agitator." The Duke of Wellington and Robert Peel, the leaders of the Tories in the Lords and in the House, faced a crisis when Daniel O'Connell, founder of the Catholic Association, won a parliamentary seat in Clare in 1828 but was barred from taking it. They guided the 1829 Roman Catholic Relief Act through Parliament on the logic that preserving the Union trumped anti-Catholicism. Many ordinary Britons, for whom hating Catholics was a matter of patriotic principle and national tradition, were appalled. Petitions and protests arrived in numbers. Some, like those sent from Bristol, Birmingham, and Glasgow, had tens of thousands of signatures. Nearly a century later Irish folklore recorded the pealing church bells and blazing bonfires celebrating "the great Catholic victory."[26]

But the Catholic Relief Act did not restore Catholic land, and it included provisions that changed the Irish political landscape. The act gave Catholics equal political rights but also increased the minimum property requirement to vote. Before 1829, qualified voters had to occupy land worth at least forty shillings in rental value per year. After 1829, the property qualification for voting increased fivefold, to ten pounds per year. Under the old "forty-shilling free-hold" rule for the franchise, landlords with political ambitions had been obliged—at least in theory—to defer to their tenants for votes. Peel and Wellington had succeeded in admitting Irish Catholics to British political life while also reducing the number of Irish Catholics able to exercise meaningful political power. Catholic Emancipation was never sold as a democratic measure. It was an invitation to the Irish Catholic middle and upper classes to join imperial politics, an invitation made at the expense of their tenants.

In 1829 the *Times* argued that religious conflict in Ireland had been blunted by Catholic Emancipation, and without sectarian resentment as a galvanising force, the dysfunctional relationship between landlord and tenant was now solely responsible for the unrest in the Irish countryside. In reality, religious divisions remained tense. In Armagh, on the eve of Catholic Emancipation, Protestant and Catholic farmers shot each other under cover of darkness. Some estimated that as many as fifty people were killed in "the hedge-firing, the Indian warfare." In County Down, a Protestant minister called down hellfire on "Popery, His Majesty's Ministers, and particularly the Duke of Wellington," whom the preacher accused of planning to usurp the throne, while the son of another preacher ostentatiously fingered a string of beads in the front row, in mockery of the rosary.[27]

In any case, Catholic Emancipation neither reversed seventeenth- and eighteenth-century conquest and dispossession nor removed the special military arrangements that facilitated the imposition of martial law. One hundred British Army garrisons reported to the lord lieutenant in Dublin Castle, who, in the face of reported outrages, could appeal to Parliament to pass a Coercion Act. Under the act, magistrates could dispense summary justice, habeas corpus could be suspended, and army regiments could occupy cities or counties. Coercion, designed for emergencies, became routine. Parliament passed no fewer than seventeen Coercion Acts between the Union and the famine.

BY 1829, IRELAND WAS INTEGRATED INTO THE BRITISH STATE and Catholics could vote and hold office. Ireland remained divided into estates according to a plan drawn by conquering armies. Irish land was still for extraction; Irish labour was still for exploitation. The Union was ostensibly a merger of sister kingdoms, but Irish society and the Irish economy were still structured by British colonial ambitions. After the Union, moreover, the Irish poor remained the object of a colonial civilising mission. The Union was seen as an engine that could transform Irish culture and subjecthood, either through slow and gradual moral reform or through rapid economic transformation.

In the 1810s, Mary Leadbeater, a Quaker diarist, healer, and woman of letters, wrote to introduce the pious British and Irish middle classes to an "authentic" world of Irish poverty, ready for gradual, homely reform under the Union. Leadbeater published poetry, criticism, collections of folklore, and translations from Latin and Greek but was best known for her collections of moralising "cottage dialogues." "The poor," one of Leadbeater's characters declares, "have not time to seek instruction in the winding walks of fancy." Leadbeater's dialogues and similar works envisioned reform as a process of meticulous cultural and spiritual uplift of the poor by the middle classes—as she indicated in the title of one of her books, moral reform was "the landlord's friend," a way to calm and enrich the countryside.[28]

While reformers like Leadbeater argued that British civilisation could best be transmitted by tutoring the poor in conduct and mores, many others imagined reform and civilisation as economic processes. In the eighteenth century, the "improvement" of land—investment to increase yields of either crops or rent—became a motto for British farmers and politicians. As Daniel Defoe wrote, "Multitudes of People make Trade, Trade makes Wealth, Wealth builds Cities, Cities Enrich the Land round them, Land Enrich'd rises in Value, and the Value of Lands Enriches the Government." From the early modern era through the eighteenth century, British

farming had evolved into a system of mostly large, highly capi-
talised farms very different from the peasant smallholdings that
prevailed in mainland Europe. Parliament passed many Acts of
Enclosure, privatising common land—"waste"—so that improving landlords could make it profitable. The consequence in Britain
was all but an end to peasant cultivation. A mere four thousand
landowners owned nearly 60 percent of Britain's cultivated land
and rented it out to commercial farmers, who employed nearly
1.25 million hired hands. The average yield of wheat per cultivated acre in Britain increased from twenty to thirty-two bushels
between 1812 and 1854.[29]

Long before the Union, the idea that improved land would help
pacify Ireland was shopworn in England. In the seventeenth century, for example, William Petty argued that if English rule could
improve Irish land, it would be a gift spectacular enough to make
up for the humiliation of conquest. It was clear to Petty that the
Irish could not improve their own land. Most Irish peasants, he
argued, squandered their wages on tobacco and ate nothing but
"potatoes from August till May, muscles [sic], cockles and oys-
ters, near the sea; eggs and butter made very rancid, by keeping
in bogs." For most of the population, Petty concluded, trade was
"little or nothing." By the end of eighteenth century, improvement
was often explicitly defined as a civilising force. Capital investment in land and profit-sharing for tenants, Arthur Young wrote,
would inspire new ideas "even in the uncultivated mind" of the
Irish labourer. "It would surely be a great piece of good fortune
for Paddy," another writer concluded, "if English cultivation could
drive all his fairies out of his head."[30]

And yet the benefits of imperial trade to Ireland were often limited, and in any case the bonanza profits available when the market was strong flowed to landlords, not to workers. Ireland became
poorer, and Irish poverty became evidence not only of a lack of

civilisation in Ireland in comparison with Britain, but also of a
bloody-minded atavism and immorality among the Irish poor. The
improvident, work-shy, and cunning Irishman was a stock character in British popular culture. Many blamed the potato for Paddy's
laziness, "whereof the labour of one man can feed forty." Others argued that Irish farming practices were primitive, and that
new technology after conquest would be a tonic. "If you could
see a Chinese or a Flemish farm," one reformer scolded, "you
would blush for your mismanagement of manure, and waste of
seed." Another urged the Irish to adopt the newer manufactured,
horse-drawn ploughs, made of iron, complaining that "the poor
man's field is only *scratched*."[31]

The imagined economic and moral causes of Ireland's failure
to thrive under the Union blurred together. British civilisation,
delivered by the Union, was in reformers' minds an unequivocal
good, a panacea. If Ireland remained poor, the logic of civilisation insisted that the cause had to be some stubborn cultural or
perhaps even racial pathology among the Irish. One observer was
disgusted at the "hundred of idlers" boozing over the corpse at
a wake, "to the loss of their families and farms that want their
work." The Lent fast and other Catholic observances, another
argued, robbed the United Kingdom "of the labour of the poor."
A third blamed the potato for affording subsistence without hard
labour, instilling among the Irish poor a "total disregard of the
value of time, a desultory and sauntering habit, without industry
or steadiness of purpose." The potato had come full circle: arriv-
ing as an expedient for landlords hoping to maximise profit from
conquered land in the eighteenth century, the crop had become
a symbol of Irish resistance to "civilisation," a cushion of easy
sustenance that protected the Irish poor from the bracing risks of
the market.[32]

"IT WOULD BE BETTER," AN IRISH FARMER GLUMLY TOLD A PARLIA-
mentary committee, "that Buonaparte never lived, or never
died." The bloom of enthusiasm for the Union that had buoyed
early efforts to "civilise" Ireland withered at the end of the war
with France in 1815. War had kept the price of grain and other
agricultural commodities high, and landlords in Britain and Ireland shared a windfall. In peacetime, the price of grain in Britain
collapsed. The Irish economy fell into a vicious cycle, the basic
structure of which had been set by conquest. Rent flowed out;
investment capital did not flow in. Ireland produced more food for
the British market, and Irish dependence on the potato deepened
as land became still more subdivided. In manufacturing, British competition swamped the small Irish sector. Economic stagnation left a growing population with fewer jobs and flat wages.
Ireland's poverty and fragility within the Union became the new
"Irish question" for Westminster, replacing the prospect of Ireland
as a potential staging ground for French or Spanish invasion of
Britain.[33]

In the 1780s, the Irish Parliament had offered bounties for farmers willing to switch their grazing land over to grain, to meet the
growing British market. After the Union, the "excitement of war
prices" added to the trend. The last tariffs on Irish grain imported
to Britain ended in 1806. Across the UK, rents increased. Edward
Elliot, a farmer in Kilkenny, commented that while he had made
money on grain, inflation also drove up his rent "to an extrava-
gant rate." After 1815, tenants had fewer means with which to pay
rents that had increased in wartime. For their part, many landlords
had spent and borrowed freely amidst the prosperous and energetic wartime market for food and other exports. The average farm
got smaller. In 1840, Irish income per person was about two-fifths
of the income in the rest of the United Kingdom—although, as

economic historians point out, basic goods in Ireland were often less expensive than in Britain.[34]

All of the United Kingdom suffered in the postwar era. After Waterloo, tens of thousands of demobilised soldiers and sailors returned to an already reeling labour market. Crime surged. The Treasury had spent nearly £1.7 billion on the wars, roughly six times Britain's total national income in 1793. Government borrowing added to the supply of circulating money. The 1797 Bank Restriction Act allowed the government to issue money without holding specie equivalent to its value, and the supply of paper money grew from roughly £8.6 million in 1797 to £25 million in 1815. The inflation that followed benefited manufacturers, who profited from high prices and cheap credit—but those high prices and low wages led to unrest. In 1821, Lord Liverpool's government allowed the Bank of England to resume cash payments. Prices fell, but bankruptcies followed as loans were pulled underwater. Meanwhile, the population of the United Kingdom grew from about fourteen million to about twenty-seven million people between 1821 and 1841.[35]

Even though high prices benefited Irish as well as British landlords, the economic structures built by the empire meant that wartime debt weighed more heavily on Ireland than Britain. Under the Acts of Union, Britain was to pay 15/17 of the expenses of the fund established to pay down the UK's national debt, and Ireland 2/17. From 1801 to 1816, Great Britain raised roughly £58 million in tax revenue each year. Ireland raised just under £5 million. Great Britain spent an average of £81 million each year, and Ireland roughly £10 million. The rate of revenue to expenditure in Britain, in other words, was 71.6 percent, compared with 49 percent in Ireland, while Britain continued to raise more than 90 percent of the UK's annual revenue. The consequence of the inequalities between the Union partners was that while British debt increased by

50 percent, Irish debt grew by 400 percent. Local taxes in Ireland increased and tax revenue fell as the Irish elite moved to London for the parliamentary year. The taxes paid by gentlemen's clubs in Dublin, for example, fell from £1,324 in 1814 to £255 in 1821 as wealthy Irishmen moved their custom to London.[36]

In 1816, the Union was renegotiated, but Ireland's financial position did not improve. First, the new terms abolished all British taxes that were not equally applied in Ireland. Second, the two countries' interest rates were equalised. The consequence was tax relief in Britain and higher interest rates in Ireland. In 1817, the Irish Treasury was absorbed into the British Treasury; in 1824, all the remaining trade barriers within the United Kingdom dissolved. The switch to a single currency also raised rents since the British pound was nearly 10 percent more valuable than the Irish pound. Meanwhile, the expansion of railroads and the rapid development of steamship technology carried Irish grain more quickly to Britain and Irish cattle and swine directly into British pens and slaughterhouses.[37]

The postwar crash in commodity prices left Ireland "in a more wretched state than any other [country] in Europe," as one farmer put it. The price of wheat fell nearly 125 percent. Farmers who in wartime had been able to sell their pigs at £4. 10s. to the hundredweight could by 1836 fetch only £1. 6s. Overall, the price of produce fell by two-thirds but rent by only a third: land that had rented at £3. 3s. per acre now went for £2. 2s. If Ireland's economy had been more flexible and diversified, falling commodity prices might have encouraged more Irish merchants to import cheaper food and to invest in new industries and new crops. Ireland's cities had some potential as industrial centres. Belfast was a centre of shipbuilding and linen manufacturing. Dublin and Cork both had populations of greater than 100,000 people in 1821, making them two of perhaps two dozen European cities of that size or greater (although they were dwarfed by the more than 1.5 million people in London, by far the largest city in Europe). The Irish economy, however, remained overwhelmingly agricultural. By 1854, out of about 20.2 million total acres in Ireland, nearly 14 million were under cultivation. According to contemporary sources, by the 1840s some 7.6 million people depended on agriculture for their livelihood, compared with about 170,000 people who lived off the proceeds of manufacturing. Historians have revised these numbers slightly upward, but there is no doubt that Irish industry was a far smaller share of the economy than agriculture. Instead, Irish capital tended to leave Ireland, and when it remained in Ireland it often went to steamship companies or industrial food processing—the physical plants that sent agricultural goods to Britain. In Clonmel, for example, new grain mills were "like the great factories . . . which we find in the English manufacturing districts."[38]

Despite falling prices, exports increased. Wheat exports from Ireland to Britain increased from 749 quarters in 1800 to a high of 661,776 quarters in 1835; oats from 2,411 in 1800 to 2,037,835 in 1840. (A quarter equalled sixty-four gallons in volume, or just under five hundred pounds.) By 1845, on the eve of the famine, Ireland each year exported roughly 250,000 head of cattle, 90 million eggs, and enough grain to feed 2 million people in Britain. Ireland supplied Britain with more than 85 percent of its imported grain, meat, butter, and livestock by the 1840s. By the 1820s, experts estimated that more than four-fifths of all Irish grain ended up in British markets. Despite endless demand for Irish products, the size and strength of British trade and banking put Irish merchants at a disadvantage. The British market set prices. Most Irish exports of grain were purchased with English bills of exchange, which could only be redeemed at face value in England. Irish grain traders had to either accept a discounted rate on their bills or else manage their money from London. Irish farmers, starved of credit, spent more to market their goods. In Kerry, for example, many dairy farmers had to transport their wares to market in Cork, seventy miles away, at their own expense. In two baronies in Kerry, the annual losses on the market value of butter were estimated at £40,000. Money paid for Irish goods was less likely to be spent in Ireland. In turn, Irish grain merchants took advantage of the vulnerability of Irish farmers, down-bidding sellers who could not afford to hold back their crops if prices were low.[39]

Furthermore, Irish agriculture generally did not attract significant capital investment. For example, farmers in the United Kingdom relied heavily on fertiliser, especially guano imported from South America. In the mid-nineteenth century, the UK imported between 190,000 and 200,000 tons of guano each year, with annual increases of as much as 20 percent. Almost all these imports were destined for England, Scotland, or Wales; Irish farmers rarely used imported fertiliser. Irish roads and canals were few and poorly maintained, especially outside Dublin and the larger towns. "There is no capital at all," one Irish merchant told a select committee of Parliament. The editors of *The Economist* were dismayed that "the soil of Ireland is cut up into patches" and was overwhelmingly occupied by labourers, rather than by capital-rich farmers in the English style. Irish living standards declined even as exports increased.[40]

Another consequence of the economic pull of the Union was more rapid deindustrialisation in Ireland. *The Economist* blamed protectionist British laws for ending the Irish wool and linen trade "by political force and fraud" and urged rapid investment and industrialisation. In 1815, "John Workman" implored Parliament to preserve some protections for Irish wool, "instead of making our weavers to eat potatoes and salt . . . to feed the weavers of England." Ireland's already unsteady textile industries could not compete with cheaper English products. In Cork, weavers complained

the "Government had taken away their trade by machinery." In
the early 1840s, a land agent noted that from a peak in 1800 of
about five thousand people employed in wool production in Carrick, County Donegal, the trade was now essentially "extinct." In
turn, Irish labourers bought many of their tools from British manufacturers, "the sickle and scythe and spade he works with, and
even his knife."[41]

The system of Irish export agriculture to Britain, like so much
else about the relationship between the islands before and after
the Union, was ramshackle and inefficient, a means of extracting
rent and labour that did not require an overhaul of Ireland's institutions. An official complained that in Ireland, "no man knows
what the produce of his farm is per acre; no such calculations are
made in this country." The oats, wheat, and barley grown in the
country, he continued, "are not considered as food by the people;
they are usually grown as means of payment for rent." Grain,
dairy, and meat, exported copiously, were usually gathered piecemeal by agents who went from farm to farm or by merchants
at fairs. Smaller cattle farmers and the many Irish agricultural
labourers who kept pigs would often sell their animals to itiner-
ant buyers, who would then drive them to Cork, Waterford, or
another port city. Exporters would buy livestock and arrange for
it to be shipped, usually by steamship and then by train, to British wholesalers. Millers bought grain directly from producers,
usually on commission or with bills of exchange. Sellers would
negotiate a minimum price, promising to deliver their grain at a
certain point in the future, and would receive at least the minimum, plus any rise in the price of grain, "a wretched mode, dic-
tated only by want of capital."[42]

By 1835, no more than one-third of Irish labourers had steady
employment. Commodity prices pushed larger tenant farmers
to save on wages by working their own fields. Cattle ranching

required even fewer workers. The consequence was less overall employment. By the 1820s, even more prosperous oat farmers in Ulster barely ate any of their crop. They sold what would have been their surplus, and "scarcely [consumed] any other food than the potato." In Mayo, farmers holding larger leases of ten or more acres, who would have been considered comfortable if not wealthy by their neighbours, ate meat only at Christmas. By the 1830s, Irish tenants were exporting "every grain of wheat and oats, and every pig." If an Irish family slaughtered their own pig, they would sell even the intestines and other offal. William Butler, who held ten acres, told a parliamentary commission in 1836 that he knew other leaseholders who had not eaten even an egg in six months. "We sell them now," he explained.[43]

Without capital and without new industries to absorb a growing population, many parts of Ireland grew poorer, especially in comparison with Britain. Extreme poverty was concentrated in Ireland's more densely populated and less fertile western provinces, Munster and Connaught—an echo of conquest, when the best eastern land was claimed for plantations. Capital flight and the pressures of rent meant that very little new land was developed in the west, even as the population continued to grow. By 1845, 43 percent of the six million acres of uncultivated land in Ireland were in Connaught, where 78 percent of the population farmed potatoes for subsistence, and where 64 percent of all holdings were under five acres. In all of Ireland there were 217 people to every square mile on average, but 386 to the acre in Connaught. Ulster was relatively wealthy by comparison, but many labourers, especially in Counties Armagh, Down, and Antrim, still faced annual food shortages each summer.

Begging became an annual ritual for many families. Carlow, Wicklow, Waterford, and Kilkenny were reputed to have the greatest number of beggars. Most, according to witnesses, were farmers,

not townspeople, "reduced persons" who had fallen into begging
when rents climbed or prices fell, or both. In Kerry, Clare, and
other western counties, many labourers spoke only Irish. As a German traveler wended his way through rural Clare, the children
who surrounded him shouted the only English word they seemed
to know: "ha'penny." A Carlow priest estimated that at least a
hundred people in his parish were beggars by profession, which
he reckoned as a 50 percent increase from 1825 to 1835. Localised
subsistence crises became increasingly common. "A famine," one
writer commented, "was always in Ireland, in a certain degree." In
1817, 1821, and 1822, bad weather harmed potato yields, leading
to localised reports of starvation. A shortage of food in Ireland,
reformer Joseph Lambert wrote, was "more a *famine* in the way of
money, as there was sufficient corn in the country."[44]

The Union had created a single market, but Ireland was still
unknown to many Britons. George IV visited Ireland once, in
1821, the first British monarch to visit since William III invaded
in 1689. Queen Victoria only visited three times in her long reign.
Ireland fascinated visitors; one tourist congratulated himself for
winning the confidence of the most indigent Irish, drinking
moonshine with a farmer or eating potatoes with a cottier, "and
[taking] a turn with him, in digging his turf." The poorest Irish,
he argued, were so unused to seeing their landlords among them
that visitors needed to slum their dress and swallow their sense of
superiority to "really" meet the Irish. Dublin was the hub of at
least thirty coach routes that radiated out around the country. But
Ireland had only seventy miles of railroad track in 1845, compared
with two thousand miles in Britain. Many coaches were in disre-
pair, and along the roads, travellers, especially in summer, were
"everywhere surrounded by a cloud of beggars."[45]

Many Irish people, however, took advantage of the Union to
seek work in the industrial cities of England and Scotland. By

1843, an estimated 120,000 Irish-born people lived in London, along with 40,000 in Manchester, 34,000 in Liverpool, 24,000 in Bristol, and 29,000 in Edinburgh. Desperately poor Irish immigrants were often despised, especially when they competed with English workers for industrial jobs, thus driving down wages. "Ireland," Karl Marx wrote with satisfaction, "has revenged herself upon England . . . by bestowing an Irish quarter on every English industrial, maritime, or commercial town." These waves of poor Irish immigrants cemented the idea of the potato as an emblem of poverty, especially among working people. In Coventry in 1835, striking hand-loom weavers carried placards reading, "Willing to Labour, but doomed to Starve." One placard was decorated with "a net of potatoes and salt." The English journalist and politician William Cobbett noted a decline in the living standards of English agricultural workers after the Union. "What, then," he asked, "do you think that he will come *lower* than to potatoes and salt?"[46]

FOUR DECADES INTO THE UNION, THE UNITED KINGDOM WAS AN industrial power and the world's largest producer of finished cotton textiles, manufactured from imported raw cotton mostly produced by enslaved labour in the United States. In Ireland, however, the poor wore homespun clothes, or else wore used clothing, including battered silk or felt hats, and French dress coats with high collars, "constantly imported from England, where the farmers wear them, but not the labourers." The Irish wore their second- or third-hand British dinner jackets to work their potato grounds, and they "mount[ed] their dunghills in a coarse and tattered ball-dress." English and British colonialism in Ireland in the seventeenth and eighteenth centuries had put the Irish economy at a distinct, and growing, disadvantage within the Union. "There is not a country in the habitable globe that could have existed so long," one Irish correspondent wrote to a British select committee, "as a skeleton whose vitals and blood have been drawn off, as this wretched kingdom; we can stand it no longer."[47]

In 1845 Ireland was on the eve of the famine, and the unity of the United Kingdom was already under duress. In Ireland, the Repeal Association ("Repealers"), founded in 1830 by Daniel O'Connell, advocated for the end of the Union and the restoration of the independent Irish Parliament of the 1780s and 1790s. In Britain, Irish poverty nagged and pulled at government business in nearly every sitting of Parliament. In Britain, as one commentator wrote, with only some exaggeration, "two-thirds of the time of the Imperial Parliament" was taken up with Irish affairs. One writer commented that British officials thought of Ireland not as a partner in the Union but as a "mere useless burden." Thomas Carlyle argued that instead of prosperity, British administration had pushed Ireland into a "perpetual scarcity of third-rate potatoes."[48]

Meanwhile, the products Ireland supplied within the Union burnished the prestige and power of British industry and of the British Empire. Meat, in particular, was a symbol of national wealth. When Smithfield Market, north of St. Paul's Cathedral, was open, tourists would visit to see thousands of cattle, goaded into wide circles, their heads facing outward for inspection by potential buyers, as well as huge pens of pigs and sheep, many of them imported from Irish farms. In the 1840s, England's per capita consumption of animal flesh was roughly 136 pounds per person per year, compared with a per capita average of 80 pounds in Paris and 89 pounds in Brussels. Meat, a political economist argued, was motivation for the British working class—the "greatest spurs to their industry" and the centrepiece of a traditional Sunday roast—and it was delivered by Irish wholesalers. In the warehouses and cellars of Cork food exporters, butter from Kerry was stored in firkins next to "masses of hams and sides of bacon . . . arranged in long rows, like octavo and folio volumes." The Irish poor usually could not afford meat of any quality. "I would like to know," a German travel writer commented, "with what feelings hungry Paddy studies these folios of bacon!"[49]

Ireland had been transformed by a combination of conquest, colonialism, and the accelerating and disruptive power of imperial and industrial capitalism into what some historians and economists have called a "small open economy"—unable to command global commodity prices but at the mercy of their fluctuations. Decades before the blight ravaged potato fields, Ireland was hungry. Demand for Irish agricultural products in the British Empire did not benefit the Irish poor. Instead, as exports boomed after the Union, Irish labourers depended even more profoundly on the generosity of the potato. Paddy was more likely to eat Irish bacon in Kandy than in Killarney. This was the fateful paradox of the Union and of its origins in centuries of violence and colonial adventuring: Irish soldiers fought for an empire abroad that subjugated and colonised them at home. By 1844, some argued that food security was the most important and contentious issue in Irish politics, above civil and religious liberties, above Repeal. To reform Ireland, what was necessary was "a remedy for famine. Yes, *Famine*! . . . Let us cease to rail at Turkish Pachas and Venetian oligarchs. The slaves of those iniquitous powers at least had food."[50]

2

WORKING FOR THE DEAD HORSE

IN 1825 EVELYN JOHN SHIRLEY BROKE GROUND FOR SHIRLEY Castle, a country house in County Monaghan, in southern Ulster. The Shirleys owned more than a tenth of Monaghan. By the later nineteenth century, their Irish estates (the family also held land in England) earned more than £20,750 a year in rent. In purchasing power today, this income would have been worth about £2.5 million. Inflation, however, does not fully capture the scale of the family's Irish wealth. Relative to the average wage in the UK, for example, the rent on the Shirleys' land would be worth about £18.6 million; relative to gross domestic product, it would be worth more than £39.7 million. These were the wages of distant conquest: Evelyn Shirley's ancestor Walter Devereux, the first Earl of Essex, had been deeded the land as a reward for service in the English campaigns in Ulster during the reign of Elizabeth I. Shirley Castle was built in a fashionable neo-Elizabethan style, with square towers topped with steeply gabled roofs. It evoked a world before the pace and pollution of the nineteenth century. Its walls were made of local stone. In the great hall, the family tree was depicted in stained glass. Portraits and pastoral scenes, including pieces by Velázquez and the Dutch old masters, hung on the walls.[1]

Beyond the castle grounds, however, Shirley's tenants lived at the mercy of the modern market. In the 1840s, an Irish family led by a man who was paid the average wage of about sixpence a day, augmented by small sums earned by his family for spinning wool and odd jobs, earned about £12 a year. In 1843, a fall in the prices for beef, pork, oats, and potatoes left many tenants in arrears on rent payments. When one tenant, Patrick Garvey, fell behind, Shirley's agent sued him, and Garvey forfeited his pig and her six piglets. The value of the seized animals did not cover what he owed. "They are cheap now," he explained. "I have no means in the world to live." Out of money, he bought seed potatoes on credit, at nearly twice the usual price. Many other tenants borrowed recklessly to hold off eviction. They asked for a discount on rent. Shirley refused. His rents were reasonable, he replied, set by the market. He did not control demand for land, nor the price of crops and livestock. "The present distress," he wrote, in a printed notice tacked up at his agent's office, "has not been caused . . . by high rents."[2]

Shirley Castle was expensive and new but designed to look old. Shirley was a modern businessman who pursued his debtors in court, watched the markets, and minded his bottom line. The lives of his tenants were similarly deceptive. Their world looked rustic and ancient but was saturated with very modern risks. The Irish poor made complex wagers on their rent and potato yields, hoping to find a marginal advantage. They knew that changes in a day's trading price of crops and livestock in London might ruin them.

They were not rooted but highly mobile, crisscrossing the United Kingdom every summer, looking for work. Irish farmers grew crops with little technology according to a venerable agricultural calendar but sold them in a fast-moving market that was acutely vulnerable to price shocks. British reformers, however, struggled to see Irish poverty clearly. As England reformed its own poor-relief system in the 1830s, British policymakers and political economists confidently diagnosed that the cause of Ireland's poverty was the inherent violence and indolence of the Irish poor, and they prescribed greater exposure to market risks to treat the symptoms.[3]

THE IRISH MARKET FOR RENTED LAND WAS CRITICAL TO THE Irish poor, who depended on access to potato ground to survive from season to season amid the rigours of an extractive imperial system of export crops and rent collection. Irish land use seemed obdurately sluggish and backward to political economists but was in reality fast, competitive, and modern. Irish landlords such as Shirley sat at the top of a pyramid, its bricks mortared together by rent. "Ireland," one historian writes, "could be described as a nation of landlords." The men at the top leased to farmers, generally through an agent. Agents further divided the land they leased, and rented smaller parcels to cottiers, who occupied rented land year-round. Agents and farmers also offered even smaller plots of land (as small as a half or quarter acre) conacre, through informal leases of ten or eleven months. Conacre (from "corn acre," but also called mock ground, dairy land, quarter land, and rood land, among other names) allowed landlords to hire seasonal labourers just in time for the harvest. In exchange, labourers taking conacre could grow enough potatoes to feed their families. It was an unequal bargain, an improvisation that kept farmers without capital from bankruptcy and labourers without adequate wages from starvation. Conacre potatoes were also the lifeline of landless labourers, sometimes called *spailpíní* in Irish (anglicised as "spalpeens"), those unable to afford conacre and forced to rent a cottage alone, or else to beg or squat. By 1845, some 2.1 million tons of potatoes, up to 75 percent of the food eaten by landless Irish labourers, were grown conacre.[4]

In the Victorian era, a very small number of people owned the United Kingdom. Just under four thousand people owned nearly 80 percent of Irish land, under two thousand owned 93 percent of Scotland, about five thousand owned more than half of England, and seven hundred held 60 percent of Wales. These large landlords generally rented their land to farmers with capital. An English "farmer" had capital to make improvements to his land, rented hundreds of acres, and employed labourers to work them. In Ireland, the average farm was orders of magnitude smaller—fifty or a hundred acres was a large farm. A tenant farmer in England might pay anywhere from one-sixth to one-quarter of the value of his crop in rent, or from one-third to two-fifths of the value of his livestock. In Ireland, rent often equalled the entire value of a farm's saleable produce. It made economic sense to subdivide land; without capital to achieve an economy of scale, most Irish farmers were pushed into what was in effect a kind of Ponzi scheme, relying on a downline of tenants to pay their own landlord, and making up any shortfalls with the sale of a pig or two each season.[5]

The market for rented land in Ireland accelerated the subdivision of farms into smaller and smaller plots. In 1845, out of the 1.6 million people counted in the census as farmers or farm labourers, some 505,000 leased plots of less than ten acres. Only 70,441 held farms larger than fifty acres, and usually not much larger. More than 650,000 labourers were not counted as landholders because they only held land in conacre. Including their dependents, as many as 2.7 million people—or more than a quarter of the Irish population—were landless, seeking conacre when they could. The poorer the province, the more intense the subdivision. In Munster, in Counties Limerick and Clare, as much as one-third of the rural population lived on a half acre or less of potato land. By 1847, in Connaught, out of an estimated 46,000 farms in the province, at least 44,000 were smaller than fifteen acres. A family of five in Cork might pay an average of fourpence (4d.) for a standard weight of potatoes, equal to twenty-one pounds. When work was available in the county, the highest average daily wage was tenpence (10d.). Potatoes were cheap—but not *that* cheap. If a family could afford conacre, it made sense to grow, rather than buy, potatoes.[6]

Middlemen, despised by Irish tenants, profited by dealing in rented land. Small middlemen were considered especially vicious because they were closest to destitution themselves, "the most barbarous class of landlords who can be described." Middlemen with larger holdings leased land for up to twelve years. They would usually farm some of their acres and would ask double the rent they paid to their landlords from their tenants. The largest middlemen were "land-jobbers" who usually held long leases and generally did not live on the land they controlled. They were speculators, and their returns could be astonishing. An Irish barrister and landowner met a cottier holding three acres whose neighbours claimed (probably with some jealous exaggeration) that he had made £400 (roughly £42,100 in today's money, measured by purchasing power, or about £377,000 relative to the average present-day wage in the United Kingdom) speculating on conacre land.[7]

It is cheap to be rich and expensive to be poor. Conacre and cottage rents were small in real terms but proportionately much greater than the rents of large farms. For example, farmers who rented two hundred acres at one pound per acre per year might sublet individual acre plots at double the price. Poverty and capital flight created other hazards. In England, farmers and their landlords might pool capital to make improvements to land, or a farmer who spent capital on, say, new equipment might receive discounted rent in exchange. In Ireland, land was almost always rented "soil only," without consideration of out-buildings or machinery. As such, if a tenant improved his land, his rent might increase. One tenant told a curious gentleman that he did not even bother to whitewash his cottage. The land-lord's agent might see it from his carriage and "think the bailiff gave him wrong information about the value, and that he had it too cheap." A farmer in Skibbereen let his pigs sleep in his cottage, rather than build a pigsty, to avoid a rent hike. Only in Ulster, where a system called "tenant right" allowed some renters to sell the improvements they made on rented land to other ten-ants when vacating a lease, were there any provisions for allowing renters to improve land without being penalised.[8]

Ireland's ruthless and competitive market for rented land was rooted in the extractive principles of colonialism. Irish labourers lived under the steadily mounting pressures of population growth and the demands of the British market for grain and meat. Rather than being distant from the United Kingdom, the Irish land mar-ket was exposed both to fluctuating commodity prices and to the business cycle. In periods of economic crisis, as in 1816–1817 and 1821–1822, up to half of Irish middlemen went bankrupt. In 1844, during a global economic depression, the number of farm-ers claiming protection under the Insolvency Act at court sittings in Castlebar, County Mayo, went from the usual rate of about twenty to more than ninety. Smaller farmers were hit the hardest. Observers estimated that 90 percent or more of insolvency claim-ants were farmers holding under ten acres, many without a for-mal lease. Some landlords used insolvency proceedings to evict their tenants, refusing to discharge their debts until they received written agreements that the tenants would leave their land and house, sometimes within a week.[9]

The lack of capital and the small average size of Irish farms also meant that most farmers could not afford to hold back their goods to wait for better prices when the market was poor. Instead, most needed to export more to make up the difference. As goods flooded the market, prices fell yet further, requiring still more exports. In 1842, the United States raised tariffs, and British investors and manufacturers panicked. Workers across the United Kingdom were laid off as production sagged. In Ireland, cottiers rushed to sell their pigs and found a weak market. The courts were full of disputes between tenants and landlords, who often sought redress when their tenants dug up their potatoes before paying rent. "I do not know which is worse for the poor farmer," a Roscommon labourer wondered, "the fall or the rise; when the market tumbles, where is the rent; and when the price gets up in a hurry, where is the food."[10]

Changes in the British market were felt most acutely by labourers taking conacre and by the landless. In 1828, landlords offering land for thirty shillings found that competition among tenants bid up the final price more than 25 percent, to three pounds, even as the local price of pigs had fallen 75 percent, sheep 50 percent, and cattle 20 percent. By the 1840s, more and more conacre rent was demanded in advance as tenants hedged against these rising prices. "Speculators," one farmer complained, "sell the poor man the very potatoes from his ground." By 1835, the average conacre crop of potatoes would sell for about ten shillings more than the total cost of rent, seed, and expenses—a tiny profit on a razor-thin margin. For a conacre farmer, a bumper crop of potatoes would *lower* prices, rendering the crop worth less than the rent. Consequently, subtenants tormented by the actions of speculators in land, rent, and potatoes had to speculate themselves, betting each growing season on whether their crops, animals, or labour would be the most valuable in order to secure land for the next season.[11]

Inevitably, many tenants and labourers taking conacre fell behind on payments. Some were threatened with eviction, a proceeding that would only very rarely remove a single tenant. The pyramid of rent meant every evicted family would pull with it a network of subtenants, as well as extended family and friends holding land in informal arrangements. In evictions filed between 1837 and 1842, a single court order might remove as many as forty or more people from leased land. Evicted tenants who refused to leave might be threatened or beaten. In Glendermott, County Derry, a farmer renting a dozen acres was ordered off his farm. Bailiffs arrived armed and began throwing furniture out of the farmhouse. One bailiff held a pistol to the farmer's head as his men pulled down the rest of the cottage and set it on fire. In County Kildare, a physician found a recently evicted family living in a ditch on a hillside. The ditch formed one "wall" and a thick pad of thatch formed the other. When the wind changed directions, the family would move the wall. They could not cover the shelter. A roof would attract the bailiffs.[12]

Eviction was fearsome, but for smaller landlords eviction proceedings could be a gamble. A more vulnerable landlord with his own landlord to pay needed cash far more than he needed a tenant removed. Many evictions were served with a notice from the bailiffs stating that "it was not the intention of the party bringing it to get actual possession . . . but to enter upon the receipt of the rents." Eviction could be a tool to clear land, but it could also be a shakedown. And eviction was not the only legal tool that landlords could use when tenants fell behind. A tenant behind on rent could also be declared to be in "distress" and have their goods distrained—that is, seized and sold—to make his creditor whole. Distrainment was nearly as humiliating as eviction. Landlords would hire keepers, who lived on the land or even in the houses of the people being processed, to make sure that tenants did not damage or sell any household goods or furniture before the distrainment was processed. Distrained livestock would be impounded and would usually lose weight and, along with it, market value. Tenants whose property was distrained could appeal, but the process took months and the necessary fees could cost more than three times the average annual profit on conacre.[13]

The constant pursuit of land, work, and cash eroded ties of solidarity among rural labourers. In some parts of Ireland, farm labourers gathered at fairs held twice a year, in May and November, where farmers could look them over in a proceeding "much like selling cattle or slaves," as one person remembered it. There were some reports of men refusing to work at harvest time for less than a shilling a day, but as one farmer put it, "anything like a regular combination among labourers does not exist here." In Irish towns, however, skilled labourers were often organised into guilds. In 1838, Daniel O'Connell, at an "ungovernably furious meeting" at the Dublin Royal Exchange, to boos and hisses, condemned tradesmen who wanted to limit the number of apprentices they took on as "combinators . . . bound by an unholy tie." Some Dubliners complained that even the porters at the quays enforced regulated prices. In Bandon, in County Cork, weavers who refused to adhere to the informal rules of wage rates and pricing might have the linen they were weaving doused with acid. In Dublin, the Board of Green Cloth regulated nearly twenty trades. In Limerick, master masons and slaters earned as much as £1 2s. 9d. per week.[14]

But Irish towns with relatively organised skilled labour were not invulnerable to the economic changes that followed Ireland's integration into the United Kingdom. Ireland's industries were dwarfed by Britain's enormous manufacturing sector. The Bandon weavers, like other skilled workers, preserved high wages with threats while there was a market for handloomed thread and cloth, but they could not compete with power looms. In Dublin between 1815 and 1836, wages in skilled trades where machinery could be used for manufacturing fell 50 percent. Relatively well-paid urban workers got poorer, just like rural workers. Free trade within the United Kingdom did lower prices, but prices fell far less than wages. For example, the cost of basic provisions like bread, tea, sugar, and potatoes fell 30 percent, and meat less than 10 percent. As manufacturing declined, much Irish industrial activity centred on preparing, packaging, or shipping food. This was a boon for townspeople, but it was seasonal. Many mills, docks, slaughterhouses, and other processing facilities followed the same calendar as Irish farms and remained open only from September to April. In Limerick, roughly eleven thousand people depended on income from this seasonal labour. The consequence was that poverty in the towns could be as extreme as in the deep countryside. Rooms thirteen feet square were rented to as many as eighteen or twenty people, who slept in shifts. Entrepreneurial urban workers might rent a room for a shilling and tenpence and then sublet the corners of the rooms to four families for fivepence each.[15]

The pressure of rent forced even the very poor into speculation. An Irish labourer without a canny awareness of the market—and without the foresight to make good bets on the fluctuating costs of food, shelter, and basic goods in relation to the size of a potato harvest or the value of a fat piglet—would slide further down the pyramid. There was no safety net to speak of, and in any case the game was rigged: the market could only get riskier with each year as market demand, population growth, and land subdivision continued. The consequence was a market that made nearly everyone poorer, their livelihood more precarious, their environment more enervated. Even an Irish farmer who could afford to rent a large farm for £2,000 a year—proof of prosperity in Britain—might live in a house without a gate, fence, or stables for cattle or horses, next to "a very indifferent garden, with nothing in it but cabbages." A farmer in County Wexford complained that farmers holding as much as fifty acres of land sold their better potatoes "to pay their rent, and of course they cannot afford to eat them." Some Irish labourers jokingly called the principal tenant's house "the mansion," but as one writer commented, it was only a mansion in comparison with "a hole dug in the bog."[16]

IN ADDITION TO BEING A "NATION OF LANDLORDS"—OR BECAUSE of it—Ireland was also a nation of debtors. And like the market for rent, the market for credit in Ireland before the famine was strikingly modern: fast-paced, expensive, and unforgiving. According to one estimate, most of the roughly £13.5 million in rent earned on Irish land in the 1840s went to service debt, both arrears of rent and advances on food and seed. To avoid distrainment or eviction, tenants would borrow money or sell their crops at a loss. Some dug their potatoes in July to sell immediately, losing up to four times the yield they might have sold in September. Others sold cows or oatmeal for half their value. In parts of County Mayo, tenants owing as much as five pounds in back rent had only rags to wear, and borrowed clothing from relatives and neighbours when they went to market. A tenant farmer considered rich by his neighbours told a journalist that he had never eaten bread, and rarely ate butter. He ate only pork so diseased as to be unsalable.[17]

Most Irish debts were reckoned in money, but few were paid in cash. What circulating cash there was tended to flow up, in payments to landlords and larger merchants. This had two consequences. First, it reinforced the power of landlords. From the top of the pyramid, they commanded not only the flow of rent but also the lion's share of hard currency. Second, it meant that people without cash needed to pay their debts with labour, land, or crops. This added another layer of complexity and precarity to the economic life of the Irish poor, whose "money" did not have a stable monetary value but had to be negotiated, and could depreciate or appreciate in response to signals from the market. A landlord owed twenty pounds expected coins or bills of exchange equalling that amount. A farmer making a deal for conacre land in exchange for a crop of potatoes would need to negotiate both over price and over the cash value of the goods they proposed to trade instead of coins or notes.

Informal credit arrangements were ubiquitous. When two farmers made a trade of items of unequal value, the difference in price, reckoned in cash, was called the "boot." Articles bought on credit from a store were bought "on tick." Animals bought at auction were "canted" and usually paid for with some money up front, called "earnest," with the rest to be paid later. Because cash did not usually circulate widely, many had to borrow when they needed hard currency. Oatmeal and potatoes were advanced on credit for as much as 80 percent interest; "the poorer the man the higher the interest." Middlemen and land agents made loans at rates as high as 60 percent per annum. Banks charged much less, about 12 percent, but only served a small tranche of Irish society, including larger farmers and professionals. Village loan sharks usually charged five shillings to the pound per year, or 25 percent. In 1822, to make credit more accessible, the government organised the Irish Reproductive Loan Fund and Central Loan Fund. But even the loan funds mirrored the pyramid structure of Irish rent. The central fund loaned out £40,000 to county trustees at 2 percent interest. The trustees loaned out units of £100 to parish subcommittees, who doled out £10 loans to farmers, payable weekly, monthly, or quarterly, at 4d. annual interest to the pound.[18]

The loan fund, for larger farmers, could be stabilising. Analyses by economic historians show that farmers who used the loan fund fared better during the Great Famine than those who did not. However, the fund was inaccessible to most. Most borrowers were required to pay back the principal in weekly cash installments, which excluded cash-poor farmers (who would need to borrow at ruinous interest in order to service the interest they already owed on their debts). Moreover, lenders usually required a letter of recommendation that attested to the borrower's good credit—a written proof of respectability and past prudence that also excluded many farmers. As a County Derry labourer, John Dermott, explained, even applicants with the means to appeal to the loan fund often used it to raise cash quickly. It took three days to apply—one to file, one for the committee to read the application, and one for the committee to pay out. Canny traders rented rooms in towns on days when the loan committees met, selling seeds and other goods to people whom they knew would soon be flush.[19]

Thus, although it was often paid in cash, rent was necessarily and deeply entangled in the web of informal credit. Irish rent was usually collected twice annually; some called collecting rent the "gale," likening it to a wind that shook their cottages and fields. Generally, landlords employed "drivers" to collect on their behalf or to serve eviction notices. An incoming gale created markets for coins and notes, as farmers scrambled to realise as much liquidity from their crops and creditors as possible. Predatory "gombeen" men (from an archaic Irish word for usury) would charge high interest on cash advances and purchases of grain, sugar, and other everyday items. The pressure to make payments also forced Irish farmers to rush to market. Dairy farmers sold butter below cost or sold low-quality "boxy" butter to make their milk stretch further.

Cattle were sometimes put up as collateral for their own fodder. Livestock were often sold at auctions held at fairs, where potential buyers would bid on cows or pigs and then borrow money to pay for them; folktales praised canny farmers who bought an animal and then turned around and auctioned it off again at a higher price. Enterprising tenants with ready cash to spare would buy oatmeal when prices fell and hold on to it to sell "on time" at a markup. They mortgaged the future to survive the present.[20]

In County Kildare, labourers called this cycle "working for the dead horse." To stay ahead of debts, and ideally to earn hard currency, many labourers and tenants looked for wage work anywhere they could find it. When roads or other public works were in the offing, an Irish engineer remarked, "every man runs to the contractor to get his name put upon the list." Irish agricultural wages were less than a third of what labourers were paid in Scotland and the North of England (although the cost of food in Ireland was significantly less). Labour for public works paid a reliable wage regardless of the season, while the wages for agricultural work rose and fell. In County Armagh, a day's labour in the late summer and autumn was worth a shilling; in the winter, a day paid tenpence. Outside Ulster, off-season wages were even lower, generally no more than sixpence a day. In some of the poorest parts of Ireland, there was hardly any work at all. In the 1830s, in the parish of Kilgeever, County Mayo, among about eleven thousand residents, there was, according to a parliamentary report, "no class of independent labourers, no employers of labour." At most, local farmers only needed thirty days of farm labour throughout the year that could be offset against rent. Some local labourers would work for as little as twopence a day, provided they also received potatoes.[21]

As with the rent economy, servicing debt required constant attention, calculation, and risk-taking. Workers with debts outstanding would do anything they could to turn over their credit

for another year. When rent was in arrears, landlords could file a
motion to evict a tenant—or they could secure a season or more of
labour at a very low price. In Kildare, a police constable overheard a
farmer settling his annual accounts. All thirteen men he employed
were in his debt, partly for rent but mostly for food advanced on
credit. The labourers took a very low wage but seemed "very well
pleased at it, as it ensured them work during the winter." Even in
Ulster, contractors rarely had ready money to pay casual labourers.
Instead, they bought food with credit—"their labour is thus anticipated, and they are never out of debt."[22]

THE POOREST LABOURERS IN RURAL IRELAND IN THE ERA
between the Union and the beginning of the Great Famine coped
with a pressurised market for rented land, and with a complex,
volatile system of debt. A landless labourer was an expert in arbitrage by necessity, speculating on the cost of rent, the market rate
for labour, and the price of potatoes to survive from season to season. The deep connections between the Irish economy and metropolitan Britain, made by conquest and colonialism and cemented
by the Union, transmitted the destructive, energetic force of
imperial capitalism into the Irish countryside. Subdivided land
and overheated rents were prime evidence of the necessary toler-
ance for speed and risk that the market imposed on the poor. But
many British critics and reformers could not see the Irish economy
clearly. They saw stagnation, atavism, and backwardness in the
Irish countryside. For example, a letter to the *Times* attributed the
subdivision of land to "the ancient division of Ireland into septs or
families" that had made "almost every Irishman feel himself entitled to hold some portion of the soil."[23]

The depths of Ireland's poverty, its lack of industrial activity and
overwhelmingly agricultural character, its alien Catholic majority,

and the strangeness of terminology such as "cottier," "conacre," and "spalpeen" made Ireland seem distant and anachronistic to many Britons. "Cottier," for example, was an archaic term, referring to peasants in medieval Germany and Scotland. Conacre seemed to many British political economists like a transitional stage between serfdom and wage labour, a phase in the development of civilisation through which Britain had already passed. The complexity and urgency of the Irish economy was flattened, for many, into a caricature of Paddy clinging to his potato, to his great detriment.[24]

The Irish economy had features that seemed to orthodox political economists to prove that Ireland had to be at a different stage of civilisation than Britain. The absence of ample circulating cash was considered especially significant. The transactions counted in money and paid in goods, land, or labour that made it possible for the Irish market to function were interpreted as barter. It was axiomatic for political economy that barter was the most primitive form of commerce. In *Wealth of Nations*, Adam Smith argued that societies evolved from barter through progressively more sophisticated and civilised media of exchange, eventually buying and selling with coined money and paper that represented its value. As Smith saw it, societies that did not use coined money—including, among others, eighteenth-century Abyssinia, where salt was the medium of exchange; societies around the Indian Ocean that used cowrie shells; and even Europe's American colonies, which used "dried cod at Newfoundland; tobacco in Virginia; sugar in some of our West India colonies"—lagged behind. A mature capitalist market economy, he insisted, proved its level of civilisation by the degree to which it used money, rather than goods, as a medium of exchange.[25]

However, the idea that economies evolved from barter to money to credit is a myth. There is no historical or anthropological evidence of any primordial barter economy. After the collapse of the

Roman empire, for example, Europe did not "revert to barter." Rather, credit, measured in nominal units of money but paid for with goods judged to be equal to that amount of money, allowed people to continue to trade when coins were rare. The absence of circulating cash was evidence not of economic backwardness but of something much more obvious: economies that used little circulating money did so because there was little money in circulation. Ireland had scant cash because the structure of the imperial economy hoovered hard currency up from the countryside. However, when seen through the lens of the conventional theory of civilisation, the tendency of the Irish poor to pay debts without cash was taken as proof that Ireland was an anachronistic exception to British capitalism.[26]

Potatoes also played a role in distorting British understanding of the Irish economy. Potato dependence was an adaptation to the demands of the market, but it seemed to many Britons to be evidence of a bloody-minded refusal of the benefits of civilisation. Potatoes did not require an extensive division of labour to grow, harvest, or prepare. Sluggish Ireland, wrote a journalist for the *Manchester Guardian*, was a warning to Britain—a premonition of what might happen if "our great seats of manufacturing industry were 'swept from the map.'" The association between potatoes, poverty, backwardness, and subjugation was as much in currency among British workers as among British theorists. If potatoes spread in England, the journalist and politician William Cobbett wrote, they would drag "English labourers down to the state of the Irish." Bread required a complex division of labour to produce, while the potato required only "lifting . . . food . . . out of the earth."[27]

Ireland was visibly and obviously poor. British critics contended that Irish poverty was old-fashioned in ways that confirmed prevailing theories of economic and civilisational development. The

Irish poor, in theory the subjects of the modern United Kingdom, appeared to live slower, simpler, less civilised lives than British workers. Ireland, it seemed, was standing still while the rest of the United Kingdom rushed forward. Perhaps it took an outsider to see things clearly. Johann Kohl, a German and the author of a widely read travelogue of a trip to Ireland before the famine, had never seen anything like Irish poverty. He travelled across the Baltic and Scandinavia, where people were poor and potatoes were a staple. But the Irish differed from the Latvian, Estonian, and Finnish peasants Kohl had encountered because their poverty seemed not ancient but *new*. The Irish lived in small, cold, wet cabins, "one shovelful of earth heaped upon another," covered with turf on the roof and with a single square hole for the door. Irish hovels were not a traditional form of peasant housing. The Irish weren't serfs living according to old traditions. Irish labourers had no national dress, no institutions of peasant life that could contest the power of their landlords, no "order or method." They weren't from the past. In Ireland, Kohl wrote, "there nowhere exists, an old fixed form in anything."[28]

IN ADDITION TO IRELAND'S VISIBLE POVERTY, ITS LACK OF CIRCU-lating money, and its potato dependence, the violence of the Irish countryside struck many British observers as evidence of barbarism. The hopeful literature of improvement produced in and about Ireland just after the Union had promised to extinguish the spectre of "poverty-stricken demoniacs" surrounding a magistrate, "with black eyes, and faces grimed with blood." When outrages continued long after the Union, they seemed to prove that there was something intractable and feral about the Irish poor. And yet rural outrages also had a role to play in the Irish rural economy. Violence was among the only tools available to most Irish tenants that could temporarily check the otherwise inexorable force of the market. Rural crime often followed the rent market; outrages were "dependent on distant market forces," as one historian describes. For example, butchers were threatened with "fire and destruction" if they took contracts to supply British garrisons in Ireland rather than Irish consumers, and rent increases could sometimes be slowed with threats. In County Tipperary, farmers were threatened with death if they sold barrels of potatoes for more than six shillings.[29]

Many counties had informal rules and norms relating to rent and land tenure that tenants and landless labourers fought to preserve. In Kilkenny, a land agent explained, "There is a general understanding that the man who charges more than £8 is a bad fellow, and ought to be punished in some way." In Killaloe, County Clare, agrarian violence in the 1820s was directed at landowners who converted their tilled land to pasture, reducing the availability of conacre. Most Irish tenants refused to speak to police. People who did give testimony against their neighbours would sometimes be imprisoned for their own safety. In consequence, many offenders were never captured, and many who were captured were never convicted. In 1844, all seven people tried for setting fire to crops were acquitted, as well as seventy-nine of ninety-two people accused of murder.[30]

Rural outrages were very often overtly directed toward preventing changes in patterns of cultivation, evictions, or rent increases. In Armagh, Lord Gosford owned more than twelve thousand acres, worth more than £13,000 a year in rent. In 1829, an engineer named William Armstrong bid for the tenancy of one of the farms on Gosford's land. Armstrong evicted a man named Michael Garvey and his sons in order to rent to a new subtenant. The subtenant was beaten bloody in midday. Armstrong also hired local men to clear boulders from the land he had leased. When

the work was done, Armstrong laid off all but five of the workers. Soon after, two hundred trees in Armstrong's orchard were
destroyed; a few months later, Armstrong discovered that the posts
of the gates and fences around his land had been smashed with
sledgehammers. On Easter Monday 1832, Armstrong's new tenant
was assaulted again.[31]

An infamous series of murders in County Longford offers
another example. Lord Lorton, the head of a distinguished
Anglo-Irish family, owned nearly seventy-three thousand acres
of Irish land, spread over several counties and worth more than
£40,000 a year in rent. In 1835, a surveyor working on Lorton's
estate discovered that parcels of land leased to two tenants had
been subdivided among at least thirty other families. Lorton asked
his agent to offer each family £20 as a premium to emigrate to the
United States, as well as the right to sell whatever crops they had
already planted, a privilege called the "fall of the house." In May,
a man named Brock, a Protestant from Ulster, leased thirty-five
acres from Lorton and his agents. A few days later he was shot
dead. Brock's widow said she saw the killer running away across
the fields. A crowd that had gathered near the body refused to pur-
sue them and barred her from going to the police. The next tenant
who tried to lease the land was beaten so badly on his way back
from the pub that "he never did any good afterwards." The next
tenant, named Moorhead, was also murdered, as were two of Lord
Lorton's bailiffs. None of the murders were solved. Even if few
were themselves willing to kill, many sympathised with those who
were willing to commit murder to stall an eviction, and most
feared revenge for cooperating with police.[32]

Along with changes to land use and threats of eviction, hunger
often provoked outrages. In 1834, in County Mayo, when potatoes were scarce and expensive, armed bands set out at night in
Erris to raid the homes of people rumoured to be hoarding food.

The chief constable of the police, William Meredith, could not conceal his sympathy with the perpetrators. "I knew nothing of the destitution which prevailed," he wrote. In the fifteen houses Meredith and his men searched, they found little more than a few boxes of potatoes, bottles of sour milk, and tattered "dress" clothes. Groping against the walls of one cottage by lamplight, a constable accidentally pushed his hand through a bundle of weeds lashed together with twine—a makeshift door. The officer could not fit through the doorway with his hat and cloak on. The police found their suspect inside, with his pregnant wife, "to be perhaps transported for an offence to which it was evident the fear of starvation had prompted him."[33]

The most feared rural outrages were the guerrilla campaigns organised by armed secret societies, of which there were many in Irish history—Whiteboys, Whitefeet, Ribbonmen, Rockites, Hearts of Steel, and others. Protected by oaths of silence and by the combination of fear and admiration they inspired, secret societies were very difficult to prosecute. Court documents revealed that the Whitefoot society swore never to speak to the police, "to wade knee-deep in Orange blood," and to "cut down kings, queens, and princes, dukes, earls, lords, and all such." The societies enforced the unofficial norms and standards of land distribution and rent—but often by terrorising and intimidating ordinary farmers.[34]

In response to the putatively uncivilised violence of the Irish countryside, the United Kingdom established its most advanced and "modern" police force, an early model for policing in Britain. Dublin had had organised police from the mid-1780s, but after the Union, the 1814 Peace Preservation Act and 1822 Irish Constabulary Act created a national force with offices in each of the four Irish provinces under central control from Dublin Castle (Robert Peel was chief secretary for Ireland for the first act and home secretary for the second; not for nothing was he identified with the "Peelers"). Under the 1814 act, the constabulary could be increased as needed with "peace preservation" paramilitaries appointed and armed by the lord lieutenant. In 1836, the Police Act created a single police force for Ireland, which had some nine thousand officers by 1845. The Irish Constabulary were large and well organised by UK standards. The principle of the liberty of the subject made most policing and prosecution a private matter in Britain, and especially in England. The Metropolitan Police were founded seven years after the constabulary and took decades to become a national force, while the constabulary was national from the outset.[35]

It might be tempting to romanticise Irish workers fighting tragic wars against their landlords. "Masses of men will almost feel that a certain amount of injustice ought to be inflicted on their betters," Anthony Trollope wrote in *The Way We Live Now*, "because the crime committed has had a tendency to oppress the rich and pull down the mighty from their seat." The men at the top of the pyramid certainly did not "deserve" their estates—many had the simple good luck of being descended from one of Cromwell's or William III's soldiers. But many accounts of agrarian crime in the archives show that the weak were punished far more than the strong by armed bands fighting in defence of customary tenancies, prices, or rents. Many more of the luckless seeking conacre were beaten than landlords or tenants; many more cottages than mansions were burned. Rural outrages might have sometimes deterred landlords from raising rent or offering conacre at higher prices in the short term, but the poor were at a permanent and structural disadvantage. To control the rate of rent or to stop evictions, outrages needed to succeed every single time. A landlord only needed to win once to set a new floor for rent or a new standard wage for employment, thereby permanently changing the economic landscape on the land he owned or leased.[36]

RURAL OUTRAGES SEEMED TO BRITISH OFFICIALS LIKE RUPTURES of sudden and frantic action in an otherwise listless countryside. Reformers sometimes complained that the Irish faced their predicament with fatalism and resignation rather than with an ambition to improve their station. This was consistent with the assumption, important to the way in which many Britons imagined Ireland and Irishness, that the Irish poor were in torpor, their bodies fed by potatoes and their minds by treason, conspiracy, and rustic superstitions. The Irish, in this worldview, were stubbornly rooted and earthy, resentful of British energy, and resistant to change. And yet almost every summer an Ireland emptied by the market of money and crops also ran out of potatoes, and suddenly "the whole country appeared to be in motion." Many men left their families and travelled to England to take in the grain harvest, returning to Ireland to bring in potatoes in October and November. Many women and children left their home villages or townlands and wandered to other counties to beg.[37]

The calculations that the poor applied to paying rent and managing debt were also useful in managing potato crops. In the summer, work was scarce, wages were low, and prices were high. When the potato crop failed in 1831, for example, the price of a stone of potatoes quadrupled between Christmas and the summer months. Even shrivelled potatoes bought in December sold for many times their winter price in July. Many conacre tenants could not afford to buy seed potatoes. When a potato crop failed, even long before the Great Famine, many faced starvation. Hunger, however, was only rarely the cause of death. Typhus and other louse-born diseases surged, and the Irish—especially children—suffered from disfiguring, agonising metabolic illnesses, including scurvy, kwashiorkor, and "famine blindness," or xerophthalmia.[38]

There were hungry years in Ireland, but the pressure of the Irish rural economy meant that for many, every summer was a hungry season. Most Irish farmers stored potatoes harvested in the autumn in pits dug in the ground and covered with dirt and straw, which they broke open as needed. In the spring they planted new seed potatoes. By the summer, the pits were empty. Some estimated that even in years of good harvest, as much as one-fifth of the population lived on the edge of famine during the summer months. As potatoes ran low, some would begin to ask for them boiled with a "bone" or "moon" left in the middle—that is, half cooked. Many believed that the "bone" took longer to digest, making it two meals in one. The chronic threat of hunger was also reflected in the ghost stories the poor told to each other when potatoes were plentiful. Irish folklore told of the *fear gorta*, the "hunger man," an emaciated ghost that roamed from house to house in times of famine, giving good luck to anyone able to give alms. Other stories claimed the *fear gorta* caused an unappeasable hunger in unlucky travelers walking in remote bogs and mountains.[39]

The midsummer countryside sometimes foreshadowed the horrors of the Great Famine. In the King's County (now County Offaly), a parish priest called on unfurnished cabins where families of six or seven slept under a single blanket and survived by "spuddling," searching cleared potato fields for overlooked tubers. In 1836, a constable saw many bodies buried in shallow graves, without coffins. In the towns, the poor clamoured outside the doors of fine houses, begging for table scraps. Urban workers rioted or attacked mills and bakeries. In rural areas, the poor foraged for roots and leaves; some attributed the diarrhea chronic among many Irish children to eating the ground-cover plants similar to kale that grew as weeds in fields of oats. In the backcountry of County Mayo, labourers would bleed cattle and boil the blood into paste. Others vowed to "kill their hunger with water" by drinking as much of it as they could. Near the coasts, people without boats or fishing gear—equipment that was often pawned in times of hardship—scraped barnacles off rocks or collected washed-up fish from beaches. In Cork, in 1831, a witness saw women, their bodies turned away in shame, gobbling the rotted stumps of cut cabbages refused by the pigs and chickens.[40]

Summer was the begging season. Because begging was considered shameful, most Irish people who needed to beg left their homes so they would not be recognised by neighbours. In County Kildare, many beggars seemed to be from counties in Connaught, nearly two hundred kilometres away. In Tracton, County Cork, as many as two hundred beggars passed through the tiny village between the beginning of summer and the potato harvest. The roads, a workhouse medical officer remembered, were full of "hordes of beggars professional and casual . . . cursing or praying with equal fervor." In Ballina, County Mayo, Mary Hanley lived through the summer by begging. She went nearly naked, wrapped in the blanket she shared with her two children every night. In good years, they might collect as much as three stone of potatoes in a day, more than enough to eat, with some left over to trade. By 1835, she reported that she would be lucky to collect a stone or a stone and a half of potatoes per day, and she pocketed at most twopence per week. "I have often made five parts of a potato," she said, "to divide it among my children." Sometimes she collected potatoes from families as alms, only to recognise *their* children begging a week or two later.[41]

In especially lean seasons, the number of beggars was intimidating. In 1827, a Catholic priest in Shanagolden, County Limerick, remembered beggars who "raised up a howling round the farmers' houses." Theft of potatoes, sometimes from fields or from closed pits, was common. Some regarded thieves as "idle unprincipled fellows, who cannot endure hunger like an honest man." Others forgave them; they knew they could easily be in their place. One labourer who had his entire store of more than twenty-four hundred pounds of potatoes stolen refused to blame the loss on the desperately poor who crossed his potato ground begging. "I don't think it was the wandering man did it," he said. "Where could he put them?"[42]

Beggars often went on the road for potatoes; others went looking for work. One labourer who left Clare most summers to make hay and dig potatoes in Tipperary and Kilkenny remarked that "one halfpenny, in addition to what we usually receive, would take us far away from home." Many walked from their homes across the country to Ireland's steamship ports, some taking small jobs on the way, or begging for potatoes to sell in order to earn enough for the passage to England for the harvest. From the 1820s there were regular steamship services to Liverpool or Glasgow offering deck space to Irish workers, alongside livestock in pens, for a roughly ten-hour journey. At the end of the season, migrant labourers would pocket a few pounds in profit, after paying for their passage as well as food and lodging in England. Many sewed the coins they earned into their trouser waistbands to keep them safe and returned to Ireland in August or September.[43]

To some, the annual tide of Irish migrant labourers was proof of the success of the Union and its civilising power. Here was a single labour market and a class of labourers willing to relocate in pursuit of higher wages. The "sea . . . no longer *separates* England and Ireland," some argued, and Irish migrants "living hard, and labouring hard" were essential to English agriculture. In 1841, more than twenty-five thousand labourers from Connaught, more than nineteen thousand from Ulster, and more than eleven thousand from Leinster made the passage from Dublin, Drogheda, or Derry. As the pressure of rent and debt increased, more men hazarded the passage. A famous hiring fair at Glasgow Cross processed six thousand to eight thousand labourers each year in the 1820s, and

at least sixty thousand in 1841. A popular air described the passage
to England:

> *I grazed my brogues and I cut my stick,*
> *In the latter end of May, sir,*
> *And down to Dublin town I came,*
> *To cut the corn and hay, sir.*
> *I paid the captain eight thirteens settled,*
> *To carry me over to Margate.*

THE SONG SKETCHES THE ITINERARY OF A MIGRANT WORKER,
from packing his boots and walking stick as potatoes got scarce,
through the hike to the docks, to the deck of a steamship bound
for England, to the fare paid to the captain—a wager on the
rewards of working a full harvest.[44]

The mobility of the Irish poor in the hungry season, along with
the small, often unventilated cabins inhabited by cottiers and
conacre farmers, made the disease environment of rural Ireland
closer to that of an urban slum than a settled farmland. Consequently, the uncertainty and hazard of the market for land and
food in the summer was compounded by the threat of epidemic
disease. Workers' bodies and clothes were almost never clean,
and typhus, caused by the bacterium *Rickettsia prowazekii*, was
endemic. The main vector for typhus, the body louse (*Pediculus
humanus corporis*) has a misleading common name. Body lice live
on clothing, crawling onto the body several times a day to feed
on blood (the head louse, *P. h. capitis*, by contrast, lives exclusively amid human hair—and does not spread typhus). When
enough filthy, infected people gather together, the insects' feces—
composed of digested blood rich with infectious bacteria—can
become airborne. Many Irish labourers owned a single suit of
clothes and a single set of linens, if they had linens at all, and they

carried them while begging or traveling to take in the English harvest. In towns, the poor often pawned their clothes for cash. Pawnbrokers did not usually wash pawned clothes but sold them to other labourers until *they* pawned them, a convenient system for lice looking for new hosts. In 1817, a County Roscommon physician found the disease "as usual, amongst the most squalid and distressed."[45]

In years when fever epidemics were especially widespread, the social fabric of the countryside began to come apart. In 1817, at the beginning of an extended typhus outbreak, soldiers outside Tullamore, in King's County, had orders to shoot anyone wandering who seemed ill. In Dublin, grifters sold "Thieves' Vinegar" and camphor as preventatives to fearful townspeople. In the countryside, some threw up mud or stone lean-tos, called fever huts, on the sides of the roads to isolate the ill. Others shared their beds with the sick. When infected people died, their bedmates were sometimes too weak to move the bodies for days. Many more were unable to gather fuel from the bogs, and desperate families "roved in troops," gathering scrub and scaling the walls of orchards and private woodlands on wealthy estates to steal fruit and cut down trees for fuel. The 1817 epidemic would last for almost two years. During that time, it sickened an estimated 1 in 8 of Ireland's 5.3 million people and killed about 45,000. In some parts of Munster at the peak of the contagion, an estimated three-quarters of the population were infected. A physician wrote, "It may without fear of any charge of exaggeration be asserted that a more general Epidemic never, perhaps, existed in any country of equal dimensions and population."[46]

Dublin, Cork, Waterford, Limerick, and other towns had fever hospitals, founded at the turn of the century, but there were fewer options for treatment in the countryside. An outbreak of typhus, cholera, influenza, or any illness serious enough to leave an infected person unable to work was a double threat to indebted labourers and tenants. In 1817 the sickly winter cut into the next potato crop, and the next begging season started earlier than usual, in May—allowing the disease to spread faster. Bedridden farmers still owed rent. One witness remembered a typical farmer who got sick and whose family was forced figuratively to "eat" their cow by selling it at a steep discount. The sick could sometimes be seen crawling to their cabin doors to eat raw potatoes left by terrified friends and family—another portent of what would occur on a mass scale during the Great Famine.[47]

IRELAND'S POVERTY, UNREST, AND SUSCEPTIBILITY TO BOTH SUB-sistence crises and epidemic disease were urgent problems in Dublin and London and investigated by many select committees and commissions. The idea, however, that the root cause of Ireland's ills was a lack of civilisation, and that any lasting cure had to reform the work ethic of Irish labourers through the discipline and risk of the free market, proved impossible to shake. Furthermore, although Ireland's economy, in all its perversity and corrosive competition, was structured by a legacy of colonialism and by an unequal Union, Irish poverty was inevitably understood through the lens of poor relief in England. In consequence, the principle that all relief ought to come at the cost of labour or risk presenting a moral hazard to constitutionally work-shy Irish labourers became the keystone for poor relief and famine relief in Ireland. The free market needed to be allowed to do its civilising work. This idea—laissez-faire—dominated British social policy in the Victorian era. As an official wrote in 1822, "The object of all should be to bring things as nearly as possible to this their natural state."[48]

And yet England itself did not, until the middle of the 1830s, have a poor-relief system that conformed to the tenets of political economy. The English system was tweaked and adjusted over centuries, but its basic principles were constant from the sixteenth century until just before the reign of Queen Victoria. England was divided into parishes, and within each parish, taxes were levied on wealthier residents and collected by a committee of local gentry, the "overseers of the poor." A resident of a parish could apply for poor relief, granted based on the overseers' assessment of their moral character and ability to work. The disabled and elderly were given either food or money or else cared for in an almshouse; the able-bodied were put to work in a "house of industry" or workhouse; orphaned children were apprenticed to local tradesmen; and the unruly and vagabond were imprisoned. Over time, however, more parishes began offering "outdoor relief," the direct provision of food, money, clothing, and other necessities to the needy. Parliament tried to manage surging demand in the eighteenth century by imposing a "workhouse test" on anyone who claimed poor relief. Under the test, claimants would have to live in a workhouse for a fixed period of time to prove that they were genuinely in need before gaining access to more complete relief. The workhouse test was cumbersome to administer. Many parishes preferred just to distribute outdoor relief. The system was riddled with holes and unevenly administered, but it had a clear principle: the poor had a right to be fed if they could not afford to eat.

The Poor Laws were assailed by political economists, who argued that the only solution to poverty was to encourage the poor to be industrious and to seek wage work. Labour was a commodity whose price rose and fell along with demand. Increasing wages to allow the poor to buy provisions was useless, since "the stone which we had forced up the hill would only fall back upon them." Instead of creating upwardly mobile and civilised workers, support given without the expectation of hard labour would turn the working class into paupers—but the Poor Laws seemed to critics to be designed to pauperise. "In general," one critic complained, "it is only hunger which can spur and goad them on to labour; yet our laws have said, they shall never hunger."[49]

The power of hunger to motivate the poor to work intrigued many political economists. The animal need for food seemed like evidence of the necessary and natural law of the market. Joseph Townsend, writing in the 1780s, insisted, "Hunger is not only a peaceable, silent, unremitted pressure, but, as the most natural motive to industry and labour, it calls forth the most powerful exertions." Over time, speculation about the motivating power of hunger and the formation of a work ethic became more systematic. "There are but two motives by which men are induced to work," the future prime minister John Russell argued in 1824. "The one, the hope of improving the condition of themselves and their families; the other, the fear of punishment." Hunger taught the lazy and indigent the necessity of industry. Satisfying base hunger also fuelled new appetites, which compounded the motivating effect. "Every taste of comfort, generated to the poor man by his own exertions," another political economist commented, "stimulates the appetite for more." As an editorial in the *Times* quipped, "*Le ventre gouverne le monde*."[50]

Thomas Robert Malthus, among the most influential political economists of the early Victorian era, was especially interested in the relationship between population and food supply. In an equation familiar to most students of economics and social policy, he reasoned that since population growth is exponential, it will always eventually outpace food supply. A civilised and well-governed society, Malthus argued, would not choose to feed the poor, since without the check of hunger, the poor would not work, but would reproduce, making a subsistence crisis inevitable. Nature, in such a crisis, would restore the balance between population and food supply through "famine . . . the last, the most dreadful resource of nature." Malthus worried that the English Poor Laws were a path to disaster, and he was even more alarmed at the prospect of Irish potato harvests permitting the population of Ireland to quickly grow beyond the carrying capacity of the land. Malthus estimated that Ireland would reach a population of twenty million by the end of the nineteenth century. The low living standards to which most Irish workers were accustomed, and the potato's abundance, he argued, would make it very difficult to reform their psychology to respond to the stimuli that motivated British workers. The Irish, he concluded, could not yet be taught; until they starved, they would not learn.[51]

These concerns about the motivation of the poor to labour, about food supplies, and about poverty shaped the reform of the Poor Laws in England and led to the creation of a Poor Law system in Ireland. As part of a wave of legislation that included the expansion of the franchise and the reform of parliamentary constituencies (1832) and the abolition of colonial slavery (1833), a Whig government heavily influenced by the principles of political economy passed the 1834 Poor Law Amendment Act. The act gave a Poor Law Commission sweeping powers to divide England into unions, rather than parishes, each administered by a committee of Poor Law guardians. The guardians were responsible for collecting taxes and administering centralised union workhouses, which operated under the principle of "less eligibility": conditions within the workhouse were designed to be worse than the most degrading and lowest-paying job outside. Necessity was often the only teacher that political economists could imagine; the poor—paupers—would only learn to be prudent if they had no other choice. The new English Poor Law was designed to deter outdoor relief and to compel the poor to look for wage work before seeking support from their local union.

Soon after the reformed English Poor Law took effect, successive Whig governments led by Earl Grey and Viscount Melbourne began to explore a solution to Irish poverty on the same principles. In 1833, a royal commission chaired by Richard Whateley, the Anglican archbishop of Dublin, began a three-year investigation into the causes of Irish poverty. The commission's reports found multiple causes, from alcohol to rural crime, but ultimately blamed the eighteenth-century land settlement for encouraging the subdivision of land. Workhouses would not deter poverty in Ireland, the commissioners argued. If less eligibility were applied in Ireland, the workhouses would have to be truly hellish to be reliably worse than life outside. Instead, the commissioners recommended that the government invest in public works to provide employment and encourage emigration to reduce the pressure on land.

John Russell, at the time the home secretary, was unimpressed with these recommendations. In August 1836, he appointed George Nicholls to conduct a new inquiry, which produced three separate reports. Nicholls, a former East India Company sea captain turned engineer and banker, had most recently impressed Russell with his work as a Poor Law commissioner for England. Nicholls concluded that something innate to Ireland itself was demotivating. When he visited English Poor Law unions with substantial Irish immigrant populations, he was told that "the Irish would endure more, and strive harder" to avoid the workhouse than many English workers. In 1837, Nicholls toured the south and west of Ireland; he purposefully ignored the north and east, which, he argued, "approximate more nearly to the English." If the poorest Irish were ready for the Poor Law, then the more prosperous counties would be as well. There was nothing inherent to Irishness, he concluded, that would be numb to the stimulus of workhouse discipline and deterrence, properly applied.[52]

Nicholls's reports affirmed Russell's preferred policy, and in 1838 the Irish Poor Law Act divided Ireland into 130 new Poor Law unions. The Irish system was a copy of the English system, save for one important difference. Despite the hostility of the Poor Law Commission to outdoor relief, the English Poor Law allowed for some exceptional circumstances when unions could give out food, money, or other support to the poor outside the workhouse. The Irish Poor Law, on the other hand, expressly forbade all outdoor relief. There were two reasons for this difference. First, theorists insisted that the Irish poor had potatoes to insulate themselves from the power of hunger, were generally less civilised, and were less motivated to work at baseline than the English poor. Second, Ireland was still subject to colonialism. Experiments in austere political economy that would not be tolerated in England could be tried in the colonial world—even if the "colony" was a part of the United Kingdom.

Nicholls—who moved to Ireland to help implement the new system—was confident that the Poor Law would begin a temporarily painful, but short and permanent, transition for the Irish economy. The path to "day-labour for wages, and to that dependence on daily labour for support," Nicholls wrote, would be "generally beset with difficulty and suffering. It was so in England." Conacre tenants, another reformer argued, were already "nearly emancipated from the soil, and far advanced towards the character of simple labourer." Hunger and necessity would complete the process once the Irish lived in a genuine free market. However harsh, the transition to the modern world would be worthwhile. Ireland would be brought sharply and quickly into the nineteenth century. The Irish labourer needed to be "emancipated" from the potato. Potatoes were food without work; satiety without the civilising fear of starvation. Without the buffer of subsistence agriculture to insulate them, the Irish poor could finally enter a world of risk, where steady employment, not access to potato ground, would keep them alive.[53]

THE SOLUTION TO IRISH POVERTY, IMPLEMENTED WITH GREAT fanfare at the end of a decade of reform in the United Kingdom, was based on a long-standing colonial assumption about the character of the Irish rural poor. Ireland, through this lens, was a kind of living fossil within the United Kingdom, a country where the majority of the poor were inert and indolent, unwilling and unable to exert themselves for wages and content to rely on potatoes for subsistence. The Irish Poor Law announced that the pressure of the market—of the risk of starvation and the necessity of paid work—was the only feasible solution to the rot in Ireland. And yet the Irish poor did not live beyond the market—they were in its teeth. The pyramid of rent, the web of debt, and the fluctuating prices of potatoes and other essential goods forced the poorest Irish labourers to be among the most aggressive and risk-taking of speculators.

The Irish system seemed simple and ancient but was new, complex, and connected to global markets. Rather than resistant to change, the Irish economy was volatile. When potato yields were good, the poor could more or less make do. When potatoes failed or markets sagged, starvation, riot, "outrage," and disease broke out. Even when the potato crop was good, many labourers were chronically hungry, on the edge of starvation every summer. Orthodox political economy, however, offered only one prescription for Ireland's troubles: to further expose the Irish to the very same markets that tore them apart. Ireland was misperceived as an anachronism, a place before capitalism that was poor and hungry because of its distance from the market. However, the very opposite was true: the Irish countryside was mired in British imperial capitalism, which was a source of its despair, not the solution to it.

For all the confidence in political economy and the healing power of the market, the Irish economy resembled the precarious future of capitalism more than its feudal past. The twenty-first-century slum in the global South was prefigured by the crowded, poor cities of nineteenth-century southern Europe—places like Naples, with little regulation, dangerous crowding, little capital investment, and a viciously competitive market for wages. Present-day slums, a scholar writes, are marked by the "overwhelming spectacle of informal competition." Moreover, faith in luck is a feature of modern slums, where "pyramid schemes, lotteries, and other quasi-magical forms of wealth appropriation" prevail among people for whom the market has brought little but pain. Crowded, subdivided, often stripped of resources by neocolonial governments and international organisations, mired with scams, slums are not places trapped in the past outside the free market. They are the product of forces unleashed by global capitalism to uproot and agitate, to energise, enrich, and impoverish. Ireland was rural, but its economy had many features of a modern slum. By 1844, nearly 2.4 million people lived on the edge of starvation every season. As one cottier put it, "The land has got the upper hand of me; I cannot manage it now."[54]

3

THE PEOPLE'S POTATO

H ERE IS A HISTORICAL QUESTION THAT COULD ALSO SET UP A
joke: How many potatoes could the Irishman eat? The answer,
repeated in many history books, scientific articles, and even tourist
guides, is absurd enough to be a punch line. According to many
sources, the average Irish labourer ate twelve to fourteen pounds of
potatoes *every day*, for as long as supplies lasted. This claim may
have sprouted from an eye-catching comment, made to a parliamentary commission amid other, more reasonable estimates, that
an Irish "working man . . . ought to have four pounds of potatoes
three times a day." Those portions would have been many times
larger than the amounts consumed by any other people that ate
potatoes as their staple. In Belgium and the Netherlands, rural
labourers ate just under two pounds a day; Scottish Highlanders,
about three. However, by 1846, the largest estimates for Ireland
had become authoritative—an outlandish zombie "fact" too compelling and evocative to die.[1]

But this claim about the Irish is false. The meals attributed to Irish workers are so physiologically unlikely as to be impossible. The average adult in the generally well-fed United States eats a total of about four pounds of food daily. An average adult human stomach has a capacity of about four litres. Given the average density of a potato, a person *could* eat about six pounds of potatoes in a meal without internal injury. While it would not be fatal to eat four pounds of potatoes three times a day, each meal would be a nauseating test of endurance. As a rare sceptic commented in 1887, "Even if [an] Irish labourer in Ireland could eat . . . 12 lbs of potatoes in 24 hours," he would be "mechanically incommoded" by the volume.[2]

Historians have been careless with this outlandish statistic because it is a very useful symbolic quantity, a blunt way of conveying the depth of Irish dependence on potatoes and, consequently, the peril of the blight pandemic that led to the Great Famine. But for the officials, politicians, and writers who repeated the claim in the nineteenth century, the idea of a heroic Irish appetite for potatoes revealed a thriving British colonial vision of Ireland. The potato had been useful to Britain's designs on Ireland in the eighteenth century—an adjunct to land subdivision, rent-farming, and aggressive exports of almost every other foodstuff Ireland could produce. After the Union, a freakish stomach for potatoes helped to explain why the supposedly irresistible and improving gravity of the market did not seem to act on Ireland and exonerated Britain of its pivotal role in Ireland's hungry seasons and hungry years.

The potato was blamed for the indolence, resistance to modernity, and preference for bare subsistence that many Britons imagined to be the cause of Ireland's poverty and failure to thrive within the United Kingdom. These assumptions made it easy for many to accept even an outrageous claim about potato eating since it proved that an inferior people were exquisitely adapted to an inferior food. During the famine, when imported American maize did not stop the crisis, officials blamed huge meals of potatoes for causing "habitual distension of the organs of digestion," thereby making a meal of maize less filling than it ought to have been. Colonial fantasies of hierarchy and civilisation enabled a belief that the Irish, like their staple, were essentially inert and earthy, a nation of potatoes.[3]

And yet, the potato was a paradox for the Irish poor. Over centuries it was a curse, but from season to season it was often a blessing. With a good potato harvest, labourers taking conacre and even the landless could shelter from the centrifugal forces applied by the market and the empire. Potatoes were generous. Before the Great Famine, an acre of potatoes could amply feed a family of six, as well as a few pigs and fowl. An acre of grain was reported to produce about 4,200 pounds of salable produce, while an acre of potatoes yielded as much as 72,100 pounds of food for subsistence. Potatoes, supplemented by milk, are a nutritionally adequate diet. The tubers are calorie dense and rich in vitamins, especially vitamin C. Potato monoculture immiserated the Irish poor, but it was also the central institution of their working, social, and family lives. The abundance of the potato was a handmaiden to colonialism, but it also allowed the Irish poor the luxury of sharing and giving charity.[4]

Potatoes were the hub of an agricultural circuit of inexpensive food, livestock, and fuel. Potatoes fed people, but also pigs—an easily fattened animal that thrived on potatoes and could almost always be sold in a growing British market. Combustible turf cut from peatlands, abundant in Ireland, provided the poor with free, or nearly free, energy. Irish families also made heavy use of straw and rushes, using the grasses for roofs, baskets, mattresses, nets, and many other objects. It might be tempting to see the rural way of life as an ancient Celtic tradition, preserved into the nineteenth century in defiance of conquest and modernity—that was certainly how many British critics saw it. However, the potato was introduced to Ireland in the sixteenth century at the earliest, and the pigs the Irish raised were, by the nineteenth century, often introduced English breeds that were destined for export to England on specially fitted steamships. Even the ingenious tools that the Irish made from woven grasses were adaptations to a dearth of other materials after the English conquest. The system was relatively new and terribly exposed. Food, livestock, and fuel were like the wobbly legs of a rickety stool. If any one of the three failed—especially the potato, the foundation of it all—the consequence was catastrophe and dehumanising squalor. "The potato," one historian writes, was "a capricious staple." But in seasons when the three legs were solid upon the ground, the Irish poor found space for leisure and the pleasures of family. This chapter sketches each leg in turn, and then shows the social and moral world built by the Irish poor around the potato.[5]

THE FIRST AND MOST IMPORTANT LEG OF THE STOOL WAS THE potato itself. Potato cultivation, like many features of the lives of the Irish poor, was easy for critics and reformers to imagine as part of an ancient way of life (as discussed in Chapter 2). Sifting colonial fantasies from material reality is critical to understanding what potatoes were to Ireland before the famine. To British eyes, the potato was bountiful and dangerously easy to grow. The crop, the political economist John Ramsay McCulloch wrote, made the Irish "content to vegetate, for they can hardly be said to live, in rags and wretchedness." In the first half of the nineteenth century, potatoes were not unique in their status of food eaten by colonised people that seemed too "easy" to be civilising. In the Caribbean and West Africa, enslaved and free labourers often ate cassava, a hardy root that colonial officials and political economists believed compounded "the natural indolence of savages."[6]

To recall, the Irish rural economy seemed old and slow to many British eyes. This was an optical illusion or a form of focal blindness, a symptom of profound confidence in the precepts of political economy, and in the improving power of markets. Since rural Ireland was generally poor, with limited infrastructure and very little capital or industrial technology, it followed that Ireland was poor because it was insulated from the energy of imperial capitalism. In reality, the Irish countryside was as much a node of the imperial network as London's docklands or Manchester's power looms. Potato culture in Ireland, like so much about the Irish countryside, looked ancient to British eyes but was in reality strikingly modern. The Irish poor established traditions and folkways around potatoes, but ultimately potato culture was utilitarian. The Irish poor grew and ate potatoes, and often only potatoes, in the most efficient, low-input, and inexpensive ways available in order to survive.

The potato, *Solanum tuberosum*, is a nightshade that is native to the Americas; it is more closely related to tomatoes and peppers (and belladonna, or "deadly nightshade") than to sweet potatoes or yams. The tuber arrived in Europe during what historians call the Columbian exchange, the introduction of dozens of agriculturally and economically useful plants to Europe after the conquest of the Americas by Iberian soldiers in the late fifteenth and sixteenth centuries. In the eighteenth and nineteenth centuries, many claimed that John Hawkins had introduced the potato to Ireland in 1565, or Francis Drake in 1573, or Walter Raleigh in 1586. More recent histories argue that the potato was likely introduced to Ireland by Basque fishermen who stopped there for water and food on their way to the Grand Banks cod fishery.[7]

In whatever way the potato arrived, Irish labourers, like peasants across northern and western Europe, quickly understood its value as a security against crop failure and the collateral damage caused by armies on the march. Potato cultivation spread at the same time as the population of Europe exploded, growing from 140 million to 266 million people between 1750 and 1850. In Ireland, from 1779 to 1841, the population increased at least 172 percent. Between 1741 and 1779 the number of Irish acres planted with potatoes was reported to have increased twentyfold—and by the 1770s, many small farmers, cottiers, and labourers taking conacre, especially in the southwest, depended on potatoes. After the seventeenth-century wars of conquest, the mounting exploitation of Irish land and labour to generate rent and food for export amid the consolidation of the British Empire transformed the Irish potato from a fail-safe crop into a staple, and then from a staple into the exclusive food of millions (see Chapter 1). "So rapid an extension of the taste for, and the cultivation of, an exotic," wrote a political economist, "has no parallel."[8]

The diet of the Irish poor was exceptional not in kind, but in intensity and specialisation—it was perhaps the most monotonous diet eaten by a population of European rural labourers in the nineteenth century. The Irish poor ate bread rarely; "they are just as much fed on flour as they are clad in jewels and embroidery," the *Times* commented. Not only labourers taking conacre but farmers leasing as many as thirty acres would have been likely to eat nearly exclusively potatoes. In many parts of Ireland, milk—or more commonly buttermilk, the fermented by-product of churning cultured cream for butter—was available for families that kept dairy cows during part of the year. In the north and parts of the east, some also ate oatmeal, at least in summer. But consumption of both dairy and oatmeal declined over time as rents increased. Farmers with milk cows would sell everything their cows produced and instead drink water with a bit of black pepper, "[tastier] than water."[9]

Irish potato fields were planted with clones (like most commercially grown potatoes today), with new tubers grown from "sets"—cut pieces of potato with one axillary bud (or "eye") to each piece. Set planting is oriented toward short-term yields. Victorian agronomists observed that the returns of intensive farming from cuttings were liable to decline over time, especially due to disease. Without a knowledge of genetics and of the role genetic diversity plays in preventing disease, many botanists attributed the decline in yields they observed to a kind of botanical senescence. As a botanist wrote in 1853, "The potato, like the tree and hen, becomes aged and past bearing." Old plants were more susceptible to diseases and pests and needed periodically to be replaced with "younger" cuttings. Seed planting rearranges a potato's genes, creating more robust and resilient plants. But planting from a seed does not necessarily produce large tubers or high yields. "Out of a vast quantity [of seeds]," farmers were warned, "you may get but a few kinds worth preserving and propagating." The poor could not afford to take the risk. They were at the mercy of their "aging" potato plants.[10]

Experimentation with potato varieties planted from seeds was a hobby for botanists, curious landlords, and larger farmers, who had income enough to buy food if a field planted with seeds did not produce a large crop. Even given these pressures, dozens of varieties of potatoes were developed. Guides to potato cultivation from the turn of the nineteenth century are full of evocative lists of cultivars: the Old Winter Red of Lancashire; the Surinam and Ox Noble of Yorkshire; the Copperplate of the Isle of Man; and dozens of Irish varieties—Commonwise, Quakerwise, Horse Legs,

Dutch Upright, Royal Early, Rocks (sometimes called Protestants), Cups, Apples, Lumpers, Pink Eyes, Leathercoats, Codders, Minions, Thistlewhippers, Weavers, and more.[11]

The poorer the farmer, the more necessary it was to find a reliable high-yield cultivar and plant it intensively until its yields collapsed. The most infamous Irish cultivar was the Lumper or Horse Potato, a large and watery spud that fed both people and livestock. Just before the famine, it was the potato most widely grown by the poor and was reputed to produce 20–30 percent more food than other varieties. Pigs and crows, some wrote, would refuse them, "until the good kind are devoured." With its soggy texture, mammoth yields, and grotesque name, the Lumper became another symbol of Irish decline, a food that "allays the cravings of hunger, and little else." The Lumper, Charles Trevelyan concluded, was "the coarsest and most prolific kind" of potato—in his view, an apt food for a prolific and coarse people.[12]

That the Irish poor depended on a potato called the Lumper when the blight struck in 1845 might seem like an irresistible detail: the lumpen Irish, dying in the lazy-beds alongside their Irish Lumpers. The Lumper grown in the lazy-bed, however, was neither more nor less susceptible to failure than other potato cultivars grown with other methods. In 1845, in Belgium, late blight wiped out the Blue, the local high-yield potato, and was equally virulent in drill-planted fields on large estates as on small farms. The weakness of potato crops was not the individual variety of potato planted or the mode of planting, but the genetic liabilities of using sets, rather than seeds.[13]

The Lumper was part of a cycle of rising and falling yields shaped by the ecology of set planting. The most widely and intensively planted "people's potato" changed over time. One botanist claimed that the Lumper had appeared in 1818 and became the dominant cultivar among the poor between 1825 and 1835, when "it was so charged with vitality that it would grow without manure in any soil." However, the Apple potato, sold to wealthier consumers by the 1830s, had been described in 1807 as "the general kind planted . . . invaluable to the poor." In 1808, the Cup was considered "not only more productive, but vastly more nutritive" than any other kind. "The cups," County Tyrone farmers claimed, "have driven hunger out of Ireland." Consequently, it is hard to be sure whether the Lumper was genuinely as unpalatable as it was reputed to be—lower-yield potatoes had a certain prestige among Irish consumers with the means to be discerning. Perhaps *any* high-yield potato was liable to be considered less tasty. By the 1830s, "this lumper, once the prince of potatoes" was already declining and in some fields producing little more than its sets in the ground. Had the blight not struck, another people's potato would have taken its place, and the Lumper might have come to be considered a treat.[14]

By necessity, potato planting was low technology, and the planting schedule was oriented toward accumulating the largest possible supply before winter. Sets of potatoes destined for the market—a smaller share of the crop, and one usually limited to farmers with enough land to take the risk—were planted in March and April and harvested in October. The "people's crop" stayed in the ground longer and was usually harvested in November. The agricultural calendar grafted the celebration of ancient holidays onto the potato harvest. Saint Patrick's Day or Good Friday often marked the beginning of planting, and the period of digging sometimes began with Garland Sunday, a day of Catholic pilgrimage in July, and ended around the time of the pagan festival of Samhain, on November 1.[15]

Important methods of potato cultivation, like the traditional holidays and observances of the planting calendar, were imperfect adaptations of ancient methods to the demands of an introduced crop and a modern market. Most Irish potatoes were planted in the aforementioned lazy-beds, a method of growing used in the British Isles since at least the late antique era, after the fall of the Roman empire. Potatoes were planted in ridges alongside trenches, where they were protected by layers of earth and manure that prevailed over "any weeds that attempt to spring up," while rain drained from the raised beds into the trenches. Lazy-beds also protected potatoes from frost, and their ditches and ridges protected the spuds from grazing cattle. A crop of potatoes could be planted twice on the same beds, with the trenches moved to where the centres of the beds had been the year before. At harvest, diggers would walk through the trenches and use long-handled spades to unearth the tubers. The lazy-bed system was relatively low maintenance, although planting and harvesting could be more labour intensive—it took about sixteen people to plant or harvest an acre of potatoes.[16]

The aesthetics and planting calendar of the Irish countryside recalled the Celtic pagan and preconquest Christian eras of Irish history, but the distribution of potato land was dynamic, shifting according to rent, crop yield, price, the indebtedness of farmers, and the amount of available manure. The volatility of the market, a farmer complained, made it "hardly possible to state a regular course of crops." Access to fertiliser was especially important. Although the nineteenth century saw the beginning of a global trade in mined guano from South America, most Irish farmers could not afford to import fertiliser and used animal dung. By some estimates, potatoes consumed up to nineteen-twentieths of Irish manure. Without manure, farmers practiced swidden: burning their land and using the ashes as fertiliser, although frequent burnings depleted the soil. Near the coasts, farmers collected and spread seaweed. When fertiliser was scarce, farmers became desperate. Near Limerick in the 1830s, labourers tore down the stone walls between fields, carted away the fresh soil underneath them, then rebuilt the walls.[17]

After harvest, Irish potatoes were almost never exported. Potatoes are difficult to store and ship, even with modern refrigeration. They require steady temperature and humidity to prevent sprouting or rotting. To keep the environment around their potatoes stable, most Irish farmers buried their crops in pits in the ground. The practice was reputed to have spread widely across Ireland after the famine of 1739–1741, when cold winters froze Irish rivers and devastated harvests. Each pit was about five feet deep and filled with dry straw or thatch at the bottom. Freshly dug potatoes were carried to the pits. Once full, the pits were covered with earth to a height "higher than what is usual over a grave," and beaten down with spades and shovels. The edge of the pit was formed into a ridge, to carry rain off the pit and to seal it against frost. When they needed potatoes, a family would break open a pit and bring in all the potatoes buried in it.[18]

Sprightly, vividly green, and gently rolling, sometimes edged with hedges and freestone walls, potato fields were beautiful. Like the pits in which potatoes were stored, they seemed like vestiges of the Iron Age preserved in the era of the steam engine. The way most Irish labourers prepared and ate potatoes conjured the same illusion. Potatoes were boiled in their skins, often in a three-legged iron pot designed to sit over an open flame. The boiled potatoes were poured into a wicker basket that served as colander and serving dish. A family would sit or squat around the basket in their cottage, sometimes with a pig rooting into the circle, and peel the potatoes with their thumbs. "They had no knives and forks," a storyteller explained, "and it was wooden spoons they used." Sometimes, farmers would make "stampy" out of potatoes, crushing and then drying them, and blending the flakes with milk or buttermilk, flour, and fresh boiled potatoes. The mixture was baked in a pan or roasted between two cabbage leaves. Irish immigrants carried these habits with them to North America. In the United States, schoolteachers were surprised that Irish immigrant children ate potatoes like bread, with their hands rather than utensils.[19]

Boiled potatoes were sometimes served with condiments known as "kitchen." Near the sea, kitchen might include seaweed, or limpets and whelks scraped off the rocks. Sometimes a salted or smoked herring was hung from the ceiling, to drip oil onto the bowl of potatoes. Herrings stretched this way were known as blind herring, or "scudum up the road" (from *scadán*, Irish for "herring")—since the herring itself was distant and notional. Kitchen notwithstanding, Irish cuisine was relentlessly bland. Many reports on Ireland in the era of the Union, however, remarked that the Irish poor seemed unusually strong and healthy. These reports have pushed credulous historians toward the idea that the Irish poor were better off in their way than the British working class, a view that indulges in one of the most durable colonial myths: that of the strapping and noble savage, uncivilised but free of the diseases of civilisation. There are plenty of eighteenth- and nineteenth-century descriptions of the Irish poor as "tall, stout, handsome fellows; the women well clad, buxom, and good looking." But considering the obvious distortions everywhere else in how Ireland appeared to many British eyes, why reject only the insults and believe only the claims that flatter the Irish (and the Irish diaspora)? The Irish middle classes, who could afford to supplement potatoes with other foods, may have been relatively hale—in 1837, a professor at the University of Edinburgh reported that his Irish students were, on average, among the tallest, heaviest, and strongest of their peers. In general, however, an all-potato diet was adequate but hazardous. In addition to suffering seasonal shortages and the threat of famine when crops failed, Irish labourers were considered prone to "acidities in the stomach, flatulency in the bowels, and other symptoms of dyspepsia." Potato-fed cattle, many believed, gave thin, watery milk and "white and tasteless butter." An exclusive diet of potatoes caused cows (and people) to suffer chronic diarrhea.[20]

By 1822, the botanist Joseph Sabine grouped the potato among the world's most important staples, along with wheat and rice. Potatoes could produce massive crops from small plots of land and mediocre soils—but their bounty could be a curse. The poorest and most vulnerable Irish farmers were trapped in a dangerous cycle. They had no choice but to put the highest-yield sets into the ground, since without the people's potato they were at risk of eviction or starvation. High-yield cultivars, however, always declined—if they didn't fail entirely. The more people depended on potatoes, Sabine worried, the more likely that a crop failure would "inevitably lead to all the misery of famine, more dreadful in proportion to the number exposed to is ravages."[21]

PIGS, THE SECOND LEG OF THE STOOL, WERE THE ONLY APPRECIATing asset available to most of the Irish population. Under the Union, Irish labourers very rarely ate pork or bacon, but they lived among swine being fattened for export. A pig's appetite and metabolism could turn household refuse—scraps of potatoes, potatoes too shriveled or insect-ridden to eat—into calories and calories into cash. Pigs and potatoes formed a circuit—and like the generous yields of potatoes, the hardiness of pigs and piglets and the efficiency with which they could be fattened were a mixed blessing. As the Irish population grew and the market for exports expanded, rent increased, land became more divided, and more Irish families depended on potatoes for subsistence; hence, more families kept pigs to sell to pay rent and other expenses. Since these pigs were fattened on potatoes, demand for land increased, which in turn increased rent—and the Irish poor went back again to the start of the cycle. Before the Great Famine, almost every Irish family kept a pig, and Britons found comparisons between the Irish poor and Irish pigs irresistible. Here again, what was treated as a distinctly Irish peculiarity—or perversion—was distinct only by degree. Pigs are symbols of good luck and wealth in China; a German expression describes a lucky person as someone who *Schwein hat*, "has a pig"; pig keeping was very common in England. However, in Ireland, as one report put it succinctly, "The pig is the main thing."[22]

Irish pork, the novelist and folklorist William Carleton wrote, could explain Ireland's place in the United Kingdom. "When pig-driving was not so general, political economy had not then taught the people how to be poor upon the most scientific principles." Carleton introduced readers to a fantastical Celtic swineherd, Phil, Professor of Pig-Driving. Phil drove legendary pigs, "huge, gaunt, long-legged, slab-sided, roach-backed, coarse-boned," able to run as fast as a mail coach. These old Irish pigs, Carleton wrote, understood Irish and Latin—and squealed to hear English. British domination, Carleton continued, forced the Irish to sell their pigs and changed the pigs themselves. The breed sometimes called the Irish Greyhound, with a large, lean frame closer to that of a wild boar, declined quickly after the Union. By 1847, experts believed that it had been extirpated everywhere but in County Galway. English breeds like the Berkshire were reputed to fatten on half the food required by Irish breeds. Under the empire, Carleton wrote, Irish pigs had become "fat, gross and degenerate . . . a proud, lazy, carnal race, entirely of the earth, earthy." Perhaps it was a good thing, he reflected, that England took them all.[23]

Irish pig exports more than doubled between the 1750s and 1770s, just as potato dependence became deeply entrenched. Paradoxically, the potato made keeping pigs possible ("It would not be worth keeping pigs if one had to buy the food for them," a farmer explained), and the abundance of the potato made keeping pigs necessary. People ate about half the Irish potato crop each year; much of the remainder was fed to livestock, especially pigs and cattle. Although cattle and sheep were more numerous, pigs were the livestock of the poor. Pigs are part of the biome of domesticated animals and plants on which we depend (and which depend on us); they are commensal, from the Latin *mēnsa* ("table"). In Ireland, the pig figuratively shared the table, eating cast-off potato scraps and other refuse. But some pigs literally shared the table (or, in the poorest cottages, the wicker bowl placed on the floor), eating and sleeping with Irish families in their cabins.[24]

Pigs are also intelligent, adaptable, and omnivorous—"notoriously ecumenical," as one historian wryly comments. "The small cost at which these animals can be reared," a pig breeder wrote in 1847, "and their fecundity and wonderful powers of thriving under disadvantages, render them an actual blessing." The animals give high yields of meat in proportion to their fodder. By some estimates an acre of potatoes could yield a ton of pork. Irish labourers could easily feed a pig or two with part of their potato crop, making pigs the most reliable means available to the poor for converting potatoes, grown primarily for subsistence, into cash. For the Irish poor, pigs were effectively stores of money, not food. A pig, one farmer explained, was like a savings bank: selling a pig was making a withdrawal against the stored value of potatoes the pig had eaten. Most labourers "would as soon think of eating the landlord himself as of eating the pig."[25]

The object of keeping a pig in the nineteenth-century Irish rural economy was almost always to sell it, not to eat it. After the Union, Ireland was "the great store house of swine for the supply of England." The same steamships that brought Irish labourers to England for the harvest brought cargoes of live pigs and salted pork. That the Irish pig was "him as pays the rint" was a well-known punch line in the United Kingdom. When a pig had been fattened for the market, farmers would either transport it to a wholesaler themselves or, more commonly, sell it to a drover at a fair or at the door of their cottage. The pig trade grew with the Union. In 1801, Ireland exported only 2,000 pigs to Britain. After the Union, officials in Liverpool, where about 75 percent of pigs shipped from Ireland were imported, counted 104,501 Irish pigs moving through in 1821, and 595,422 in 1837. Many were loaded onto railway cars bound for Manchester, where they were trans-shipped to regional markets. A pig breeder wrote admiringly of a drover who was able, with his dogs, to drive 14,000 imported Irish pigs to markets in the West of England in 1830. Still, despite the strong market for pork in Britain, buying a piglet on credit to fatten on potatoes, as many did, was a risk. An outbreak of epizootic disease among pigs could wipe out a year's rent. Experts estimated that about 10 percent of Irish pigs died of disease each year. Diseased pigs could still be sold, but at a loss.[26]

Pig keeping, like potato culture, was structured by the demands of the market. Irish families lived in famously close proximity to their pigs out of necessity. Building a pigsty might lead to an increase in rent, and pigs were valuable. If a pig needed shelter, it came inside. Many Irish pigs lived in intimacy with labourers and their families. Some writers described the pig "as much a domestic animal as the dog," taken to be sold at fairs on leashes by Irish children. Irish pig keeping, like Irish potato cultivation, was often misunderstood by Britons. Potatoes were relatively new to Ireland. Irish peasants had adapted the lazy-bed system to the cultivation of an introduced crop. Many Britons, however, considered fields of potatoes in lazy-beds to be an eternal feature of Irish life. Likewise, a new system of pig husbandry—of Irish landraces replaced by introduced British breeds, and bred almost exclusively for export—was reimagined by British observers as an Irish national tradition. The "Arab has his horse," wrote one observer, "the Greenlander his dog, so has the Irishman his pig." It was rare to see a cabin or farmhouse without a pig or two nearby. Some pigs let themselves into cabins—the bottoms of wooden front doors were sometimes dented or splintered by rooting pigs. On Irish roads, pigs wandered freely. Cottiers and labourers taking conacre were sometimes prosecuted for the damage caused by their free-range pigs, and many cut piglets' snouts or pierced them with a ring to curb rooting.[27]

The proximity between the Irish poor and their pigs invited invidious comparisons between the animal and the human. The Irish way of life, to William Cobbett, "as to food, is but one remove from that of the pig, and of the ill-fed pig too." The *Times* described UK government support for Catholics as "pearls before swine." Paddy, his lazy-bed, and his beloved pig were stock figures in jokes and tall tales. One writer chuckled to remember a pig that had eaten all the clothes in a woman's washtub. In another anecdote, almost certainly a joke, a landlord who had installed floorboards for a tenant in his farmhouse asked why the family's pig was sleeping in the best room: "Because, plase your honour, it has every conveniency a pig could want."[28]

Pigs have had a long, often uncomfortable proximity to humans—they are omnivores like us, intelligent and social like us. Pigs are often used to teach human anatomy, and their organs can substitute temporarily for human organs in transplant surgeries. Pigs and humans readily swap pathogens like influenza, and human flesh is reputed to taste like pork. Pigs, symbols of wealth and luck to some, are to others symbols of the uncanny and diabolical. Eating pork is taboo in Judaism and Islam—pigs are considered unclean animals, scavengers liable to break open graves and eat human corpses, making the people who eat pigs unclean by transitive property. In a miracle narrated in the three synoptic

Gospels of the New Testament, Jesus drives demons out of the body of a man and into a herd of pigs. The idea that a pig could be possessed by demons as readily as a person echoed in Irish ghost stories. In the tale of the Black Pig, or Dolocher, the spirit of a murderer and rapist who killed himself in a Dublin jail possessed a pig that hunted in the city's lanes at night.[29]

Proximity to pigs was more than a symbolic danger. The intimacy of Irish pig keeping and the uncanny similarity of pigs and people meant that diseases passed easily between the two species. Influenza probably swept through both people and pigs in Ireland at the same time, and epizootics "of remarkable fatality" struck Irish pigs in 1751 and 1764—coincident with reports of especially virulent and widespread human flu epidemics. But the pathogen that epitomised the relationship between Irish people and their pigs was *Taenia solium*, the pork tapeworm whose life cycle can carry it through both porcine and human bodies. A pork tapeworm infection begins with a human ingesting pork infested with encysted larvae of the tapeworm, called cysticerci. The larvae grow into adults in human intestines. The adult worms reproduce only in human guts, both by laying eggs and by detaching proglottids— segments of their horrible, annellated bodies. Both the eggs and proglottids pass in the stool, and when pigs eat human feces, the eggs migrate through the walls of their intestines into muscle tissue, where they become cysticerci and begin the cycle again.[30]

The Irish often used the word "measles" to describe infestation of pigs with cysticerci. An Irish farmer's adage stated, "Every pig has its measle." *Trichinella spiralis*, the roundworm that is the most common cause of trichinosis in pigs and humans, also spreads through larvae encysted in muscle tissue. In contrast to Irish pigs, kept individually and in close contact with human feces but fed mostly on a diet of vegetable matter, pigs from the larger, more industrialised farms of the United States were far more likely to be infected with *Trichinella*, as overcrowding and feeding pigs with scraps of infected raw meat increased the likelihood of infection. By 1879, German authorities estimated that as many as 20 percent of American hams showed evidence of trichinosis.[31]

It would have been difficult or impossible to distinguish among the causes of measly pork. However, given the nearly all-potato diet of most Irish pigs, *Trichinella* was likely rare among them. Regardless of the species of worm, ridding pigs of the cysts that made their meat squishy, pale, and unappetising (as well as infectious, if eaten undercooked) was of urgent economic importance. Tapeworms, as well as their proglottids and eggs, are visible to the naked eye. Nineteenth-century veterinary researchers reconstructed the animal's life cycle and concluded that pigs "reared in small lots by poor people" were the animals most likely to be infected by eating human waste. A single person with a tapeworm could infect many pigs; a tapeworm can produce as many as eighty-five million eggs in its two years of life. Experts in the bacon trade estimated in the early 1860s that about 0.10 percent of English and Scottish pigs were visibly infected with cysticerci. Among Irish pigs, the rate of infection was between 3 and 8 percent.[32]

Sick pigs were treated in Ireland with many of the same medications as humans—although the animals were considered "intractable patients." The measles were treated with "aperients such as salts, sulphur and antimony," the toxic compounds humans took to kill intestinal worms. It could be difficult, however, to tell if a living pig was ill. Only very severe infestations, most common in pigs that were already in poor health, caused visible symptoms like swelling or ragged breathing. "I have seen pigs," a public health officer commented, "in whose flesh cysticerci abounded, in apparently the most perfect health and very fat." To determine if a living animal was infected required palpating the tongue, eyelids, or other parts of the pig's body not sheathed in thick hide, and small farmers had every incentive to hide a pig's illness. In response, Irish pork merchants hired "measle triers," who would—at their own peril—subdue pigs to check their tongues for cysts. If the trier found cysts, the price would fall. If the seller protested, the measle trier might wrestle the pig again and cut into its tongue to show the farmer the cysts and larvae.[33]

Finally, pigs have another important similarity to humans: they are dangerous. In a twenty-first-century case report of an adult man killed by a pig, the corpse had "numerous, dispersed severe blunt force injuries" from the pig's kicks and headbutts, as well as multiple shattered bones and bite wounds to the head and arms. The man was dead and his body pulped long before the pig stopped its attack. Pigs have forty-four teeth, with six incisors and two long canines that project from the lower jaw as tusks. Boars grow longer tusks than sows, and farmers generally removed them or pared them down to reduce the risk of a serious bite or goring. "Swine," a breeder admitted, "are very difficult animals to obtain any mastery over, or to operate on or examine. Seldom tame or easily handled, they are at such periods most unmanageable, kicking, screaming, and even biting fiercely." Pigs, especially large males, another breeder wrote, are "by no means a safe animal to venture near at any time."[34]

The Irish themselves joked about the pigs who "paid their rent"— not every Irish joke was told by Britons at Ireland's expense. British readers, however, were less likely to grasp the gallows humour in Ireland's pig tales. The Irish poor lived in intimacy with pigs *because they had to*. Reformers warned parents never to leave children alone with pigs, especially sows nursing piglets. A father who napped while his toddler played with a litter of piglets awoke to "the poor little thing . . . all in a gore of blood, and its face so eat by the nasty sow, that the life was out of it, sure enough." Anyone vulnerable could be attacked by a pig if they were unlucky. In a famous letter from Dublin, Frederick Douglass described meeting a beggar whose face had been partially eaten by a pig while he was passed out from drink, leaving a half-healed wound that revealed parts of his skull. The potato could fail and collapse a family's prospects; a pig could kill a child, maim an adult, destroy a home. The Irish poor depended on both from necessity.[35]

THE THIRD LEG OF THE STOOL WAS THE DRIED PEAT THAT IS IRE-land's most abundant biofuel. Peat, like potatoes and pigs, was part of rural life across northern Europe—but also like Irish potatoes and pigs, peat became a symbol of a degeneracy deemed especially inherent to Ireland. Peat bogs are cold, oxygen-poor, and acidic. They inhibit bacterial growth and consequently can preserve organic matter for centuries. The bodies and artifacts found in Irish bogs by nineteenth-century archaeologists inevitably invited comparisons between Irish and British progress in civilisation.

In 1821, on land belonging to the Bellew family (who owned more than ten thousand acres, worth more than £5,000 a year in rent), a curious amateur archaeologist found a human body nine feet below the surface of a bog. "It had all the appearance of recent death when first discovered," he wrote, "but on exposure to the atmosphere it decayed rapidly." Before the corpse deliquesced, the dead man's face looked handsome, "of foreign aspect," and he had black shoulder-length hair. He had been wrapped in what looked like a deer skin and buried with long poles on either side of him. The raw and hairy hide, its discoverer concluded, was an "instance of ignorance and barbarism that could hardly have occurred out of Ireland." The body, probably from the Iron Age, seemed to show that just as the modern Irish were out of step with the modern British Empire, the ancient Irish were also less civilised than pre-Roman Britons, who wore tanned leather.[36]

A peat bog is an ecosystem formed in cold, wet soils and dominated by mosses from the genus *Sphagnum*. Dense layers of moss slow down the process of decomposition, trapping carbon dioxide. Living plants in peat bogs trap more carbon through photosynthesis than the decaying organic matter below them can release. Peatlands are carbon sinks; the trapped carbon in dried peat is what makes it burn. The methane that bubbles out of peat can spontaneously combust, the inspiration for legendary creatures, like will-o'-the-wisps, that carry lights to lure the unsuspecting into the wet, cold darkness. Peatlands cover about 3 percent of the earth's terrestrial surface and about one-seventh of Ireland's. Globally, they might hold as much as 21 percent of all plant-stored carbon.[37]

Ireland was substantially deforested by the seventeenth century, partly because of military demand for wood. By the eighteenth century, wood was so scarce outside the cultivated woodlands of the wealthy that logs were more easily gathered, preserved, from peat bogs than cut fresh from forests. One Roscommon field was guarded by a scarecrow built of wood salvaged in this way, resembling at a distance "women occupied in weeding." Deforestation transformed the fabric of everyday life. Before, most Irish cottages had been constructed of wattle and daub, spread over frames of coppiced hazel and roofed with thatch. When wood became scarce, labourers began to build with stone. Inside many Irish cottages, straw and wicker furniture replaced wood. The "traditional," sparsely furnished stone structure was an adaptation to environmental change. Deforestation also changed Irish energy consumption, and peat became essential to the rural economy. Unlike stone houses, peat had been in common use for many centuries. However, turf cutting, reported from at least the seventh century, rapidly increased as forests declined, and peat became the main fuel almost everywhere in Ireland. In places where bogs were scarce or depleted, the poor foraged for blackthorn and gorse to burn.[38]

Historians estimate that about 90 percent of Irish turf was cut
either for personal use or for very local markets. Ireland has far
fewer reserves of coal than Britain, and little coal was imported,
especially before the famine. In 1838, for example, the Dublin
Steam Packet Company used peat in the engines of its flagship,
Royal William, and steamships sailing on the Shannon also often
burned turf. Before the Irish rail network was completed, a year's
supply of turf was about 40 percent cheaper than coal. Even Irish
cities burned peat. Dublin was supplied with turf from the inland
Bog of Allen, Limerick from bogs near the Shannon. Although
there were a few industrial turf collectors, most of the trade was
local, small scale, and low tech. Turf cutters would usually cut and
dry turf and sell it to the owners of horse or donkey carts to haul
to barges on rivers and canals that would carry the fuel to towns
and cities.[39]

Like potatoes, peat was abundant—but, unlike potatoes, peat
could not really be said to fail. "An economical system of cutting
turf has not been adopted," a writer commented, "because the supply was deemed inexhaustible." Even so, the growing Irish population and, after the famine, the gradual industrialisation of peat
cutting began to encroach on what had seemed to be a limitless
resource. It was estimated that between 1814 and 1907, something like eight hundred thousand acres of Irish turf were burned.
Although peat could not fail in the same sense as a crop, a peat
shortage was a catastrophe. Peat helped keep Ireland's economy
from dissolving in the decades before the famine. The fuel was so
essential that it could not be exploited on an industrial scale. Any
industrial collection of peat threatened the well-being of the poor.[40]

Peat bogs are archives, natural records of changes in climate and
flora. They preserve ancient pollen as well as particulate matter.
Animal carcasses, wooden and metal objects, and stores of provisions all survive well in peat—caches of butter are among the most

common finds in Irish bogs, as well as weapons, clothing, and cookware. The rarest and most spectacular discoveries are human corpses: at least eighty have been found in Irish bogs since 1750. In the nineteenth century, landowners and amateur archaeologists often found entire trees under the moss, as well as Stone Age and Iron Age hand axes and pots.[41]

When Arthur Young visited Ireland after the American Revolution, he noted that men draining a bog had found plough marks fifteen feet beneath its surface, as well as the foundations of houses and cattle pens. The Irish poor rarely ploughed their potato grounds in the eighteenth century, and only larger graziers could afford outbuildings for livestock. Diggers also found massive sets of antlers—the remains of either Irish elk, a species entirely extinct, or European moose, a species long extirpated from Ireland—as well as trunks of oak, yew, and fir. Ireland had once had farms and forests, Young concluded, as well as game and lumber, but the lazy modern Irish, content simply to burn the turf for cooking fires, never restored this prosperity. The old trees and plough ground seemed to testify to a squandered time of plenty.[42]

THE THREE-LEGGED STOOL OF THE POTATO, PIG, AND PEAT MADE commercial agriculture possible on divided and capital-starved Irish land, but also structured a moral economy that often clashed with the market economy. Large yields on small land reinforced the governing paradox of Irish economic life under British colonialism. Potatoes, pigs, and peat were abundant, and their abundance nourished a culture of generosity, egalitarianism, and strong family bonds. At the same time, abundance could abet exploitation, extraction, and immiseration. As James Fintan Lalor wrote during the famine, "The potato was our sole and only capital, to live and work on, to make much or little of;

and on it the entire social economy of this country was founded, formed, and supported."[43]

Oral traditions and folklore about potatoes emphasise plenty—there are stories of people who had so many potatoes that they could eat and give away as many as they wanted and still leave unused mounds in ditches for the crows. Recall the lurid overestimates of Irish average potato consumption—tall tales that turned the abundance of the potato into evidence of Irish strangeness. Abundance was antithetical to political economy. Scarcity meant risk, and risk meant growth and civilisation. The abundance of potatoes, inconstant and seasonal though it was, afforded the Irish poor the ability to have something that few Britons, even among the middle classes, enjoyed. Irish men and women could marry and have children without worrying about feeding a growing family, as long as they had access to land for potatoes. Irish labourers had time at least periodically for leisure—dances, fairs, weddings, funerals, sports, and feast days. A family holding conacre, after a good harvest, could give potatoes as gifts and be generous with beggars. Potatoes allowed the poorest Irish enough to *give*.[44]

The gift economy in the Irish countryside was like a lake forming after a deluge in an arid place: a seasonal oasis of comity, pleasure, and plenty that filled and then evaporated. The overall economic order of the Irish countryside was viciously competitive and moved in time with British and global markets for grain, livestock, and meat, but a gift economy upends that usual capitalist order. Without scarcity, as a botanist writes, "wealth is understood as having enough to share, and the practice for dealing with abundance is to give it away." In other words, beneath the scarcity-bound material economy of the Irish countryside lay a moral economy where abundance was the rule and hoarding potatoes was a sin.[45]

The market for potatoes was far less competitive and far more local than the market for export crops. Farmers in Wicklow, for example, considered it impossible to turn a profit on potatoes, no matter the demand, if the market was more than forty miles away. Customary rules governing the export of potatoes, even for short distances, were enforced first with moral suasion and then with violence. In summer, and when harvests faltered, labourers would sometimes threaten anyone trying to carry potatoes outside a given parish or townland. Most farmers, especially in times of scarcity, would only sell their potatoes by the "basket," a quantity of about 125 pounds. Beggars would often sell smaller quantities as they walked through the countryside. Labourers often bought from beggars, who charged more per potato but sold in quantities that the poorest could afford to buy. Rural "outrages" (see Chapter 2) were sometimes directed at potato sellers who asked more than the normal price. This hostility to profiteering is echoed in folktales. In one story, a potato seller who did not get the price he wanted for his crop threw the surplus into a river. During the Great Famine, he was "the first to die with the hunger."[46]

The wealth afforded by a good potato harvest could be rare and was almost always temporary. A few good seasons might lift a labourer taking conacre into a more secure cottier tenancy, but an injury or a twist in the market or a change in the weather could put a family right back where it started. A "good name" was often more valuable and permanent, and giving gifts built a reputation. Many beggars received a standard two handfuls of potatoes, and on many days in summer, twenty or more families of beggars might call on a farmer. "There is a strong dislike," an observer commented, "connected with [farmers'] religious sentiments, to making any calculation of the amount which they 'bestow for God's sake.'" A farmer with an especially good harvest might give away as much as a shilling's worth of potatoes in a day without thinking of the cost. In summer, begging was considered shameful enough that women and children would travel to other counties rather than be seen on the roads near home. But at harvest, it was understood that potatoes from neighbours were for the asking. In good years a person might collect five or six stone of potatoes each day throughout the roughly two weeks of the harvest. "People are very liberal when they are digging," one worker explained, and would give potatoes even to a man with a full bag, "as they know he is making a little store to keep the family in, of a hard day in winter." The abundance of potatoes was "a common fund upon which every person in distress has an acknowledged claim."[47]

Openhandedness was a prized virtue among the Irish poor. However, potatoes given as charity during the day were some-times stolen back at night. A poor farmer taking conacre was expected to give potatoes without an eye on his own inventory, but widespread theft of potatoes shows how an act of public generosity could be privately and clandestinely revoked. Giving potatoes freely held communities together, but a gift could also be a performance to save face or preserve a good name. Human beings struggle with contradiction far less than the social sciences predict. A man might have given his potatoes without a thought to his own subsistence and then just as earnestly slipped out at night to fill his pits for the winter. In any case, potatoes were reg-ularly taken under cover of darkness, "not from immoral feeling, and never to procure their being sent to prison for food." Cows were also secretly milked in their sheds by the hungry. The gift economy of the potato was both beyond the market and pro-foundly influenced by market pressures—for land, for food secu-rity, and for rent.[48]

The abundance of the potato secured subsistence and acted as a platform on which many other social institutions and cultural forms were built and maintained. A secure supply of food afforded labouring people in Ireland the chance to marry earlier, with less worry about family survival. One baffled Irish landlord told the royal commission that a conacre tenant on his land had "asked me to lend him £2 to pay the expense of his wedding. I asked him how he could marry under such circumstances; and he said that he had got a quarter of an acre of potato-ground from a farmer, and that he could therefore reckon on potatoes enough to keep a wife." The plenty of the potato allowed even the very poor to marry if they chose to, and to unite families that might otherwise be flung apart. At fairs, families would often arrange marriages, negotiating over dowries that might include access to a lease or to conacre land, pigs or piglets, furniture, or farm implements.[49]

The Irish were scolded in Britain for their imprudent marriages and their many children. But for people working as subsistence farmers and wage labourers—people with nothing else but relatively reliable and plentiful food—a large family was a meaningful kind of wealth. As one Briton wrote, "In the number of their children do the Irish peasantry rejoice." Children were "their wealth and [they] look upon their offspring as the resources from whence in age and in sickness they must derive their subsistence and their happiness." The wealth children represented, like the potato itself, was both inside and outside the market. Children were useful labourers, to be sure. However, Irish families were large not only because tenants and labourers taking conacre needed more hands. A large family was also a form of abundance, made possible by the abundance of the potato. Children were a symbol that the calculus of supply and demand, at least in one small but infinitely important way, couldn't touch and warp *everything*.[50]

The paradoxical abundance of Irish leisure and family life also offended some British visitors, who saw in it only further proof of

Ireland's incorrigible backwardness. The idea that the rural economy had made the Irish, in a strange way, too likely to behave as though they were rich enough to be idle repeated itself in British ethnographic writing about rural Irish culture. "The town of Limerick," a visitor wrote, "was like a fair . . . thousands of people idling about in the streets and at night getting up party fights, and they were leaving their food, which in a few months they will be begging from England, to rot for want of exertion, *because it was a holiday!*" Some observed that the Irish would walk seven miles after a workday to go to a wedding or party or dance. An Englishman, one commented, "is not so lively; but then a hard day's work with him is certainly a different affair from what it is with *Paddy.*" Reformers argued that wakes for the dead had become "parties of pleasure for the living." Wakes required tobacco, including a plate of snuff placed on the stiff body itself, and alcohol to keep the mourners from sleeping through the night so they could protect the corpse and the person's soul. These were "luxuries"—what were the Irish doing to *earn* them?[51]

Irish dress, like wakes and parties and fairs, also came to be seen as suspiciously fancy for a people mired in poverty. Once again, appearances were deceiving. As wool and linen manufacturing declined after the Acts of Union put British and Irish producers into more direct competition, Ireland made less and less fabric. British cotton clothing was rare among the Irish poor (if not among the wealthier classes), and light cotton was unsuitable for heavy everyday use by agricultural labourers in a cold, wet climate. Instead, the Irish poor usually wore homemade wool clothing, although some, especially men, wore used clothing, including more formal garments that had been cast off and repaired many times. Landlords sometimes donated used clothing to their tenants, garments that circulated through families and pawnshops. Women often wore coarse flannel petticoats, sometimes dyed red or blue, and short jackets that resembled the Spencer jackets popular among women in Regency-era England. In some parts of the west, people bartered yarn stocking for canvas, candles, butter, eggs, and other articles. In the summer many went without shoes or socks. The Irish poor, in other words, wore the clothes they could find, could make, could afford, or were given, but reformers found the Irish tendency to wear long, battered tailcoats especially galling. The coats "impede the limbs in walking, and are altogether cumbersome and unsuitable." The Irish, critics concluded, should change their clothes to avoid anything but "what is necessary for cleanliness, and for neatness and decency of appearance."[52]

The abundance of the potato, though it was often unstable and always temporary, also galled British observers. Regardless of the distant cause, the potato was a symbol and an engine of the problem. In Ireland, a fellow of the Royal Society argued, "the potato has begotten millions of paupers who live but are not clothed, who marry but do not work, caring for nothing but their dish of potatoes." The potato and its moral economy seemed to represent the Irish themselves, "fecund, rooted in time and place, and mired in the past."[53]

THE FALL OF THE PEOPLE'S POTATO ALWAYS THREATENED A CRISIS, and by 1842 a farming guide warned that "great failures have taken place in the potato crops within the last few years." Although farmers knew that every cultivar would eventually begin to fail, many despaired. "Our great Creator," one explained, "is not pleased with us; He wishes to punish us and to show us we are under his scourge." The Irish dependence on the potato had become so profound that a serious food shortage seemed all but inevitable. The three-legged stool that supported both the Irish export and rent economy and the moral economy of the Irish poor was at risk of collapse.[54]

As the first chapters of this book explain, the elements of Irish economic life that seemed precapitalist—wages paid in land, rent paid in labour, widespread subsistence agriculture—were adaptations to a competitive market structured by the dispossession and exploitation that followed the conquest of Ireland in the late seventeenth century. But colonial eyes could not see the forest for the trees—or the potato fields for the stalks. What was new looked old, and what was roiled by the market looked still. The hostility of many political economists to the ambiguities of the potato and to the stubbornly anti-modern and anti-market forces in Ireland that potatoes appeared to represent made at least some look forward to a catastrophic potato failure that would shock Ireland out of its torpor.

When the blight pandemic spread to Ireland, the crisis was neither entirely unexpected nor entirely unwelcome among British officials and commentators. As the next chapters show, the legacies of the long, violent, and contentious history of Britain and Ireland—as well as deeply held ideas about empire, civilisation, and the market—shaped how the government of the United Kingdom responded to the failure of the Irish potato crop. When the potatoes failed, the *Times* published an editorial that recalled ideas about the Irish appetite. In England, the editors wrote, "hunger would have been (as elsewhere) the herald of comfort," a spur to effort, innovation, and, eventually, prosperity. The Irish, though, had no stomach for hard work, only for potatoes. "When the Celts once cease to be potatophagi," the editorial concluded, "they must become carnivorous. With the taste of meats will grow the appetite for them." The argument, bitterly and accurately summarised by the American abolitionist Asenath Nicholson, was simple, circular, and devasting: for the Irish worker, "lazy, dirty, and savage as he is, the potato is a boon which is quite too good for him."[55]

Charles Trevelyan, with less venom than the *Times* but with
an equal sense of the inevitability and potential *utility* of Irish
starvation, summarised the problem of the potato in his trium-
phalist history of British responses to the blight, *The Irish Crisis*
(first published in 1848, when the crisis was far from over). In
the end, the potato had "no value in the market." Consequently,
the Irish poor could not sell potatoes and save for a rainy day or
even buy the cheap comforts of the British poor—their sugar
and coffee, cheap clothing, and cheap bread. They could not join
the civilised world. "What hope is there," he asked, "for a nation
which lives on potatoes?"[56]

4

PEEL'S BRIMSTONE

IRISH FARMERS STARTED TO DIG UP THEIR POTATOES IN AUGUST 1845, many weeks earlier than usual. Potatoes are hardy, but experience had taught the farmers that when an individual plant was diseased, the sickness could spread very quickly. The blight that had struck North American fields the year before and had flattened the Belgian and Dutch harvests through the summer was spreading in Ireland. The disease proliferated astonishingly quickly, turning potato stalks "black as ink." The smell in stricken fields was overwhelming, "unusual, close, malarious."[1]

The blight was dire and unwelcome, but not a surprise. A potato disease was spreading in Europe, and many expected it would reach Ireland. Furthermore, potato crops were fickle. Irish potatoes had failed in 1817, 1822, 1831, 1839, and 1842, causing localised famine and precipitating outbreaks of typhus and other epidemic fevers. In response to these repeated crises, the government had developed a template for famine relief, based on the principle that a well-calibrated market would allow the Irish poor to survive until the next harvest. First, to secure the food supply, the government proposed to buy, import, and sell either cheap food or seed potatoes. Second, to provide work for the unemployed, the Irish Board of Works was given permission to invite county and barony committees of landlords, professionals, and clergy to propose public works projects to the Treasury, and the Treasury was given the power to loan and grant money to the Board of Works to pay wages at emergency worksites.

In 1845, Ireland was not unique in Europe in its dependence on intensively planted potatoes, a vulnerable agricultural ecology. And yet, though blight destroyed nearly all the 1845 potato crop across the Low Countries and a large proportion of the crop in Germany and the Baltic, far more people died or were displaced in Ireland than in any other blight-stricken European country. Political history, not natural history, turned a potato failure into a famine. Outside Ireland, there were other crops for the poor to eat—and there were governments less fearful that generous relief would turn the poor into paupers.[2]

The first wave of the blight, in 1845–1846, overlapped with one of the most important transformations in British politics since the Union. In 1845, Prime Minister Robert Peel broke with many members of his own party and moved to repeal the Corn Laws. The laws, passed at the end of the Napoleonic Wars, protected the price of British grain from foreign competition and shored up the economic and political power of aristocratic landlords. After repeal, Peel's followers broke with the rest of the Conservatives and eventually joined the Whigs and Radicals in a new, free-trading Liberal Party. More cautious Whigs allied with protectionists to reconstruct the Conservatives. Although Peel claimed that the Irish crisis was the reason for his decision to tack from protectionism to free trade, the drama that filled the

House in the spring of 1846 muffled reports of mounting chaos and panic from Ireland.

WE NOW KNOW THAT *PHYTOPHTHORA INFESTANS*, THE CAUSE OF late blight, is not a fungus but a fungus-like oomycete, a relative of fungi and algae, that favours wet conditions. Oomycetes cause other serious plant diseases, such as sudden oak death, which threatens old-growth oak in California, Oregon, and elsewhere. Oomycetes are often known as water moulds, although many species (unlike *P. infestans*) do not prefer wet conditions. All oomycetes are rugged and can survive shocks that would easily kill their host plants. *P. infestans* spores, for example, can survive freezing and drying and can remain dormant for years. Late blight can easily spread from stored potatoes, or even from infected soil or the seeds of other crops that happen to carry spores.[3]

In ideal conditions, the blight oomycete's entire reproductive cycle takes less than five days, and each lesion on an affected leaf can release up to three hundred thousand spores per day. Most ecological invasions require multiple introductions of the new species. However, samples from European potatoes preserved from the 1840s show that every sample's genetic code contains a distinctive haplotype—an inheritable and distinct group of chromosomes, used by geneticists to trace lineages—tracked to the Toluca Valley in Mexico, where potatoes grow wild. Incredibly, this means that the European late-blight pandemic *might* have been caused by the arrival of a single blighted cargo of potatoes, or even just one blighted potato or preserved spore that then cloned itself by the quadrillions.[4]

The names of several cultivars of potato introduced to Europe in the early 1840s by Belgian farmers looking for varieties resistant to dry rot, another potato disease, make allusions to Peru and the Andean cordillera. From this, some experts have inferred that the blight arrived in Europe via Mexico from a beachhead in Peru, either on potatoes or in shipments of guano. There is plenty of circumstantial evidence in the historical record to support this theory. An oral history of the famine blames guano, "imported for the first time from South America," for the blight's arrival. A history of the famine published in 1875 speculates that the blight in Ireland was most virulent in fields that had been previously planted with wheat and fertilised with imported guano. If guano was indeed the source of blight, it would be a cruel irony if Ireland, one of the only potato-growing regions in Europe generally too poor to import fertiliser, was the place where the blight proved most devastating.[5]

Although it appeared to be an act of God, a disaster as unavoidable and unstoppable as an earthquake, the late-blight pandemic was an unintended consequence of the increasing integration of global commerce. Potatoes kept as food for sailors and seed potatoes of new varieties ordered by farmers were stored in the holds of newer, larger, and faster steamships. Fertiliser mined by indentured Chinese contract labourers on arid islands off the coast of Peru—islands that had been visited for millennia by seabirds, which deposited phosphate-rich guano in layers many metres deep—allowed farmers across North America and Europe to increase yields. Farms separated by oceans became ecological neighbours. In these globalising conditions, *P. infestans* arrived in Ireland, where the agricultural ecosystem might just as well have been designed for its comfort. Storage of potatoes in dirt pits allowed a few spores settled on a potato to colonise an entire season's supply. The economic structure of Irish agriculture made it impossible to create firebreaks against the disease by replanting potato fields with other crops. The pathogen thrived everyplace in Europe where poverty encouraged intensive potato planting. In

Belgium the blight was worst in poor and densely populated Flanders, where 25 percent of rural households were landless and where the average family farm was too small for subsistence.[6]

Blight was reported in New England and eastern Canada in 1844. Belgian farmers first noticed widespread blight in mid-July 1845, near Courtrai. A few days later, farms across the border in the Netherlands reported cases. Belgian and Dutch authorities panicked. Blight destroyed 71 percent of the Dutch and 88 percent of the Belgian potato crop in 1845. An estimated three hundred thousand people died of starvation and hunger-related illness across the Netherlands, Belgium, and Prussia. The blight spread across the European potato belt, from the UK to European Russia. London newspapers reported on food riots in Prussia and Poland, and on emergency restrictions of grain exports in the Ottoman Empire. Potatoes shipped from England to Belgium went into steamships healthy and sound and rotted before the end of the short voyage. Authorities feared that consumption of diseased potatoes would lead to cholera outbreaks, or worse.[7]

In England, farmers in Northamptonshire, Huntingdonshire, and elsewhere reported that the blight struck potato stalks that grew in clay and prime soil alike, and in well-drained as well as boggy fields. The disease appeared to spread from the leaves, down the stem, and into the tuber. Some speculated that potatoes had somehow been infected with a cattle disease. Others thought the blight was a "gangrene" or "cholera" of the plant, because the stricken potatoes smelled putridly sweet and fecal.

The *Gardener's Chronicle* reported the appearance of the blight in Ireland in August 1845. By this time, in London's Covent Garden, every greengrocer found that at least some of their inventory had been reduced to a pulp by black mould. Within a few weeks, naturalists had isolated the organism consuming potatoes. It looked like a fungus. Most botanists and mycologists assumed that something in the climate had killed the potato, and that the "fungus" they found growing throughout was an opportunistic organism that decomposed plants that were already dying or dead. Although under a microscope the pathogen seemed to have "an appalling character," astonishing scientists with "the fecundity and power of so small and apparently weak an object," it was considered the consequence, not the cause, of the disease.[8]

Decades before the germ theory of disease became widely accepted, in the 1840s most infectious diseases were thought to be caused by climate. Diseases like malaria ("bad air") were blamed on miasmas of rotting animal and vegetable matter. Some scientists blamed the blight on static electricity, generated by steam locomotives pulling trains across Britain; others blamed emissions of toxic gases from hidden volcanoes, venting into the soil from deep beneath the earth. Perhaps tiny insects were eating the crops, or imported fertilisers had poisoned the soil. One researcher argued that weather conditions caused the juices of the potato plant to curdle into a thick, proteinaceous "vegetable casein" similar to the additives used to coagulate milk for cheese-making.[9]

The most sophisticated climatic theories presumed that the cause of the blight was excess water. When the blight appeared in Europe, although biologists and chemists had not yet fully explained photosynthesis, it was common knowledge that plants exchanged water, oxygen, and carbon dioxide when exposed to sunlight. A prizewinning essay noted that a potato plant in full flower had a root system whose length totaled nearly a third of a mile and that contained at least twenty-four thousand filaments and pores for taking in water. It was reasonable to conclude that lots of rain and little sunlight would be "unfavorable to the motions of the fluids or to the action of the cells" of the potato plant. Among the major contributors to the debate, only M. J. Berkeley, an Anglican priest and mycologist who later wrote an

important textbook on British fungi, hypothesised that the fungus
was actually killing potatoes itself.[10]

Robert Peel, following the Belgian, Dutch, and other governments, organised a scientific commission to report on the disease
and to scour scientific journals for potential treatments. Peel's commissioners estimated that at least half the Irish crop was lost. They
also discovered something worse: potatoes stored in pits were also
susceptible to blight. In previous potato failures, there might not
have been a large quantity of harvested potatoes, but those that
were harvested remained edible. In 1845, every new pit broken
open might prove to be rotten—causing scenes of incomprehension
and mourning dramatised in one of the most famous paintings
to depict the Great Famine, Daniel Macdonald's *An Irish Peasant
Family Discovering the Blight of Their Store* (1847). Since the blight
could affect stored potatoes, it was impossible to predict how much
food Ireland would need to survive until the next harvest. Some
landlords criticised the commissioners as alarmist, but most understood the threat. "When the evil day of scarcity does come," Lord
Heytesbury, the lord lieutenant, wrote, "it will probably come with
fearful rapidity."[11]

With the blight accelerating, and based on the vague consensus
that the cause of the disease was excess moisture, the commission
published its official advice to farmers in late October. Above all,
farmers were told to keep their potatoes dry. Potatoes should be
harvested in dry weather. Blighted potatoes needed to be sorted
and separated. The commission recommended that blighted potatoes be set aside to make starch for glue and shirt collars. Sound
potatoes, in turn, should be stored not in pits but in pyramidal
piles, with flat layers of potatoes insulated by layers of ash, lime,
or dried turf, and the pyramid's sloping sides structured "like the
roof of a cottage cut into steps." Potatoes should be kept in these
mounds until it was time to eat them. "Recollect," the commission

warned, "that if they get damp nothing can make them keep." It is not clear how many Irish labourers, especially those who spoke only Irish, heard the recommendations. The pamphlets were distributed through the Royal Irish Constabulary's field offices— there were only so many constables, and the report was only published in English. *Punch* teased the commission for its "speculative wisdom" and for preaching "in an unknown tongue . . . fifty impossible remedies to the wondering peasant."[12]

The commission's public reports were sober but reassuring; privately, the commissioners were alarmed. One suggested to Peel that the government secretly arrange with British consular staff to purchase seed potatoes in the drier parts of the potato belt, like northern Spain and Portugal. "The case is much worse than the public supposes," he wrote. In Schull, County Cork, and even on the small islands off the southern coast, all stored potatoes "without one single exception" were beginning to rot. A priest in Kells, County Meath, estimated that one in twenty families would be out of potatoes by Christmas. And yet even as the crisis deepened, the priest noted, exports kept moving out of the county. He saw at least fifty dray carts full of grain on the road to Drogheda, "thence to feed the foreigner."[13]

ROBERT PEEL HAD SPENT HIS ADULT LIFE IN PARLIAMENT. THE son of a wealthy family in the textile trade, he became an MP in 1809, at twenty-one years old—"nursed in the House of Commons," sniped an enemy. Peel was considered "an adopted member of the aristocratic commonwealth," a manufacturer's son consistently on the side of the landed. To critics, Peel was two-faced and amoral, always "willing to give what it costs nothing to withhold." To supporters, he was pragmatic. Sir Lawrence Peel, in an admiring biography of his grandfather, described him as a careful reformer, "fearful, lest the new wine should burst the old bottles . . . proud to be of the people, their friend, and never their flatterer."[14]

Peel recognised the arrival of the blight in Ireland as a very serious crisis that would require a coordinated national response to prevent a famine. However, for Peel and his cabinet, discussion of relief policies was shaped by other controversial issues, including the mounting Irish campaign to repeal the Acts of Union and the prospect of ending the Corn Laws in favour of free trade in grain. These issues, intertwined historically and politically, formed a tangle that could easily bring down a government.

During the era of the Acts of Union, William Pitt the Younger had sold the prospect of a United Kingdom by promoting the mutual benefits of open trade between Britain and Ireland. Pitt had also favoured free trade more broadly. Lowering tariffs would reduce prices for consumers, and suited an expanding commercial empire defended by a mighty navy. During the Napoleonic Wars, wealthy landowners benefited from high prices for their produce regardless of tariffs. But when the wars ended, the coalition of landlords that had prospered during the conflicts was exposed by a sudden fall in commodity prices, especially grain. In 1815, Lord Liverpool's Tory government passed the Corn Laws to shore its aristocratic political base and to preserve the wartime unity of Irish and British landholders.

After Pitt, although the Tories had strongly supported the Union, the party divided on Catholic civil rights. However, overwhelming pressure from the Catholic League pushed the prime minister, the Duke of Wellington, to pass Catholic Emancipation in 1829 (with Peel's help managing the House of Commons). In November 1830, Wellington resigned, facing demands for the reform of Parliament and bringing the Whigs, under Earl Grey and Lord Melbourne, into power. The Whigs passed a suite of reforms, including the 1832 Representation of the People Act (the so-called Great Reform Act), which redistributed parliamentary constituencies to better reflect the distribution of the UK's population, shuttered "rotten" and "pocket" boroughs controlled by small numbers of voters, and introduced modest increases in the franchise.

The Whigs had their own Irish problems. After Catholic Emancipation, Irish rate-paying tenants, supported in the House by a group of Irish MPs dedicated to the repeal of the Acts of Union, resisted the tithes demanded by the UK government to support the Anglican church of Ireland, sometimes with violence. In 1834, as the tithe war grew, Lord Stanley, then colonial secretary, urged Grey to pass a Coercion Act. The lord lieutenant, Lord Anglesey, preferred a compromise that would preserve the tithe but share it between Anglicans and Catholics. When this cabinet dispute was leaked to Parliament, Stanley resigned, followed by Grey. Robert Peel briefly became prime minister, leading a short minority government supported by Whigs loyal to Stanley. When the Tories failed to gain a majority in a general election, Lord Melbourne, the home secretary during Grey's premiership, became prime minister. But the Whigs, shaken, had lost cohesion and momentum. And then Melbourne, too, was defeated by free trade. In 1841, his government was overturned on a proposal to lower duties on foreign sugar and timber, and to change the duty on foreign grain by setting it at a fixed rate that would in practice be a discount. Melbourne resigned, and Peel became prime minister.

Peel's administration, like every administration since the Battle of Waterloo, needed to navigate a safe path through both free trade and Irish issues, each with its own pitfalls and powerful constituencies. Peel was vulnerable to both protectionists and so-called Ultra-Tories within his own party, who vehemently opposed Catholic Emancipation. On free trade, Peel preached protectionism while making incremental changes to grain and sugar tariffs.

Supporters praised him for doing more to "free trade from the fetters which shackled it" than any prime minister in a century. Peel was deft at adapting his opponent's policies to his own purposes. He had opposed Catholic civil rights when his rival, George Canning, supported them, and then he carried the 1829 Catholic Relief Act himself. Now he promoted a trademark Whig policy from the Conservative benches. Peel, some said, had "caught the Whigs bathing and walked away with their clothes."[15]

The future of the Union itself was also on the parliamentary agenda. As chief secretary for Ireland under Lord Liverpool, Peel had created the Peace Preservation Force, the paramilitary group that enforced the law in Ireland before the creation of the Royal Irish Constabulary. Now, in the 1840s, the Repeal Association was organising "monster meetings," usually held in the open air and attended by many thousands of people. Daniel O'Connell and the other leaders of Repeal were committed to promoting Irish national autonomy and legislative independence under the Crown, and to agrarian and constitutional reform, not revolution. But despite—or perhaps because of—these relatively conservative political ambitions, O'Connell enjoyed mass support. And so, although Repeal was officially nonviolent, the monster meetings were spectacles, featuring music and quasi-military parades, shows of Irish unity that hinted at the potential for rebellion. Without amplification, most people attending the meetings would have had very little idea what was being said—but the meetings themselves were an argument, and a threat.[16]

Peel let them happen. On August 15, 1843, at the Hill of Tara, the old seat of the High Kings of Ireland, O'Connell led his largest meeting yet. The *Times* estimated that more than a hundred thousand people attended (a number impossible to verify). The speakers from the provincial chapters of the Repeal Association arrived in procession, led by trumpeters on horseback, a harpist in an open horse-drawn carriage, and a full marching band supervised by mounted parade marshals wearing white rosettes. The meeting had been advertised with placards bearing the Repeal slogans: "Hurrah for Repeal—Victoria our Queen—our watchword 'Liberty' and Ireland for the Irish." The *Times* warned that the meetings would lead to insurrection. If they were not stopped, the Irish might support "a system which, they argue, cannot be illegal, because it is not checked by authority, and cannot be dangerous, because it is not opposed by force." Did O'Connell think *he* was the High King of Ireland?[17]

O'Connell and other leading Repealers planned another meeting, for October 8, at Clontarf, a suburb of Dublin. O'Connell's rhetoric had grown increasingly vehement. He argued that Parliament's right to sit derived from the ancient witan, the Saxon council of nobles and bishops that had advised the English Crown for centuries before the Norman Conquest. Queen Victoria, by this logic, could call an Irish Parliament without consulting Westminster. Moreover, if O'Connell was right, the Act of Union would have to be considered unconstitutional under the "real" Saxon principles of English government. Peel called O'Connell's bluff: the Clontarf meeting was banned as seditious, and crowds were warned to stay away by bills and placards around the city. Curious Dubliners crowded newspaper offices and the government's printshop. O'Connell had no appetite for armed rebellion. He called off the meeting, although he considered the threat to send in the army a "base or imbecile step" on the part of the lord lieutenant. Meanwhile, when rowdy Repeal supporters assembled at Clontarf, ready for a riot, they found an empty field.[18]

Peel had set a clever trap. O'Connell looked weak. In early 1844, however, the government, eager for a final defeat and humiliation of Repeal, pressed its attack too far. O'Connell and his son

John were arrested and convicted on charges of conspiracy. The men were sentenced to a year's imprisonment, but released on appeal to the House of Lords. O'Connell was paraded through the streets of Dublin, his reputation repaired. However, the unity of Repeal was fractured. Now even the Repealers faced an "Irish question." Conservative Catholics distanced themselves from more militant, secular, and nationalist activists. Peel exploited this fissure. In 1845, in an ambitious plan for the legislative session, he proposed to increase government funding to Saint Patrick's College, the Catholic seminary founded in 1795 in Maynooth, and to establish secular Queen's Colleges to provide nondenominational higher education in Ireland's three largest towns outside Dublin (the colleges opened in 1849 and 1850, in Belfast, Cork, and Galway). O'Connell bitterly opposed the Queen's Colleges as threats to Catholic higher learning. His rivals supported them in order to build a more inclusive Irishness on the model of European Romantic nationalism. O'Connell called his Irish critics from within Repeal "Young Ireland," an allusion to Giuseppe Mazzini's republican "Young Italy." The nickname, meant as an insult, was adopted as a badge of honour.

Peel's biographers often debate when and how he decided to abandon protectionism in favor of free trade, as well as the extent to which Irish affairs influenced his conversion. Regardless of the specific proportions in the mixture, Peel was mindful of both and triangulated his policy between the two explosive political issues. The Duke of Wellington told a friend that "rotten potatoes have done it all, they put Peel in his damned fright, and both for the cause and the effect he seems to feel equal contempt." But Peel's mind had changed apace with the prevailing opinion in the House of Commons. Every year from 1837, Charles Pelham Villiers, a Whig MP and a member of the Anti–Corn Law League, proposed a new motion for repeal of the Corn Laws, and every year the majority opposed to repeal got smaller, falling from more than 300 in 1842 to 132 by 1845. Free traders, one of Peel's biographers wrote, "were weak in the House but they felt themselves strong in the empire." As Britain consolidated its place as the centre of a global network of settlement and trade, it followed that free trade and liberal commercial policy would only become more popular, even at the expense of the traditional aristocracy.[19]

As the summer ended, reports from Ireland confirmed a growing subsistence crisis. Much of the potato harvest was lost. The government would need to do *something* about the failure, Peel insisted: "Letting things take their own course seems to me impossible." Relief, Peel reckoned, would probably fall to the government to finance. Peel did not expect much private charity to be forthcoming. The British public, he believed, had soured on Ireland after Clontarf. Relief would need to be local to Ireland and publicly funded—ideally by Irish taxes.

Initially, the government rebuilt a familiar system on a much larger scale. A central Relief Commission, to be based in Dublin, would coordinate with parish and county relief committees, distributing food to be sold and reviewing requests to fund public works projects. Peel summoned the cabinet on October 30, 1845, to explain his plan, which overlapped with a play against the Corn Laws. Russia, Belgium, and the Netherlands, he pointed out, had already opened their ports to imported grain, waiving or reducing tariffs. The Corn Laws, he argued, would need to be temporarily suspended to lower the price of grain across the United Kingdom. On November 6, Peel proposed an order-in-council to open ports to grain at a much lower duty, to be followed shortly after by measures to allow maize into the UK virtually duty-free, part of a schedule of lower duties on all other grains. Peel next asked the Baring brothers' banking firm to open secret negotiations to purchase £160,000 of maize from the United States, to be sold in Ireland.[20]

In early November, a delegation led by O'Connell presented an alternative plan, backed by the Dublin Corporation, to the lord lieutenant in Dublin. The corporation proposed that the government halt all grain exports from Ireland and prohibit distilling and brewing for the duration of the crisis, while also opening Irish ports to duty-free imports of colonial grain. They also proposed relief committees in every county to organise public works and maintain stores of food. The plan would be paid for with a 10 percent tax on residents, increased to up to 50 percent on absentees, along with a loan of £1.5 million, borrowed with the rent from Irish forests—owned almost entirely by the aristocracy—as collateral. The lord lieutenant, Lord Heytesbury, demurred—as O'Connell must have known he would. On December 8, at a meeting of the Repeal Association, O'Connell declared that if the Irish Parliament were to be restored, "the abundant crops with which Heaven has blessed" Ireland would be "kept for the people of Ireland" and the Irish Parliament would provide ample food and employment. These proposals were met with indifference or derision in Britain. *Punch* drew O'Connell as a giant potato, "the real potato blight of Ireland."[21]

Peel continued to press his cabinet to at least temporarily suspend the Corn Laws. On November 22, however, Lord John Russell, the former home secretary and now the leader of the Whig party, forced the issue, publishing a letter from Edinburgh declaring his support for free trade in grain. Peel found himself in a very difficult position. Rather than surprising the Whigs with a proposal to wind down the Corn Laws, which would have forced Russell to support the government, Peel would now seem as if he were taking policy advice from the Leader of the Opposition. The threat of being embarrassed by the Whigs outweighed other considerations and may have pushed Peel to introduce his plans as quickly as possible.[22]

Only two days before Russell's letter forced Peel's hand, the Irish Relief Commission opened. The government planned to establish depots to sell imported food beginning in May 1846. Local committees were expected to buy maize from the depots in bulk and sell the grain to the poor in increments of up to seven pounds. In the end, the UK government spent more than £185,000 buying maize, with the expectation that about £130,000 would eventually be repaid. The money purchased more than forty-four million pounds of maize, which was reckoned to be enough to feed about 490,000 people for three months. On public works, the government spent £452,727, of which it expected £226,363 to be repaid through taxes on Irish land. The government also issued an additional loan of £133,536, to be repaid in full. Surveying for Board of Works projects cost another £7,840.[23]

Peel's Relief Commission, a product of mainstream British politics and political economy, offered a chance to prove the superiority both of free trade over protection and of British management of Irish affairs. Relief, at first, was an argument for the Union, a large-scale project meant to show British compassion and to educate the Irish poor in civilisation. In February 1846, *Punch* adapted a nursery rhyme to Irish circumstances: "The butcher, the baker, the candlestick maker / All jumped out of a rotten potato"—a playful adaptation of the sentiment among some in the United Kingdom that a widespread potato failure might be *good* for Ireland. The "rotten potato" might force the Irish to abandon their staple and begin a new era. If that happened, *Punch* predicted, "Paddy shall enjoy his own pork. . . . Let the little children of Ireland be taught the above-named doggerel as a household song of comfort and thanksgiving."[24]

Opening a free trade in grain to Ireland would allow the government to follow the orthodoxies of political economy and expand Irish markets. Although Peel admitted that "there is such a tendency to exaggeration and inaccuracy in Irish reports that delay in acting upon them is always desirable," the news from Ireland seemed very bad. "The removal of impediments to import," Peel wrote, "is the effectual remedy." But Peel's ambitions risked scuppering his government. Charles Greville wrote in February 1846 that despite Peel's small movements toward free trade, and despite having "the potato famine as a base for his operation, he cannot do what he does now without entirely breaking up his party."[25]

The most novel part of Peel's plan, the bulk purchase of maize, often known as "Indian corn," "Indian meal," or cornmeal, shows how ideas about labour and political economy and free trade overlapped in relief policies, and how relief was meant not only to halt starvation but to reform Irish economic life. Maize, crucially, was not grown in Britain. No one in Parliament had much to lose from the opening of a market for a new grain compared with the competition with foreign importers that would follow a reduction in tariffs on wheat or oats. Even better, maize might persuade Irish labourers to abandon potatoes as subsistence, a change that political economists predicted would encourage the Irish poor to buy grain instead, civilising Ireland through the opening of a new market for British grain. Maize would also open a new trade with the United States, "another ligament for uniting the two countries." Maize was a critical rotation crop in the southern US, generally tended, like cotton, by enslaved labourers and poor sharecroppers. Intensive cropping of cotton followed by maize consumed and depleted the soil but produced two very saleable harvests. Antislavery Britain bought a lion's share of American cotton; why not maize as well? Maize, boosters argued, might also independently improve the work ethic of Irish consumers. Enslaved workers in the United States and the Caribbean, a pamphlet crowed, believed "rice turns to water in their bellies and runs off, but Indian Corn stays with them and makes [them] strong to work."[26]

Neither Peel nor any of his enemies imagined that the blight would last longer than a season. Some traditionalist Tories even considered the blight to be a hoax, perpetrated by Whigs and Repealers to discredit or destroy the Union. The Dublin *Evening*

Mail declared in November 1845 that the potato shortage had
been exaggerated to intimidate landlords out of collecting rent.
The Duke of Wellington considered the blight an instance of an
old problem. When potatoes failed, Irish labourers had to work
for rent, but they weren't used to spending cash for food, and so
needed to be paid in rations: "This is the real difficulty in Ireland."
Other Tories were sceptical of the reported extent of the crop failure, but hopeful that Irish estates could be converted from potatoes
to pasturage or grain. John Wilson Croker, an Anglo-Irish writer
and former lord of the admiralty, proffered an arch quotation from
Virgil's *Georgics*: "The great Father himself has willed that the path
of husbandry should not run smooth." The blight was a challenge
to improve Irish agriculture and teach the Irish to make bread that
required "the plough, the harrow, the reaper, the carter, the bailiff,
the salesman, the miller," and to banish "single-handed Paddy who
makes a hole in the ground to receive half a potato."[27]

On December 4, 1845, as leading Tories publicly doubted the
depth of the crisis in Ireland, the *Times* made known that when
Parliament returned in January, the members would be asked to
consider the repeal of the Corn Laws, with immediate effect. The
report hinted that the cabinet was unanimous. The *Times* piece,
perhaps placed by Peel, warned Tories that if they did not support
a Tory move toward free trade, they would find John Russell in
power. Furious at the leak, Stanley resigned. On December 11,
Peel also resigned. However, Russell could not persuade the new
Earl Grey, son of the former prime minister, to join a cabinet and
was unable to form a government.[28]

Amidst this political intrigue, the question of whether free trade in
grain would actually benefit Ireland had all but disappeared, a casu-
alty of intense public interest in the backroom drama surrounding
the Corn Laws. Rising prices for food in England after a year of poor
grain further tipped the political balance, as cheaper imports would

lower prices for English consumers. But there was very little infrastructure to import grain to Ireland—Irish farms exported wheat
and oats, and rural Ireland had limited facilities for marketing grain
directly to consumers. Even with lower prices wholesale, it would
be expensive to transport grain to the parts of Ireland that needed
it most. A flood of grain could not feed all of Ireland if there was
no way of distributing it. Protectionist Conservatives fell in behind
Lord George Bentinck. Before 1846 he had been mostly silent in the
House, preferring to manage his stable of racehorses. Now, inflamed,
Bentinck rallied Tories with claims that Peel was exaggerating the
extent of the potato crisis. One Irish Tory agreed, scoffing that "fever,
dysentery, and death" were "a kind of normal state" in Ireland.[29]

"Peel's famine," as Bentinck called it, was "an enormous lie" to force
free trade through the House. Through the winter and into the spring,
the protectionist Conservatives, especially Bentinck and the young
Benjamin Disraeli, recognised that the balance of votes in the House
of Commons meant that repeal of the Corn Laws was inevitable, and
they used the debates to grandstand and to promote their own careers.
In the meantime, crime associated with famine conditions was increasing in Ireland, and the lord lieutenant requested the power to declare
martial law in districts with high rates of outrage. Coercion Acts and
protectionism to keep grain prices high had once unified the Conservatives. As a pamphleteer quipped, "Shooting men in Ireland seems
indeed the inseparable corollary to starving them in England." But in
1846, although an unusually punitive Coercion Bill easily passed the
Lords (among other provisions, it called for a curfew that only applied
to tenants and labourers, on pain of seven years' penal transportation),
Peel's enemies among the Whigs, Repealers, and protectionist Conservatives in the Commons introduced amendments and procedural
motions to slow its progress and embarrass the prime minister.[30]

Peel was tied to the Coercion Bill, and it began to pull him
under. The protectionists threw their arms around Peel in support,

the better to stab him in the back. Well aware that Peel's majority was fragile, they needled the prime minister for a vote on the
legislation, and asserted that any outrages that happened while
the bill was under debate would be blood on Peel's hands. "From
never having spoken," a colleague remarked of Bentinck, "he never
now does anything else." Even if he had a majority to pass the
bill, Peel knew that the protectionists and Whigs had every reason to draw out the process, further humiliating the government.
In April, Daniel O'Connell gave a long speech, from the usual
place occupied by the Leader of the Opposition. Disraeli wrote
that O'Connell looked sick and was nearly inaudible, except to the
front benches. "It was a strange and touching spectacle," Disraeli
commented. Most of the House saw a "feeble old man mutter-
ing before a table" and pretended to listen only out of respect for
O'Connell's decades of service in the House.[31]

Peel was reeling. The fox-hunting protectionist Tories were
"eager to run him down and kill him in the open." Finally, on
June 25, Charles Buller, a liberal Whig and barrister with close
connections to the British administration in Canada, gave a speech
opposing coercion and the structure of the Relief Commission. He
reminded the House of the £20 million raised as compensation for
former slaveholders after the abolition of colonial slavery in 1834,
and offered that "if a grant of money was required to put down
Irish misery, the House would not hesitate in voting it . . . to a
nation to whom they had behaved worse than even to the Africans." But as he paused, messengers from the Lords entered the
House; the Corn Laws had been repealed, pending royal assent.
Buller kept speaking, but no one listened. The House, exhilarated,
called for a vote on a reading of the Coercion Bill. The motion
failed. A few days later, Peel resigned.[32]

The debates over the Union, the Corn Laws, and the Coercion
Bill wove in and out of the question of how to address the blight

in Ireland. Moreover, the debates took place according to the rhythms of the UK legislative calendar, not the Irish agricultural calendar. In consequence, Parliament debated measures to respond to developments in Ireland that had happened months before, and then made plans based on guesses about crop yields that could only be verified months later. Parliament's sittings, alliances, and pre-occupations left legislators perpetually lagging behind the crisis, while market ideology limited the options available for relief. The debates might have focused on Irish affairs, but on the ground in Ireland, Peel's Relief Commission proceeded unsteadily, out of step with events in Westminster.

ON OCTOBER 14 AND 15, 1843, ABOUT A WEEK AFTER PEEL rooked O'Connell at Clontarf, two letters from Ireland written by "Philalethes" appeared in the *Morning Chronicle*, a London paper. Philalethes ("lover of truth," a common literary alias at the time) had spent six weeks in Ireland following the progress of the Repeal campaign. Although he had left Ireland before the monster meet-ing, which had ended with confusion but no violence, the letters described an explosive, seditious, and revolutionary undercurrent to Repeal. The letters reappeared in other British and colonial newspapers—they were quoted in full, for example, in an April 1844 edition of the *South Australian*, published in Adelaide.

Philalethes argued that for Daniel O'Connell, the monster meetings were mostly self-promotional bluster. However, for the Irish Catholic majority and the people whom Philalethes considered to be their *real* leaders—a cadre of fanatical Catho-lic priests—Repeal was a call to arms. Philalethes described his sense of isolation in Ireland, where "English travellers have been as rarely seen . . . this year as white men in Timbuctoo." He was con-vinced that farmers were stockpiling weapons. Poems published by

Catholic intellectuals and ballads sung by labourers presaged war. The United Irish rebellion would repeat itself. Noticing an absence of public drunkenness at country fairs, Philalethes reminded readers, "The same untoward quiet preceded the breaking out of the last rebellion." Drunkenness was a vice, but so was sobriety when practiced by the Irish. Philalethes predicted a civil war, in which "one or two millions might be spared with advantage . . . the country would be for the survivors."[33]

These letters, by the standards of the British writing about the Irish, were unremarkable. What was remarkable, however, was that Philalethes was Charles Trevelyan, the senior Treasury bureaucrat who would preside over the implementation of Peel's famine-relief program—and every other phase of famine relief from 1845 until the end of the crisis. When the letters appeared, O'Connell had just been arrested, and the government was anxious about the consequences. When Trevelyan had returned from Ireland, he reported to Robert Peel and the home secretary, James Graham. Trevelyan's motivation for publishing his letters seemed to be to shame the government for not doing more than disrupting the mass meeting. The letters implied that Catholic priests ought to have been rounded up and arrested. Regardless of Trevelyan's intent, Graham and Peel were livid. "He must be a consummate fool," Peel wrote.[34]

Trevelyan almost certainly embroidered the letters. He may have been misled by the people he met in Ireland, who might have been happy to tease and mislead a sanctimonious Englishman. "We are not without our suspicions," the editors of the *Morning Chronicle* wrote, "that 'Philalethes' . . . afforded his share of amusement to 'the boys.'" Or like a present-day newspaper columnist who voices his beliefs through an invented person—a taxi driver, a newsagent—Trevelyan may have invented the conversations he reported. What is eerie, however, is Trevelyan's willingness to find comfort in the possibility that mass death might cure Ireland's economic and political ills.[35]

In many histories of the Great Famine, Charles Trevelyan is the villain, the "virtual dictator" of the relief program, "the personification of free-market economics as a mask for colonial genocide," a tight-fisted hand to the grindstone who considered the blight a divine punishment. That reputation is bolstered in popular culture. In the song "Fields of Athenry," written by Pete St. John in 1979 and likely to be sung whenever Ireland plays England at anything, the hero is sent to an Australian prison colony because he "stole Trevelyan's corn." But Charles Trevelyan was not a Napoleonic figure, bending the Treasury around his ambition and will to power. He was a skilled bureaucrat whose faith in liberal political economy and laissez-faire, individual discipline and prudence was consistent with his devout Protestantism and faith in the "natural" laws of the market.[36]

Trevelyan served at the government's pleasure but had powerful patrons—it is remarkable that he wasn't sacked or demoted after his 1843 letters embarrassed both the prime minister and the home secretary. Trevelyan was a protégé of the great liberal writer, legislator, and lawyer Thomas Babington Macaulay, and also his brother-in-law. Trevelyan had started his career in the empire. His father was an archdeacon in Taunton, from an old Cornish gentry family, and his mother the third daughter of a baronet, and the Trevelyans had claimed to own hundreds of enslaved people in Grenada. His widowed mother received a share of nearly £27,000 in compensation under the 1833 Abolition of Slavery Act. Educated at a grammar school and at Charterhouse, Trevelyan finished his education at the East India Company's college, Haileybury, and entered company service in Bengal in 1826 as a clerk and translator.

In India he acquired a reputation for aggression and self-righteousness. Posted to Delhi, he attracted attention for

publicly condemning the corruption of his boss, Sir Edward Colebrooke, which led to Colebrooke's dismissal from the company.
Trevelyan was only in his early twenties when he caught the attention of T. B. Macaulay, the law member of the Governor-General's
Council and the architect of English-language education in India.
T. B. Macaulay was the son of Zachary Macaulay, the former governor of Sierra Leone and a leading figure in the antislavery movement. Trevelyan courted and married Macaulay's sister, Hannah
More Macaulay (named after the Evangelical reformer and abolitionist Hannah More, a close friend of Zachary Macaulay's—there
was room in an antislavery dynasty for the son of a slaveholding
family). Trevelyan was known as a "stormy reformer" and sportsman, fond of the perilous blood sport of hunting wild boar with a
spear from horseback. Macaulay was amused by Trevelyan's intensity. "He has no small talk," Macaulay wrote. "His topics, even
in courtship, are steam navigation, the education of the natives,
the equalization of the sugar duties, [and] the substitution of the
Roman for the Arabic alphabet in the Oriental languages."[37]

In 1840, at age thirty-two, Trevelyan was appointed assistant
secretary of the treasury, a senior non-ministerial position. The
promotion may have been made at Macaulay's recommendation.
Macaulay had returned from India in 1838 to serve as MP for
Edinburgh, had been appointed to the Privy Council, and was
secretary at war in Lord Melbourne's cabinet. In addition to his
work at the Treasury, Trevelyan wrote pseudonymous letters on
many subjects as both "Philalethes" and "Indophilus." He did not
fear reprisal from his political bosses, because of either his patron
Macaulay or his oblivious self-confidence—or both.[38]

In Ireland, Trevelyan, a gifted writer, coordinated the
famine-relief effort through thousands of letters, overseeing the
bureaucratic design and execution of the plans developed first by
Peel and then by John Russell's ministers. However, save a brief

trip to Dublin, Trevelyan never visited Ireland during the famine. He managed the crisis as though it were a tabletop game, conducted by correspondence. This distance and confidence in the minutiae of Irish affairs were not unusual among British administrators. Ireland was an uncommon destination for British tourists, but readers could be forgiven for assuming that every person who visited Ireland after the Union wrote a book about their journey. In addition to the many works of travel literature penned between the Union and the famine, Parliament published reports and evidence from no fewer than 114 commissions, and 61 special committees struck to report on conditions in Ireland. All these printed words, one scholar observes, were a "paper landscape" that for many Britons was more real than actual Irish soil.[39]

Trevelyan held the views typical of a British liberal in the early Victorian era, and especially those of the pious and reform-minded Evangelical Anglican liberals predominant in antislavery and missionary organisations. Governments existed, Trevelyan wrote, to allow private individuals to live and work "with freedom and safety," and little else. A government, he continued, should not do the work of "the land-owner, merchant, money-lender, or any other function of social life." In his 1848 memoir of the famine, Trevelyan recognised it as a "sharp but effectual remedy by which the cure" of Irish backwardness would be accomplished. "God grant," he wrote, that the promise of the Union might be fulfilled by "the generation to which this great opportunity has been offered."[40]

For most of the Great Famine, government relief programs were administered by the Treasury and the Commissariat Department. In 1845–1846, the Relief Commission was an umbrella over these institutions as well as over the Coast Guard, the Royal Corps of Engineers, and other government departments. Trevelyan liaised between these agencies and the Treasury, which oversaw and audited spending. The Commissariat, a branch of the Treasury usually responsible for supplying imperial garrisons, supervised the distribution of food by a network of depots overseen by the Coast Guard. The Commissariat also oversaw the public works programs operated by the Irish Board of Works. True to the laissez-faire ethos, *markets*, not communities or individuals, were the primary object of relief. When the price of potatoes or oatmeal rose too high, relief officers would release funds or maize, in doses titrated to protect merchants from government competition and Irish labourers from the temptation to idle on the government dole. In principle, if the markets for food and labour were correctly managed, individual families would be able to find their own work and food.

At the beginning of the crisis, Trevelyan sent the leading commissary officers copies of Edmund Burke's *Thoughts and Details on Scarcity*, written in 1795 and published posthumously in 1800. Burke wrote the pamphlet after a crop failure in Ireland, to persuade William Pitt to refrain from interfering with the markets for grain by capping prices or restricting trade. It wasn't government's job to directly feed the hungry, Burke wrote. To "provide for us in our necessities is not in the power of Government." Agriculture, Burke argued, was no different than any other branch of commerce, and supporting agricultural prices or wages would be a disaster. "The whole of agriculture," he wrote, "is a natural and just order." Several officers commented on Burke's pamphlet in their letters to the Treasury, although they might have been humouring or flattering Trevelyan. "Mr. Burke's remarks you sent me are most just and statesmanlike," one officer wrote. "But I will not write more on the subject, or I will never finish"—a terrific excuse for a student who has not done the required reading.[41]

Long after the famine, an enemy described Trevelyan as "trained to vigilance and circumspection among a dangerous population in India." Although he worked for a domestic ministry, Trevelyan saw Ireland through a colonial lens, as an alien, uncivilised

Celtic fringe of the United Kingdom. The Treasury's partner, the Commissariat, organised into military ranks, was responsible for paying, lodging, and provisioning troops across the empire. It was primarily a colonial organisation, supporting British garrisons. In 1824, commissary officers who would later be assigned to Ireland served in Barbados, the Cape Colony, Bermuda, and Canada. Many had served in the Napoleonic Wars, when military logistics were stretched to the limit.[42]

The Irish headquarters of relief were in the Custom House in Dublin, the Georgian architectural masterpiece on the banks of the Liffey. The logistics of the relief effort were demanding. The Commissariat corresponded with more than a thousand individual relief committees, managing both orders for maize and requests for public works. With regard to the latter, the officers were inundated with applications—for bridges, roads, church repairs, new locks and canals on the Shannon, and more. With regard to the former, to distribute maize the commissary established a network of depots, each one under the supervision of a commissary-general or deputy commissary-general. The central depot, in Cork, established on the premises of a Royal Navy magazine, received unground maize from America, to be parched and ground in Cork's industrial mills.[43]

From Cork, steamships delivered corn to depots at Limerick, Dublin, Westport, Sligo, and elsewhere, each of which was responsible for selling wholesale maize to local relief committees, in quantities up to twenty tons. The depots, supervised and guarded by Coast Guard officers, also sold packages of up to seven pounds of maize to individuals and families. "The multitude and eagerness of the parties crowding round the doors," one officer wrote, "are difficult to describe." The staff of the Irish Constabulary, with its eleven thousand officers, were given additional pay to work for the Relief Commission in distributing maize, and the Royal Corps of Engineers supervised many public works sites. Depots began opening in April and May 1846, first in Limerick, Cork, Galway, and Westport, followed in May and June by openings in Dublin and Dundalk, and then in Waterford. Only Sligo remained closed until later in the summer. The depots processed more than 67,000 pounds of unground maize, 26 million pounds of cornmeal, 1.18 million pounds of oatmeal, and nearly 14,000 pounds of ship's biscuit.[44]

As the plan rolled out, commissary officers struggled with the relief committees. The first deliveries of maize arrived in February 1846, but the supplies were put in storage in the government's network of depots. Commissariat officers complained that the committees refused to believe that the supply was finite and that the government intended to hold back grain until they considered distributing it to be absolutely necessary. Although commissary officers wrote more than fifty letters to local committees to explain the rules of the system, one officer reported that many continued to send carts to the shuttered grain depot.[45]

The relief committees themselves varied widely, from effective and decisive to inept and grasping. Generally, they represented the landowning and professional classes of the baronies. They included ex officio the lieutenant or deputy lieutenant of the county, the officer of the Board of Works, Catholic and Protestant clergy, the chair and guardians of the local Poor Law union, Coast Guard officers, and magistrates. The lord lieutenant was also allowed to appoint anyone he chose to a relief committee. In towns, they included mayors and aldermen, clergy, Poor Law officials, and magistrates.

Relief officers complained that local relief committees did not know, and refused to learn, the rules governing the food and work programs. But many also struggled with their own conscience; some violated commission rules out of compassion. Trained to haggle with purveyors and contractors and to provision armies on a tight budget, the Commissariat officers were professionals in austerity. But refusing soldiers and officers was easier than refusing starving or typhus-stricken families. They stood between the starving and food, and some gave it away. Trevelyan reminded them in letters that their quotidian work of making inventories, corresponding with local committees, paying out grants for public works, and selling meal in bulk had a grand purpose. The Irish poor needed to be led away from potatoes.[46]

When one officer gave away a few bags of meal, Trevelyan fired off a message to Randolph Routh, one of the commissaries-general leading the administration of the relief program, reminding him to keep his men in line. "Our plan," he wrote to Routh, "is, not to *give* the meal away, but to *sell* it." If the Irish came to depend on free corn, the plan would fail. In June 1846, a request to distribute free food was denied: "Gratuitous relief demoralizes the people." It was maddening, heartbreaking work. One officer, working in King's County (County Offaly) in April 1846, was confounded by the command to separate "normal" hunger and desperation from hunger and desperation caused by the failure of the potato.[47]

Maize recommended itself to Peel and others because it was a grain abundant in the Americas and rare in the United Kingdom. But what made maize appealing to politicians designing a relief program—its price, its connection to the markets of the United States, its scarcity in British and Irish markets—were precisely the things that made it alien to the Irish, who had little idea how to cook or eat it. A few of the commissary officers who had worked in Canada and traveled in the United States had eaten cornbread or grits and understood how to prepare cornmeal, but they were a small minority in a populous country. Trevelyan sent out copies of pamphlets with instructions on how to parch and grind kernels into meal, but his instructions were secondhand. Some of the Irish called maize "Peel's brimstone" because of its yellow colour and infernal British origins.[48]

For Irish consumers, the problem with cornmeal was that it was prepared almost like oatmeal, but not quite—and small differences in preparation made cornmeal cooked like oatmeal inedible. Oatmeal made into oatcakes would adhere on a griddle after being mixed in cold water, but cornmeal cakes prepared this way would fall apart. Cooking cornmeal, like oatmeal, into "stirabout" porridge by steeping it in cold water, then bringing it to a boil would create a yellow paste with the consistency of mortar.

In short, maize was presented as a gift from Britain that the Irish were expected to buy—a gift that looked like sulphur and turned into thick, disgusting glop in water. It was an alien food chosen *because* it was alien. The government and local authorities did offer incentives to use maize—a baker in Dublin was awarded a medal for baking cornbread. But prisoners in a Limerick gaol rioted when offered cornmeal. Routh hopefully noted that at least some of the Irish believed it prevented fever and that it was "a good working food, and not accompanied by heart-burn." Rough and ill-prepared cornmeal scoured the intestines of many who ate it. Some feared it; some imagined it had been sent as a joke or as a killing blow. But "when hunger had progressed a little," as Asenath Nicholson wrote, "these fears subsided, and they cared neither what they ate, or who sent it to them."[49]

The government's plan to import maize had always been intended to prime the ignition of private trade that, eventually, would take over and replace government trade. Later in the famine, the disconnect between the immediacy of the crisis and the British government's preoccupation with protecting the future of Irish markets and preserving the work ethic of starving recipients of relief would become grimly risible. But in 1845–1846, few imagined the blight would come back at all, much less come back the next season, and worse. In principle, it made sense for the government to open a trade in cornmeal for a season and attract other importers, while remaining in the market to prevent profiteering during the potato failure. Then, when the crisis passed, the government could withdraw and count on the laws of political economy to regulate the market fairly and profitably for both importers and consumers.

And the plan worked, up to a point. Following the government, private merchants began importing their own maize. There were fairly minor logistical struggles; for example, both private and government buyers complained about the fragile barrels American merchants used to pack the grain, with thin staves and loose hoops. If a stevedore stumbled with a barrel, the "eggshell packages" would spill out their contents. Irish consumers reportedly preferred the cornmeal sold by the government, which was packed in sacks stamped with the royal coat of arms. Despite these issues—the kind that the Commissariat's officers were trained to resolve—relief officers overall were pleased with the effects of the initial distribution of maize in the countryside. Some believed that the corn had persuaded Irish farmers of the government's compassion and support: "They have seen, and are not slow in declaring, that in a great emergency they are not neglected."[50]

In the first wave of the blight, in short, the gulf between the laws of economic life and government faith in them, and inchoate, unpredictable reality was only beginning to open. The first wave was not as severe as the waves that followed, and Peel's relief measures worked reasonably well to prevent mass death (especially by comparison with the winter of 1846–1847). Across Ireland's 2,056 administrative divisions, only a few divisions in Ulster and Munster did not report any blight. Seventy-two percent of divisions reported crop loss of at least 30 percent, 14 percent reported crop loss of over 50 percent, but only 5 percent reported crop loss of 70 percent or more. Counties including Antrim, Clare, Kilkenny,

Monaghan, and Waterford lost about 40 percent of the crop, while in Armagh and Wicklow, almost no potatoes were lost.[51]

The death toll in the first wave of the blight was significant, but small by comparison with subsequent years. Overall, it is not clear exactly how many people died in the Irish Great Famine; scholars agree that at least one million people died by starvation and hunger-related diseases between 1845 and 1851. It is clear from partial demographic evidence, and a wealth of anecdotal evidence, that 1846–1847 and 1848–1849 were especially deadly. Consequently, because proportionally more people died in later waves of blight, many historians consider Peel's relief plan to have been at least a qualified success. Local relief committees, for the most part, were satisfied with the government's plan, and said so in letters. Folk histories of the famine suggest that many believed that the meal had been sent from the United States by Irish immigrants and other Americans as donations, and that relief committees had seized these gifts to sell to the poor. "Sad to say a ship load of American corn coming to Ireland," one oral history explained, "would pass ship-load of Irish corn going out of the Irish port to England." Other folk histories claimed the "English Government bought all the grain of the country for a very small price" and then sold it back to Irish farmers at extortionate rates. What looked like successes in letters from relief committees in making a market and winning the hearts and minds of the Irish poor was likely much more complicated in reality.[52]

The first wave of the blight was incomplete and uneven—and in areas where it was intense, the countryside was volatile. In many parts of Ireland, stores of Indian meal were full, and the 1845 harvest had been a vintage year for oats. But prices were rising. In Drogheda, even skilled workers earning six shillings a week found themselves spending all their wages on rent, turf, oatmeal, cornmeal, and milk. Potatoes were unaffordable, even where they were available. In one jurisdiction 1,250 people requested workhouse relief, more than three times the capacity of a midsize Irish workhouse. There was heavy pressure on the government to permit outdoor relief under the Irish Poor Law. The Relief Commission refused, demurring until Parliament could decide the questions when "its judgment will not be influenced by the contemplation of peculiar and unusual distress among the poorer classes of the country."[53]

Food riots broke out. A mob attacked ships carrying grain down the Suir from Clonmel to Waterford at a bend in the river near the village of Kilsheelan, in Tipperary. A terrified magistrate aboard a grain barge leapt into the river and swam to safety. About fifteen kilometres from Kilsheelan, in Fethard, government stores were looted by rioters.[54] Afterward, barges on the route were escorted along the banks by horse-drawn cannon, fifty cavalry, and eighty infantry. A drove of pigs seized during the Clonmel riot was held hostage; the mayor of Clonmel was offered the pigs in exchange for prisoners. Commissary officers were angry. "If there were a doubt in any reflecting man's mind," one wrote, referring to Trevelyan's recommended reading, "on the correctness of 'Burke's Thoughts and Details on Scarcity', he need only come to Ireland." Army officers were loath to guard the government's warehouses without additional hazard pay.[55]

Each layer of the Relief Commission had a different perspective on what it was expected to prevent. In England, Trevelyan and other Treasury officers worried that the plan for Ireland would fall apart. In 11 Downing Street, the office and London residence of the Chancellor of the Exchequer, relief was meant to be a temporary therapy, a means to forestall starvation and encourage reform. In Dublin, at the Custom House, Routh and other Commissariat officers worried about maintaining fiscal and logistical discipline in correspondence with many hundreds of often

unruly and spendthrift relief committees. Individual relief officers, in turn, worried about what would happen if they ran out
of meal or money. Some worried that society would collapse, that
"there would not have been an animal left alive in the country,
nor a mill nor a store unpillaged." They also occasionally worried
that the Irish poor were too far outside "the circle in which commerce revolves" to benefit from relief, that they might "starve in
the midst of plenty." Trevelyan acknowledged the need to make
exceptions to his rules "where it is evident that the consequence
of our insisting on the strict execution of our rule would be that
the people would starve." Whatever it cost, he wrote in another
letter, "the people must not, *under any circumstances*, be allowed
to starve." Trevelyan did not clarify how officers could determine
when the line between ideological discipline and human decency
had been crossed.[56]

PUBLIC WORKS PROGRAMS RAN PARALLEL TO THE DISTRIBUTION
of meal. The free trade in American grain was to be bolstered by
a program that would put the Irish to work. Free trade, within
the moral universe of political economy, was natural and improving. Opening grain markets would encourage Irish labourers to
buy their food—an engine of civilisation. Labour, in turn, was
also considered civilising. A working person, after all, could not be
truly poor; only a dependent pauper could be. If opening the grain
trade could permanently transform Irish trade, perhaps a program
of labour for cash wages could permanently alter the Irish work
ethic.

The Board of Works, a long-standing Irish government department, gained a new file under the Relief Commission. Like the
meal program, public works were intended to prevent graft and
self-dealing by the wealthy in famine-struck districts. Local relief

committees, under the auspices of the Board of Works, were permitted to hold presentment sessions to hear bids for projects that could employ the indigent. The projects would then be forwarded to the lord lieutenant's office for preliminary approval, then forwarded to the Relief Commission in the Custom House for a second signature, then forwarded to the office of the Board of Works (also housed in the Custom House), then approved by a military or civil engineer. The commissioners of public works were besieged with letters complaining about the process, as well as petitions from landowners "objecting to the lines in which the roads are proposed to be made, as destroying ornamental or highly-cultivated land."[57]

Presentment sessions were meant to be organised at the barony level, but many parishes held their own competing sessions. Landowners and prominent tenants used the sessions to try to fund projects to increase the value of their land; they made presentments "conducted more with a view to private, than public interests." Local feuds spilled over into debates about which projects to propose and which to fund. The Treasury sent angry letters to remind local committees and engineers that any public works were for the relief of distress caused by the failure of the potatoes. But as one of the officers explained to Trevelyan, "Farmer, priest, landlord, and tenant all make strong attempts to squeeze something out of the Government purse. It is very difficult for the Lord Lieutenant, under the applications and statements made to him, to resist ordering works." Most of the relief-era public works projects were known as "jobs"—graft or pork, roads either to nowhere or to the doors of the local landlord's or agent's house.[58]

In April, a mob in Carrick attacked the people selected by the Board of Works, smashing their tools and complaining about the low rate of wages, tenpence per day. At Clonmel, the army was called in; the Cork relief committee imported corn directly from

Liverpool after the relief board refused to sell them more than fifty sacks of twenty stone each. The workers at Carrick wanted to be paid at least 1s. 6d. per day. Strikes on the relief works were common. The daily average of workers steadily grew from 36,308 in the week ending July 4, to 83,781 in the week ending July 25. Predictably, public works peaked in July along with the sale of maize. In June and July 1846, the government issued as much as 233 tons of meal per week; some subdepots sold as much as 20 tons in a single day. In the end, the 1845–1846 works cost Parliament £733,372, half given as a grant and the other half as a loan, supported by £98,000 in donations. Each local relief committee had its own agenda for spending the money, and the Relief Commission complained that the rapid growth of public works was "not an index to the state of distress, or to the amount of employment necessary to be given to afford relief."[59]

To get a job on the public works, a worker needed a ticket from the relief committee. Work tickets were valuable assets and quickly became a medium of exchange. "Employment," an officer wrote, "cannot be found for the numbers that will require it." Unscrupulous relief committees distributed tickets to favoured tenants or sold them to middlemen. Just as police and army officers guarded maize stores, they also guarded cash—locked boxes of silver coins holding up to £1,000—which had to be sent with clerks to pay the public works wages in more remote Irish regions that lacked banking facilities. But like the spread of the blight itself, the 1845–1846 public works program was regional. Nearly a fifth of the work took place in County Clare, and another fifth in Counties Limerick and Galway. In comparison, fewer than two hundred people were on the payroll in Dublin, and fewer still in County Donegal.[60]

The public works program ran far ahead of the Treasury's hopes for an orderly labour market. If the concern of the commissary was to use "the market" to the benefit of the Irish, the Board of

Works was supposed to prevent landlords from improving their land for free or cheaply. "The scarcity is so extensive," Trevelyan wrote, "and the habits of the country are so peculiar, that our plan of relief, whatever it may be, ought to be such as will admit of a clear and easy distinction being made between what is indispensably required for the relief of the people suffering from scarcity, and what is demanded under the pretext of that scarcity, in order to forward the interested views of various parties."[61]

The clash between the pragmatic needs of the Irish poor and the settled ideology of poor relief put relief officers' efforts in knots. The closer officers got to Irish rural poverty, the more complicated and impossible the situation seemed, and the less it resembled the clean logic of political economy. Presentment sessions seemed to show an Irish gentry eager to enrich itself at the government's expense and abdicate its responsibility to employ the poor. The labour market, in turn, seemed to show that Irish workers would take the path of least resistance, choosing low-paid public work over better-paying private employment.

The Relief Commission also faced an unexpected new problem. The usual flow of migrant agricultural labourers to England had stopped. English farmers complained, and the commissioners in Dublin and London assumed that "every labouring man in the country was directed to look to the Board of Works for employment." The Lords of the Treasury concluded that "people employed on the Relief Works have indulged in habits of indolence, preferring the receipt of an eleemosynary allowance under the name of wages" to better wages for private work in either Ireland or England. The Treasury demanded that relief officers inspect local public works projects, and that local committees only dispense tickets to workers with no other means of support; the tickets had to be signed by two members of the committee and issued only by the secretary of the relief committees.[62]

The gulf between the idea, or ideal, of what relief was meant to do and what the potato failure had done grew wider month after month. The relief system was elaborate and bureaucratic—an impressive example of Victorian administrative energy and acumen. But Ireland was too big and populous and the Relief Commission too small by comparison to survey or relieve the entire country, even during this first, partial wave of the blight. In Limerick and County Clare, as much as one-third of the population was estimated to have neither food nor money. Smaller farmers, those holding under fifteen acres, could not afford to employ labourers. Without wages, and out of fear of blight, the number of people taking conacre had fallen 75 percent. A Mayo newspaper wrote, "We have heard of the *appointment of commissioners*—of the *renting of stores*—of the *arrival* of Indian corn and American flour, but we *cannot discover a single instance of any starving family being relieved*."[63]

Villages and towns fell through the cracks. In Claggar, a village in County Meath, deliveries of meal were infrequent, and the meal that was delivered was wet and mouldy. Workers who ate the mouldy meal became violently ill.[64] As in previous food shortages, epidemics broke out among the hungry, tired, and filthy. Many workers suffered from diarrhea and dysentery, "painful and violent griping, with other violent symptoms" in acute twelve-hour bursts, which officials blamed on eating blighted potatoes. In Glownton, County Cork, medical officers noticed a 40 percent increase in dysentery. Some officials observed an unusual "gastric fever," and many were struck both by terrible gastrointestinal distress and by colds and flus, which circulated readily. As during the 1817 typhus epidemic, whole sick families crowded into beds. In County Wexford, in addition to diarrhea, skin diseases increased as much as a hundredfold. There was a spike in petty crime, especially theft and intimidation.[65]

In 1846, the price of potatoes climbed beyond what many Irish families could afford. In some markets the price of Lumpers had increased as much as 350 percent to the hundredweight. But the hungry still wanted potatoes, and many could not afford or could not acquire meal. In March 1846, in Cork, in the Fermoy Poor Law Union, dozens of women and children followed behind the plows, "quarrelling for the rotten potatoes" that had been left in the ground at the harvest. In Tyrone, the last potatoes went into the ground as seed. In Wicklow, a local committee reported that the majority of the people kept eating "food totally unfit for use." In Galway, people had begun to starve to death. In Limerick, committees heard reports of cattle poaching. In Mountmellick, County Laois, families were seen eating the foul runoff from a starch yard.[66]

In England, as the first season of the blight came to an end, English workers were growing resentful of the attention paid to Ireland and Irish questions. The blight had devastated English potato fields as well, and the combination of expensive food and sagging industrial productivity squeezed the English working class. A Newcastle paper inveighed, "Already villages are sickening with the attempt to use the tainted wreck of the crop. Already cholera and typhus are the fearful companions of want." If grain and work were scarce in England, how were industrial labourers "to feed the Irish millions, when they cannot get bread for themselves? Is it just that they should be the victims of so absurd and cruel an experiment?"[67]

Perhaps under pressure to declare victory, Trevelyan assured the government that the north of Ireland was virtually secure, thanks to government control of prices through cornmeal distribution. The south had also been saved, he continued, by "the assistance afforded by the Government, either directly, or by means of money, meal, or employment; or indirectly, by the stimulus and organization which has been given to private effort." But Routh, on the ground in Ireland, worried that the celebration might be premature. July had been worse than June, he wrote. The pressure on the government depots was enormous and growing. If the public learned that the government was finished, prices would quickly rise. It wasn't the end of the struggle, he wrote; it was "the crisis of the struggle."[68]

FROM THE OUTSET, FAMINE-RELIEF POLICIES WERE WOVEN ON A framework of contradictory principles. Officials were wary of any intervention that might directly relieve the suffering of Irish individuals or communities. Irish civilisation—reckoned as market participation and disciplined labour—seemed too flimsy to allow for the provision of food or money to the starving without asking for work in exchange. Markets, however, required extensive husbandry and intervention—paradoxically, to safeguard laissez-faire principles from the hazards posed by the Irish poor, who were left to find a "natural" path back from starvation. Famine-relief policy was designed to create conditions that would, in theory, impel the Irish to use the market to help themselves. Ecological crises are almost always enmeshed in a complex web of man-made social, economic, environmental, and technological forces. The famine had its natural causes, but it was neither wholly "natural" nor inevitable. The depth of British faith in the market, however, meant that the politics of famine relief had been wholly naturalised. Moreover, long-standing and bitter controversies in Parliament over the Acts of Union and free trade shaped Peel's famine-relief policies in predictable ways. Ironically and tragically, it was the government response to the arrival of the blight that proved to be, in a sense, inevitable.[69]

Peel's plan had its virtues, but it was designed to work for one season of crop failure, not longer. Moreover, as a letter to the Cork relief committee explained, relief had prevented starvation but might have set the stage for sequelae of multiplying crises. Workers whose potatoes failed were still bound to work for their landlords, but now they had no potatoes to offset low wages or to account for the many days' labour they owed in place of cash. They bought their meal, but "whatever money they raised by the sale of their pigs, sheep, and by pawning their bed and body clothes, except the squalid rags they now wear, is exhausted." Workers had no money for food, and their employers had no money to pay them with even if they had work to offer—which they didn't. They "must either starve or rob." When seed potatoes were imported to Wexford and Sligo, no one would buy them. Farmers were reluctant to plant potatoes, and even more reluctant to offer conacre. Rent evaporated. Far, far more terrifying, however, were the rumours that the new crop of potatoes was already blighted in the ground. In mid-August 1846, amid those ominous signs, the first Relief Commission concluded its business. Things were about to get far worse.[70]

5

THE END OF THE WORLD

EARLY IN WILLIAM CARLETON'S NOVEL *THE BLACK PROPHET*, A melodrama set during the 1817 potato failure, the "prophecy man" Donnel Dhu sees a rainstorm and predicts starvation. The water, he explains, will kill potatoes and soften the earth for grave-digging. The heavy clouds are "death hearses movin' slowly along." The novel appeared in serial in the *Dublin University Magazine* between May and December 1846. A pastiche of childhood memories from 1817 and reporting from 1845, Carleton hoped *Black Prophet* would make the suffering of the Irish poor vivid to his readers, with fictional scenes presented "in the midst of living testimony." However, by midsummer, long before the conclusion appeared in print, it became obvious that the blight had returned, just as virulent as the past year's and more widespread. Fewer potatoes were in the ground, and a greater proportion of planted potatoes were destroyed. Inspecting a field in August, a relief official found few potatoes larger than a marble. The familiar putrid smell was everywhere.[1]

In the winter of 1846–1847, rural Ireland became a hellscape, shocking and incomprehensible. An estimated four hundred thousand people in Ireland died of causes related to the loss of the 1846 potato crop—thousands by starvation, and hundreds of thousands by disease. The bonds of social life dissolved. Mobs of the hungry marched on worksites and government offices. Parents watched their children die and were too weak to properly mourn them. Children watched their parents die and were too weak to move their bodies. Those who could fled Ireland, a panicked beginning to one of the largest waves of European migration in the nineteenth century.[2]

Everyday life collapsed, and famine-relief efforts stood in pathetic contrast. Ireland did not suffer in secret. Thanks to faster communications by steamship (and occasionally telegraph—though telegraphy was quite new in 1846) and the widespread syndication of articles from London newspapers across the British Empire, in the United States, and beyond, the world knew about the ongoing catastrophe in close to real time. Moved by images and stories of Irish suffering, people and organisations around the world donated money and goods to the relief effort. In counterpoint to this public openhandedness, the Whig government that replaced Peel's Conservatives, led by John Russell, fixated on the moral hazard of eleemosynary aid—of giving relief without labour in exchange, even to the starving. Faith in the civilising power of austerity and even deeper faith in the power of markets remained core principles of the response to rapidly deteriorating conditions.

Some historians speculate that had Peel remained in power, Ireland might have suffered less in 1847. This argument echoes wishful thinking from the Irish intelligentsia of the 1840s, some of whom argued that the Conservative prime minister had "recognized the duty of government to feed the people to the utmost extent." However, differences between the Tory and Whig approaches to relief were practical, not principled. Where Peel emphasised managing the food supply, Russell focused on labour. The 1846 Labour Rate Act, which established a new famine-relief system based at government-sponsored worksites, passed quickly in August, before the parliamentary recess. Public works, financed primarily by Irish taxpayers, would provide Irish labourers the means to buy the food that free trade would bring to Irish ports. By raising local taxes to pay for public works, the slogan went, "Irish property would support Irish poverty." Reasoning from the principles of political economy, Russell's government hoped that the famine would make Irish workers more dependent on wages.[3]

The Labour Rate Act was written to make public works a last resort. The law echoed the workhouse principle of less eligibility by limiting access to public jobs to those labourers unable to find work from private employers and by mandating that public wages always be set lower than the lowest local private wage. Despite these provisions, by March 1847 more than seven hundred thousand people had jobs on the works, supporting millions more. Facing ballooning costs and few returns, and thrown off-balance from the spring of 1847 by a financial crisis, the Whig government declared an end to the famine as a national emergency for the United Kingdom. Local authorities in Ireland, rather than national bodies like the Treasury, would be responsible for famine relief. The government quickly wound down the public works and sponsored a temporary program of local soup kitchens, financed directly by grants and public donations. At their peak, the kitchens distributed daily rations to some three million people. The poor—those who did not die or flee—spent the winter growing weaker and fighting for work, and the summer shuffling in line for soup.

The tragedy of Black '47, as it came to be known by many, is not that the government of the United Kingdom did nothing, but that it did so much to so little effect. The British government recognised the depth and urgency of the crisis. What 1847 shows instead is the poverty of an early Victorian political imagination that could only see a solution to famine that depended on market principles and the disciplinary power of supply and demand. When the Irish poor did not behave in ways that confirmed the predictions of political economy, it was the people, not the predictions, that needed correction. Under famine conditions, relief plans that required work in exchange for food or money left the people vulnerable to die first. The potato famine reached ghoulish depths in basements and hovels and fields, places hidden from officials supervising worksites and soup kitchens. People on the margins—the disabled; the very young and the old; the geographically, socially, or politically isolated—were helpless. One relief officer estimated that in his district no more than one out of every seven destitute people earned wages, and that hundreds of people with jobs on the works ate nothing from morning until nightfall. Although some died on the works, most died in secret. "The imploring look or the vacant sepulchral stare," of the starving, one witness wrote, "once fastened upon you, leaves its impress for ever."[4]

AFTER PEEL RESIGNED IN JUNE 1846, LORD JOHN RUSSELL became prime minister. Russell, the third son of the Duke of Bedford, was, like Peel, a career politician. Like Peel, he entered the House of Commons at twenty-one. Russell, a slight man belittled by critics for his "solemn gibberish," became prime minister while still wounded and gun-shy after his failed attempt to form a government in December 1845. Russell was unsure if he could control his cabinet, much less his backbenches. To keep his government together, Russell needed the consistent support of a core of free-trading "Peelite" Tories.[5]

Russell was confident that without the Corn Laws in place, trade would supply Ireland with enough cheap grain to meet demand. "A government," *The Economist* concurred, "may be perfectly easy while it is totally ignorant of the source whence the people's food is derived." Russell also insisted (correctly) that Peel's large-scale purchases and imports of maize were never intended to be permanent. Russell's ministry scaled down the government's grain-buying and marketing, keeping open only the depots in the most impoverished southern and western districts. "This is a special case," Russell admitted, a chance for Parliament to show "the poorest among the Irish people that we are not insensible, here, to the claims which they have on us." But those claims had natural limits, he argued. Even in the face of desperate need, relief had to be parsimonious, to prevent the Irish poor from swapping dependence on potatoes for dependence on the government. "The infliction of Providence," Russell reflected, would be worth the pain, if the consequence was a transition to dependence on wage labour.[6]

Free trade could not bring grain into Ireland fast enough to meet profound need—and it was ironclad doctrine that Ireland export food while waiting for grain from the United States and Black Sea ports. That Ireland should continue to export cash crops despite the near-total destruction of its subsistence staple was the same principle, on a macro scale, that demanded that the starving work for money and food. It was better to endure famine in the near term than to retreat from the rigour and civilising power of the market in the long term. Laissez-faire, as usual, required bureaucracy. The public works established under the Labour Rate Act were designed to be self-limiting; the lower-than-average wages mandated by the statute were meant to deter people from seeking public works jobs if other employment was available. Works were funded by loans that would have to be repaid from local taxes, to encourage landlords to offer private employment. Russell's government spent four times as much on relief in nine months as Peel's government had spent in over a year.[7]

The global market for grain in August 1846 was very different than it had been a year earlier. Lower tariffs made transatlantic trade cheaper. The grain supply, however, was constrained by limited infrastructure. Though there may have been enough grain for sale on the world market to satisfy every buyer, there were nowhere near enough quays to load it or ships to carry it. In the United States a similar number of merchants and shipping firms were filling many more orders, and British buyers competed with other European governments. The cost of freight doubled in Europe and tripled in the United States. The price of grain in ports on the Danube and in the Black Sea more than doubled. This bottleneck in supply created a bubble in grain prices, which worsened the Irish food supply crisis. There were accounts, possibly apocryphal, of ships laden with wheat crossing and recrossing the Irish Sea, killing time as merchants watched prices rise. In Sligo, as many as ten thousand barrels of maize and other grains were kept in warehouses to appreciate. As for demand, it was endless. "Ireland would swallow all that could be thrown into it," Charles Trevelyan wrote, "and remain still unsatisfied." The government's rules for marketing grain, meant to protect private trade, set the price of grain from government stores based on local markets, which increased the price of grain sold by the Commissariat by as much as 30 percent.[8]

The remaining government depots received hundreds of requests for grain from relief committees and workers. In autumn 1846, officers struggled to explain why the government was selling grain at nearly the same price as profiteering merchants, and why most of its supply was still on American docks. The poor battered at the doors. "I never witnessed anything like it," a Catholic priest wrote of a night he spent inside a locked storeroom near Loughros, County Leitrim, "and hope I never will again." A crowd of as many as a thousand people attacked the Cahersiveen depot, in County Kerry, smashing at the barred windows and heavy doors with crowbars until the storekeepers surrendered and gave out meal and biscuit. In Blacksod Bay, County Mayo, occupants of some twenty small boats pulled alongside a schooner, boarded it, and carried away seventy tons of meal.[9]

By mid-1847, however, the government's faith in the capacity of free trade to supply grain to Ireland was partially vindicated. Food came in quantities, albeit months after the crisis had begun in earnest, and the bubble burst—the price of maize, for example, fell from £19 a ton in February 1847 to about £7 six months later. In the first six months of 1847, nearly 2.85 million quarters of grain (nearly 79 million pounds) worth nearly £8.8 million had been imported. Ireland, Lord Clarendon wrote, had a market that was "freer, cheaper, and better supplied, than that of any country in Europe where distress prevailed, and where those measures of interference and restriction had been unwisely adopted which were successfully resisted here." To free-traders it was a victory, proof that markets *could* supply cheap food, and that Providence rewarded patience.[10]

A good supply of food in the ports, however, did not mean a good supply of food in the backcountry. In many remote parts of Ireland, the Commissariat stores had been the only facilities with the capacity to bring imported grain to market. Yet they were mostly closed by the time affordable grain arrived on Irish shores in 1847. Said one official, "The machinery necessary for the new state of things does not exist." Even in the coastal towns in the west of Ireland, where depots were open, there were few commercial mills able to grind maize. "The ordinary mercantile machinery," Trevelyan worried, "even of the greatest trading nation in the world, is unequal to such a novel emergency." Even when there had been enough grain on the market months earlier, there were not enough ships to carry it to Ireland. And now, when there was enough grain in Irish ports, there were few ways to carry it to the people who most needed it.[11]

The pressure of famine conditions compounded these complex logistical problems. Even in places with plenty of grain and the means to market it, social collapse kept food out of the market. Warehouses, wagon trains, farms, and stores were robbed in daylight. In Tralee, County Kerry, a crowd ransacked the town and the ships in the harbour, taking bread, bacon, and other food. Farmers and shopkeepers sold off their whole stock as fast as possible to prevent theft, which temporarily lowered prices but emptied inventories. The Irish clung to "a general expectation, or rather desire" that the government continue to bring grain to sell to the starving.[12]

In practical terms, before this grain arrived there was *nothing* to eat for many of the Irish poor. People ate the eggs of wild birds, seaweed, grass, leaves, roots, carrion, and dirt while waiting for supply to catch up with demand. For the 1846 harvest, only three hundred thousand acres of potatoes had been planted—a seventh of the acreage planted in 1845, and the smallest planting since perhaps the mid-eighteenth century. What food there was in Ireland was still sold by farmers to pay rent—the rent market did not stop, even at the nadir of the famine. Slightly better-off tenants sold their oatmeal but could not afford to eat it.[13]

Ireland continued to export food. In 1846, 3.3 million acres were planted with grain, and Irish farms raised more than 2.5 million cattle, 2.2 million sheep, and 600,000 pigs. Waterford alone exported more than 20,200 barrels of wheat and nearly 59,000 barrels of oats from May 1846 to February 1847. Despite the continuing flow of exports from Ireland, 1847 was the first year since 1842 when imports of grain exceeded exports, with Ireland exporting about 1.96 million quarters of grain (mostly wheat and oats) and importing about 4.52 million quarters (mostly maize). Ireland remained a net importer of grain until at least the early 1850s. This shift in the balance of exports was caused by the effect of famine conditions on the availability of labour to sow and reap, not by farmers holding back their crops or selling them on the Irish market. As one of the leaders of the Young Ireland movement reflected, Irish trade was wholly dependent on British demand. "England has bound this Island hand and foot," he wrote. "She robs the Island of its food, for it has not the power to guard it."[14]

Livestock exports testified to this geography of suffering. From 1846 to 1847, exports of Irish cattle fell 8 percent and of sheep 58 percent, while the number of pigs exported rose 23 percent. Sheep and cattle were the livestock of wealthier graziers, who could afford to husband their flocks, wait for prices to rise (and perhaps take advantage of the glut of imported grain to use as fodder). The poor, however, were liquidating their assets, trading the certainty of a small return on a pig against the possibility of a total loss. In Cork alone, thirty-one thousand pigs were brought to market, nearly five times as many as in the years before. This was not an unfamiliar phenomenon in Irish agriculture. Past shortages of potatoes and increases in rent had often forced Irish farmers without reserves of cash—that is, most Irish farmers—to sell their crops and animals at a steep discount, flooding markets and driving down prices even further. "The pig can no longer find a home in the Irish cabin," mourned the author of a guide to commercial pig breeding. Without potatoes to feed them, and in desperate need of money for imported grain and rent payments, tens of thousands of hungry pigs, "half-famished animals" with "semi-wolfish eyes," were exported. In some parts of Ireland, piglets could be had for a sixpence each—no one could feed them, so no one would buy them.[15]

As ever, there was food in Ireland—but not for the hungry.

WITH THE FOOD SUPPLY LEFT TO THE MARKET, THE GOVERNMENT focused on encouraging the poor to find wage work. Although the Labour Rate Act established public works on an unprecedented scale, the act also included provisions that, paradoxically, were supposed to *deter* Irish labourers from taking on publicly funded work. In each district, works were paid for with government loans, to be repaid by local taxpayers who owned or leased land worth more than four pounds in annual rental value. Labourers were to be paid at least twopence less than the average local daily wage. As a Whig MP explained, when the "maintenance of the poor was not derived from the land," society was "in an unnatural and in a diseased state." The works were a treatment for the "social body" of Ireland rather than for individual starving workers.[16]

The idea that wage labour was civilising had anchored one of the Whigs' signature policies of the 1830s: the abolition of chattel slavery in the colonial empire. Under the 1833 Abolition of Slavery Act, the majority of formerly enslaved workers in the British Caribbean were declared to be apprentices. They were expected to work for a wage during "free" time while also continuing to work without wages for the people who had once claimed to own them. In theory, apprentices would learn the value of time and of money, and would ensure "the continued cultivation of the soil, and good order of society, until all classes should gradually fall into the relations of a state of freedom." The Irish poor, who were fair-skinned Europeans and had never been enslaved by the modern English or British Empires, were considered to be higher in the imagined hierarchy of civilisation than formerly enslaved people in the Caribbean, but perhaps not by much. Teaching the Irish to prefer wages to potatoes for subsistence, Russell wrote, would impel them "to study economy, cleanliness, and the value of time; to aim at improving the character of themselves and their children."[17]

Every new public work required approval from the lord lieutenant and the Treasury. The Treasury expected loans to be quickly repaid, in half-yearly installments and at rates of interest as low as 4 percent and as high as 20 percent. Relief committees were told to keep lists of the destitute, subject to auditing by relief officials. The free market and its natural healing properties were administered by nearly twelve thousand clerks and officers. Their workload was astonishing. In the field, officials supervised worksites, liaised with relief committees, managed lists of approved workers, audited accounts, arranged for security for engineers and pay clerks, negotiated with subcontractors, arranged to distribute food from commissary stores, and more. Each was also expected to file regular reports. An average of eight hundred letters a day came through the Relief Commission offices, with a peak on May 17, 1847, of 6,033.[18]

There was an odd symmetry between the harried paperwork of relief officials and the listless manual labour of the people employed on the public works. Both groups moved through a bureaucracy designed to make sure that no hungry person got something for nothing. In folk memory, relief work was nothing more than "digging holes and filling them up again." Labourers did the purposeless work, and relief workers wrote the reports that proved the work had been done. In addition to requiring a staff of thousands to facilitate and manage wage labour, the Labour Rate Act forbade "productive works," or public works that might enhance the value of private land. On October 5, 1846, faced with heavy criticism, the government climbed down from this part of its policy. Henry Labouchere, the chief secretary for Ireland, wrote a circular letter (the "Labouchere Letter") that allowed productive works so long as the costs were eventually repaid by landlords.[19]

Labourers resented the low wages offered on the works. In Clover Hill, County Roscommon, three hundred people surrounded a surveyor and threatened to kill him, convinced that he had told the Board of Works that tenpence a day was the usual private wage in the county, in order to set their wages at eightpence. Wages were set by the market price of labour, not of bread or potatoes—and private wages (if there were any on offer) remained low, even when the price of food increased. Many worksites were especially tense in the autumn of 1846, when grain prices were very high and before famine conditions deteriorated to the point where labourers were too ill and hungry to strike collectively or to attack a foreman or engineer. Ratepayers, in turn, resented being taxed for projects they believed ought to be paid for by the entire taxpaying public of the UK.[20]

The public works were shambolic as well as bureaucratic. Presentment sessions to propose new projects often dissolved into rowdy chaos. Labourers packed the meetings, and grand jurors hastily approved proposals, regardless of cost. The Anglo-Irish politician and Treasury official Thomas Spring Rice compared the initial wave of presentment sessions to the Australian gold rush, a stampede "to the diggings." In Kilmacthomas, County Waterford, a large group of unemployed workers crowded the presentment sessions to demand food and fixed prices for essential goods. Sixty dragoons sent to restore order were overwhelmed and had to call for reinforcements. When the leader of the mob, "Lame Pat" Power, was captured, the soldiers were pelted with rocks by the crowd and in turn fired warning shots. Even when they were not shouted down at packed meetings, many grand juries approved nearly every project they were presented with, however implausible or expensive. These proposals, when sent to Dublin for approval, were rejected or reduced. Anger at the government grew. It was easy for relief committees to paint the Board of Works as tight-fisted and intransigent. Taxpayers could claim that *they* had been generous while Dublin Castle and the Treasury had been miserly.[21]

As more worksites opened, relief officials worried that too many workers would abandon farm labour in exchange for jobs on the works. A shortage of agricultural workers would prolong the famine and potentially destroy the export trade. Many grand juries assumed that they would never really be asked to repay the loans they were rapidly accumulating. Commissary-General Randolph Routh warned that unless the Labour Rate Act were amended to allow the government to seize the property of individual ratepayers who defaulted on their rates, the government would never be made whole. Thomas Carlyle complained that presentment sessions would vote away £28,000 in a morning's work ("English have plenty of money") and complain when the bill came due ("Had we known that!").[22]

POTATOES WERE ESSENTIAL TO RENT, ESSENTIAL TO EXPORT AGRI-culture, and essential to family and social life. Without them, social and economic life in rural Ireland imploded. In this period of utter misery and desperation, the public works provided a scant but relatively reliable income to people able to get on and stay on the rolls of eligible workers. Despite the emphasis among the leaders of the Relief Commission that the public works were to be a school of industriousness for the Irish poor, there is ample anecdotal evidence that most workers who managed to get on the books did as little as they could possibly do to keep earning wages without being sacked. Political economy predicted that higher-paying private employment would draw down the numbers on public works, but the general crisis suppressed the private labour market. For their own security, larger farmers reduced their operations. It seems most Irish workers understood "that the work was provided for the people and not the people for the work." Why would someone exert themselves to earn a pittance while starving to death? Canny landlords, in turn, used the works to shelter their money. They spent government loans freely and deposited their own receipts in savings banks. Weekly deposits doubled in many counties, an increase driven by wealthier tenants, professionals, and middlemen, not landless workers. One relief official despaired that the didactic purpose of the public works had been turned inside out. Employers and workers had each abdicated their place in the social order, taking "the whole moral training of the people out of the hands of society at large" and imposing the burden "upon the Government."[23]

Labourers on crowded worksites oscillated between enervation and irritability. Workers sat around waiting for shovels, wheelbarrows, or gunpowder to use for quarrying. Historians have criticised the works for having too many staff, but in truth there may have been too few to manage the crush of mostly adult men (but also some women and boys) looking for jobs on more than five thousand worksites. One official wrote that the crowds were so large that staff were "completely in their hands." The Board of Works, an overwhelmed official wrote, employed more men "than the whole British Army all over the world." Theft by workers as well as supervisors was ubiquitous, and illicit distillers enjoyed a thriving trade. Pay clerks, perhaps in exchange for a kickback from the receipts, sometimes distributed wages from "offices" set up at the makeshift bars that mushroomed around worksites. When wages were due, paymasters sent identical carts onto the road at the same time, of which only one was laden with cash, in the hope that the decoy would be robbed instead.[24]

The famine destroyed mutual support and solidarity in the countryside. The works program was dominated by the stronger and better-connected among the poor—the able-bodied, the relatively better-off, the cunning, and the lucky. Larger tenant farmers, according to reports from the Board of Works, negotiated with their landlords to have their sons put on the rolls. Regulations required that even people without any access to land prove they could find no other employment before being eligible for a job on the works. Those with land needed to prove their hardship to an even greater extent. In practice, oversight was uneven—excessively scrupulous in some cases and absent in others. The system thrummed with graft and favour-trading.[25]

The rush to the public works was inexorable. Gentlemen complained that they could not find tradesmen to mend their shoes and coats. Some ratepayers complained that the staff of the Board of Works were too cowardly to stare down the numberless poor; others considered relief officers pompous idiots methodically laying out roads that could just as easily be plotted by "a countryman with a straw rope." The Board of Works, in turn, complained about ratepayers, especially those who played the role of the "spouting patriot" at presentment sessions, loudly condemning the government and the Relief Commission "through the broken pane of glass to the poor creatures outside." Many migrant workers in Britain returned to Ireland, giving up an end-of-harvest windfall of several pounds or more for a few coins paid for the pretense of work. One contractor in Dundee complained that in a single day, twenty workers, all of whom earned a minimum of sixteen shillings a week, quit to return to Ireland.[26]

To orthodox political economists, this was irrational, barbaric. No civilised man would sacrifice a high wage paid for skilled work to earn pennies breaking rocks. The migration back from England proved, Nassau William Senior wrote, that the Irish needed coercion to be industrious, since they would give up well-paying work for "an eleemosynary allowance, under the name of wages." And yet, returning to Ireland made perfect sense from a worker's perspective. Migrant labourers had gone to England to earn security for their families. They returned to Ireland for the same reason. The market moved faster for the poor than for the rich. Just as Irish farmers sold their crops even when prices collapsed in the years before the Great Famine, during the famine, Irish labourers could not afford to wait to be paid. In October 1846 there were no potatoes, and a few pence every week was worth more than five pounds in a few weeks or months. The government, however, was anxious to encourage workers to plant potatoes and grain for the 1847 harvest. In response, in autumn 1846, the government and the Relief Commission agreed that instead of daily wages, wages on the public works should be paid by the task.[27]

Working by the task or by the piece was not an innovation in Irish labour; it had been common in Ireland before the famine, especially among workers taking conacre. Under the conditions of Irish labour before the famine, task work was worth the effort. However, risking exhaustion, injury, or illness labouring harder or faster under a task-work scheme during famine struck many as an intolerable threat. Riots broke out. On one Skibbereen site, four hundred men went on strike after being told they would have to work by task. When threatened with removal from the lists, they attacked the overseer, who "had to run for his life." At a Coshlea presentment session, a grand juror blamed a Board of Works surveyor for the rollout of task work. The surveyor, named Kearney, was "hunted like a mad dog by the whole country population" and only escaped death by leaping into a speeding carriage. In Tipperary, workers rioted, declaring they would never give the government "the sweat of their bodies," even for double wages. In Limerick, nine hundred workers marched to the courthouse, brandishing shovels and spades and pickaxes and chanting, "No task work!"[28]

For their part, Relief Commission officials struggled to maintain their sanity as they coped with shifting and sometimes ambiguous regulations; febrile, hungry, and sometimes violent labourers; and intense pressure to keep costs low. Like many British colonial officials in the early Victorian era, many of the staff hired for the works were half-pay military officers, from the ranks of the Royal Navy, Royal Marines, and British Army.

They were hard men, but the works were an exceptionally difficult assignment. One official, after cutting names from a relief
committee's list of approved workers, was asked where he was
staying, so the committee might "send the . . . dead bodies in
carts" and leave them at his door. "I cannot see my way out of
this labyrinth of work," another officer wrote. The day before, he
had signed sixteen thousand tickets for labourers on the works,
and had gone to bed at 4:00 a.m. before waking with the winter sunrise four hours later. The job was "one long continuous
day, with occasional intervals of nightmare sleep." Many officers
resigned; others did the minimum to draw their pay. Officials in
Dublin worried that unless something changed, there would be
no qualified engineers available to survey new worksites. In Galway, an officer shot himself in the head, but the bullet glanced
off his skull, ripping through his nose and cheek. He was alive,
but his colleagues were sure he would try again.[29]

In Ireland, both the unemployed and hungry rural majority and
the thousands of officials and engineers sent to manage them were
depleted and disoriented by the depth of the crisis. The reports
from the public works were grim, but Parliament had few alterna-
tives to the system on offer, even from the Opposition. The famine,
the Tory leader George Bentinck declared, was "a calamity unex-
ampled in the history of the world" that required abrogating "the
severe rules of political economy." He was probably right in principle. However, the policy he and his party proposed as an alternative to public works—a massive loan tender to pay for railway
construction in Ireland—was insincere and self-dealing. Railway
construction appealed to the Irish middle class, who saw rail as a
symbol of modernity and independence and a good investment.
Landlords also liked the potential rewards of railway construction
and were eager to have railway shareholders absorb the risk, and
cost, of employing the poor. The government objected that a great

deal would be spent on materials and equipment, not labour, and that speculators would be the greatest beneficiaries. The plan was crushed in the House, but—like the fantasy of an alternative timeline where Peel, rather than Russell, served as prime minister through 1847 and rescued the Irish with a steady supply of cheap cornmeal—Irish railway investment became a Great Famine counterfactual, symbolic of another reality where the right kind of capitalists saved the day with a spectacular private alternative to the moribund public works. The railroad idea "was, indeed, a brilliant bubble," the *Bristol Mercury* wrote.[30]

By March 1847, the public works system was still growing. Designed to save money, it had run for seven months and cost the government more than £944,000—about £102.4 million in today's currency when adjusted for inflation alone. However, if reckoned in proportion to increases in gross domestic product, a government project on a similar scale to the 1846–1847 public works would cost the United Kingdom more than £3.83 billion if launched today. The public works were designed to encourage unemployed labourers to seek private employment, but by March, more than 708,000 people were on the lists. Based on the population from the 1841 census, the works employed as much as 26 percent of the population of County Clare, more than 20 percent of the population in Tipperary and Roscommon, and about 15 percent in Counties Cork, Galway, and Mayo. The average labourer supported a family—and often also an extended family. In Ireland's poorest counties, the works effectively had become the only reliable source of income. The Board of Works had lost control. "What was possible and practicable with 50,000 men," an officer wrote, "is no longer so with seven times that number." Nearly every worker was getting weaker, and injury was a death sentence. As one relief officer wrote, idleness was no longer a problem. Instead, he wrote, "there is a *physical incapability*."[31]

Hundreds of thousands of workers and their families had become completely dependent on public worksites for survival, the opposite of what the policy had been intended to encourage. "It is impossible," an officer conceded, to "limit . . . the dependence of the people upon the Government." Russell and his cabinet looked for a way to take the costs of famine relief off the government's balance sheet and transfer responsibility for relief to local authorities. Relief officers, inspired by the work of the Quakers and other groups, pressed for a plan that would directly feed the hungry. Russell and his cabinet resolved to allow direct aid in the short term and to devolve the relief program to the Poor Law unions before the next harvest. A Board of Works official, relieved, insisted that Poor Law guardians had always been "the natural channel for investigating distress." Charles Trevelyan concurred. More spending, he wrote, would "exhaust and disorganise society throughout the United Kingdom, and reduce all classes of people in Ireland to a state of helpless dependence." Even if the potatoes kept failing and the people kept starving, the famine could no longer be a crisis for the United Kingdom.[32]

IN THE WINTER OF 1846–1847, ON THE PUBLIC WORKSITES, IN drafty cabins and wind-bitten lean-tos, in crowded urban rooms crammed with families, hundreds of thousands of human bodies were eating themselves. Starving bodies and minds are ill-suited to hear a gospel of industriousness and forbearance. Without sufficient nourishment, the body can no longer metabolise, converting food to usable energy, and it shifts to catabolism, consuming first fat and then muscle to keep the brain and vital organs functioning. Over days or weeks, the starving person becomes irritable, weak, and tired. Ideas of food and eating become intrusive obsessions. The heartbeat accelerates and breathing becomes shallow.

Some people develop a constant thirst. Some become constipated; others develop chronic diarrhea. Children's bellies swell, as do the ankles of both adults and children. Skin flakes. Hair falls out or turns white. Starvation puts pressure on the heart and kidneys, weakens the immune system, and slows wound healing. Starving people usually die of organ failure or infection.

The effects of fasting on the body were the object of scientific curiosity throughout the nineteenth and early twentieth centuries. "Hunger artists" who starved themselves for a living were a fixture in carnival freak shows. Nineteenth-century physicians understood the stages of starvation and that starvation was psychologically as well as physically harrowing. Twentieth-century experiments showed even more starkly the changes in motivation and mood that accompanied catabolism. In 1944 and 1945, at the University of Minnesota, thirty-six men, conscientious objectors conscripted into the Civilian Public Service (CPS) in lieu of military service in the Second World War, volunteered to endure semi-starvation for six months. Ancel Keys, an expert on nutrition who developed food rations for the US Army, was the lead researcher on the project, which is often called the Minnesota Starvation Experiment. Keys has a seedy reputation—he relied on the CPS as a source of human subjects for experiments that included exposing test subjects to extreme cold, months of enforced confinement to bed, and diets deficient in specific vitamins.[33]

Nutritionists and physiologists place the Minnesota Starvation Experiment in a canon of research on the biochemistry of ketosis (the metabolism of fat instead of glucose for energy) and other metabolic processes. However, in its own time, the experiment's findings on the psychology of starvation were considered as significant as those on metabolism. Test subjects never suffered malnutrition; they were fed a restricted but nutritionally complete diet intended to cause them to lose 25 percent of their body weight

over six months, considered a safe proportion that would simu-
late starvation without putting the subjects at risk of serious illness. Although the men were not at risk of actual starvation, they
reported increasingly strange eating habits—taking hours to eat
small meals, licking dirty plates, "[toying] with their food, making
weird and seemingly distasteful concoctions." Some, for example,
crushed potatoes, jam, gingerbread, and sugar into a paste and
spread it on bread. "Hunger! Hunger! Hunger! They wondered
whether this horrible nightmare would ever end."[34]

Now consider the effects of starvation—the physical debil-
ity and decay, paranoia, depression, and desperate, manipulative
solipsism—spread across a population of millions that had already
endured a year of chaos, epidemic disease, and widespread food
shortages. The everyday activities of household economy—cutting
turf; weaving grasses into tools and furniture; maintaining iron
tools, thatch roofs, and stone walls—slowed or stopped as people
grew weak and hungry. "Society stands dissolved," wrote James
Fintan Lalor. It was a horrific time, recorded in the archives in
nightmarish impressions. Families fell apart. Children were abandoned. Bodies rotted on the ground, gnawed by dogs and rats that
were hunted, in turn, for meat. In the last years of the blight, especially in 1848–1849—a year that in some counties was nearly as
bad as 1846–1847—the utter destruction caused by famine was
visible in the workhouses that became centres for organising relief.
In contrast, during Black '47, the worst happened in "derelict cabins and overgrown lanes," in the places where the most vulnerable
tended to live.[35]

A medical officer remembered a thousand men marching on
Skibbereen, "once stalwart . . . now emaciated spectres," with spades
and shovels on their shoulders, "in the glitter of a blazing sun." In
Schull, County Cork, a relief officer looked the other way when
locals slit open bags of grain and gathered spilled meal and flour

off the ground. Commissary-General Richard Inglis found a young
woman collapsed on a road. Her family had died in the weeks
before. Unable to move their bodies, she watched as rats and insects
"nightly held their disgusting banquet." The dead were buried without coffins or thrown unburied in ditches. In February, a farmer
named Thomas Millar was arrested for trying to sell the corpse of
his seven-year-old nephew to an apothecary in Youghal. Typhus,
relapsing fever, dysentery, cholera, and flu broke out. Even those
who could afford grain did not always have the means to cook it
because cutting and drying turf consumed too much energy. Crime
increased dramatically, from eight thousand reported offences in
1845 to twenty thousand in 1847—and unreported offences must
have been orders of magnitude higher. The rate of robbery, theft, and
other crimes against property, with or without violence, rose especially sharply. A carman pulling a load of flour from Derry had his
skull broken with a rock. Another carrying money was ambushed
by three men whom he fought off with a whip. The offenders could
not be traced.[36]

The Irish poor were notorious in Britain for making a "poor
mouth," that is, exaggerating their poverty to grift the English.
In 1846–1847, however, reports—especially from Skibbereen,
the County Cork town whose name became a synecdoche for the
worst of the famine—drew attention and sympathy, even from
Britons sceptical of Irish hyperbole. In December 1846, Nicholas
Cummins, a magistrate from Cork, wrote a public letter to the
Duke of Wellington that was widely reprinted, including in the
Christmas Eve edition of the *Times*. In a village near Skibbereen,
in an apparently deserted cottage, he found "six famished and
ghastly skeletons" covered in a horse blanket—a man, a woman,
and four children. They were feverish and barely responsive. To
Cummins's shock, some two hundred people soon emerged out of
other cottages, "delirious, either from famine or from fever. Their

demoniac yells are still ringing in my ears." He turned, ready to run. A woman who appeared to have just given birth, her breasts bare, her newborn in her arms, and her bloodied thighs half covered with a sack, grabbed his collar. He fought her off and fled. The next morning, Cummins returned with an escort of police. The party opened one locked house to find two frozen, rat-bitten corpses. Outside, a woman dragged the corpse of her twelve-year-old daughter, naked, into the street and covered the body with stones.

Cummins implored Wellington to deliver his letter to Queen Victoria: "She will not allow decency to be outraged." He begged the duke, as commander-in-chief of the British Army, to remember his own Irish origins and the many Irish soldiers under his command, "the gallant Irish blood . . . lavished to support the honour of the British name." He described how an old man had died next to his son, who was too weak and too traumatised to move him; the body was "nearly putrid when discovered by the dispensary doctor." Ireland had served the British Empire, Cummins insisted—now that loyalty should be repaid. Irish folk memory dramatised Skibbereen and the impression the town's desperation made on the British public consciousness. A ghost story claimed that when Queen Victoria—who did visit Ireland, but in 1849, not 1847—stepped off her yacht in Cobh, she saw an inscription that read, "Arise ye Dead from Skibbereen, / And come to Cork to welcome your Queen." Terrified, she turned around and sailed back to Britain.[37]

The days were dull and dreary, but also agitating and unsettled. As the Minnesota experiments showed, starvation tends to produce a mental state that combines irritability and apathy, weakness and anger, and "overpowering frustration." Hunger made sufferers sluggish and inert, except when the boredom and pain of sitting in a cold, wet cabin watching children shiver or shit blood grew intolerable. "Groups of men and women almost naked" were seen along the roads, "running up and down in a frantic state (as if they were all the inmates of a Bedlam, from which they suddenly burst forth, impatient of restraint), crying to every person they meet for bread." Folk memory of the famine is wild and hallucinatory. In some stories, people eat grass and turn green after death. In others, Catholic priests curse their parishioners for going to Protestant churches for food. In another story a man is pronounced dead, and just as he is about to be put in the coffin, he calls out. The doctor tells him he is lying ("The doctor knows best"), and the man is buried alive. Folktales of the famine also celebrate rough justice—the good are rewarded and the greedy and unscrupulous punished (in reality, the unscrupulous were probably more likely to survive). An old woman in one story, "who had a stocking full of gold hidden," tries to boil the gold, like cornmeal. A landlord who tips an evicted woman's pot of cornmeal stirabout onto the ground is cursed, and after his death he haunts his land with a heavy iron pot hung forever around his neck. In another, a woman found dying in a chapel yard perishes with her mouth full of banknotes. A virtuous woman boils a pot of stones to make her crying children believe a meal is coming. When the woman empties the pot, a pile of fine, whole potatoes spills out.[38]

In an editorial, the *Times* condemned what the editors took to be the self-destructive laziness of the Irish in the face of starvation, their "national thoughtlessness, the national indolence." The Irish appetite, trained on apocryphally gargantuan servings of potatoes, needed to be reformed. The famine might be a work of Providence after all, if it could encourage the Irish to want more than potatoes. "When the Celts once cease to be potatophagi," the editors wrote, "they must become carnivorous. With the taste of meats will grow the appetite for them." "Potatophagi," with its ancient Greek flavour, was an allusion to the English myth that the pagan

Irish had been cannibals before their conversion to Christianity. In a widely reprinted Puritan tract about the Irish, published just before the Cromwellian conquest, they were "anciently called Anthropophagi, man eaters." Conversion, the use of "potatophagi" implied, had only swapped an obscene appetite for human meat with an obscene appetite for potatoes.[39]

Cannibalism was a common metaphor for class conflict in Ireland during the famine. An inspecting officer wrote, "If the graziers do not break up some of their farms to allow employment the labourers will eat the farmers, and the farmers will eat the landlords." But real cannibalism is famine's open secret: there are few recorded famines without at least rumours of the desperate eating human flesh, sometimes that of people already dead, sometimes freshly killed. It seems to have been rare in Ireland, but not unheard of. "People killed and ate anything they could catch," a folk history relates, "pigs, rats, cats, cattle, sheep, and finally their own children." There are references to mothers eating their infants and to fathers "known to make a wolfish meal" of dead children. In May 1849, in Ballinrobe, County Mayo, a priest reported that a starving man had eaten the heart and liver of a man who had died in a shipwreck. Later, a relieving officer reported that a man had seen the same man "cut up a shipwrecked human body," apparently intending to eat the thigh, until his neighbours stopped him.[40]

As food dwindled, disease surged. Many clergy and gentry who volunteered in hospitals contracted typhus and died. The more profound the epidemic and the more severe the lice infestation, the more flecks of typhus-infected louse feces scatter in the air, turning an insect-borne disease into an airborne disease. The Society of Friends gave clothing away to the poor to try to reduce lice infestations. Many pawned the new clothes to buy food. The Irish poor well knew that the dirty clothes of a feverish person needed to be cleaned or destroyed, and that the clothes that had belonged to the sick had "the venom of the sickness in it" and could easily make others sick. But what could they do? Without the means to wash, much less replace, louse-infested clothes, most wore what they could scavenge, weighing the possibility of contracting an epidemic fever against the more immediate risk of death from exposure. Typhus and other illnesses, as one historian puts it, "pauperized, when they did not kill." Weekly mortality rates in workhouses rose from about four in one thousand in October 1846 to twenty-five in one thousand by April 1847. Most of the (at least) one million Irish fatalities in the course of the famine died not of organ failure caused by starvation but from infectious diseases worsened by hunger and wasting. Of 140,000 reported deaths in 1840, starvation was listed as the cause of death in 17 cases. In 1847, out of 250,000 reported deaths (the real death toll was much higher), 6,000 were attributed directly to starvation. Scurvy and other syndromes caused by malnutrition were common. In Mayo, between 1846 and 1850, historians estimate, about 41 percent of all deaths were "hunger-sensitive," and another 30 percent were partially hunger-sensitive. In Clare, about 65 percent of deaths were either wholly or partly sensitive to hunger, and in Tipperary, 66 percent.[41]

To fight epidemics, relief committees had the power to build temporary hospitals, ventilate and cleanse cabins, and bury the dead. During the crisis, at least three hundred hospitals and dispensaries opened, taking in some twenty-three thousand patients. However, fever hospitals were targets for sabotage. Many believed they accelerated the spread of disease; some suspected they were part of a wider plot to exterminate or expel the poorest Irish labourers. In Killeshandra, in summer 1847, a mob attacked a field hospital and promised to pull down any "fever shed" built in the district. In Tipperary, priests condemned the local fever hospital from the pulpit and prayed to "see grass growing at the door of the hospital." In Donegal the poor built huts out of sod and wood to isolate the sick—similar to shielings, the rough shelters used by shepherds—and pushed food through the doors with the long-handled spades used to dig potatoes. Digestive diseases and accidental poisoning killed many others. People ate wild plants, decomposing carrion, the eggs of seagulls and other birds, moss, uncooked seaweed, cats, worms, insects, dogs, and rats. Livestock that had not been sold or slaughtered died as quickly as their owners. In Claremorris, the flayed corpse of a horse was left on the road. Relief officers found a family of eight eating its rotting flesh. In County Sligo, orphaned children gnawed on the bones of a pig that had died in an outbuilding. Grinding hunger and disease stripped relationships down to a bare and cutthroat struggle, "a sordid avarice, and a greediness of disposition to grasp at everything in the shape of food."[42]

The famine killed the weakest and most vulnerable. The strong were more likely to survive, and survivors were likely to flee. Among the one million excess deaths (that is, deaths above the expected annual average number) from 1846 to 1851, the fewest were among people ages ten to fifty-nine. They composed some 68.5 percent of the population but roughly 40 percent of the excess deaths. Children died at the highest rate; carpenters built special two-and-a-half-foot coffins for babies. There were too many deaths for individual burial plots, and some workhouses dug mass graves eight bodies deep. Religious rituals all but stopped. Rumours circulated about reusable coffins, their bottoms supported by hinges and hook-and-eye clasps, that could be carried to graves or to large pits, and the bodies dropped through the trapdoor into the hole.[43]

The scenes in the Irish countryside, reported with unprecedented detail and often accompanied by graphic and affecting sketches, reinforced the idea for many British readers that the Irish were a people foreign to British modernity. In March 1847, the *Times* condemned "the astounding apathy of the Irish themselves to the most horrible scenes immediately under their eyes." Instead of British spine and resilience, "all that we read of in [Ireland is] . . . Turkish or Chinese fatalism, of the indifference to life on the banks of the Ganges, or the brutality of piratical tribes." Irish suffering was marshalled to reinforce and retroactively justify conquest. The Irish *needed* management and always had. The Great Famine had proved the case. Britons would never starve, one commentator wrote, because they had "landed two or three merchants on the banks of the Hoogly, and in a century called India our own." The degradation of the Irish invited comparisons with the most oppressed victims of British imperial and colonial rule. The "wasted remnant" of the Indigenous peoples of Canada and the "degraded and enslaved African," a Quaker philanthropist wrote, were appalling to consider, "but never have I seen misery so intense, or *physical* degradation so complete, as among the dwellers in the bog-holes of Erris." A relief committee official placed the Irish between civilisation and barbarism, with "neither the pleasure of savage liberty, nor the profit of English civilization."[44]

The horrors reported from Ireland shocked the world. Donations of food and money arrived in unprecedented quantities. From spring 1847, many of those donations went to support an ambitious program of soup kitchens that gradually replaced the public works. The soup kitchens were a rare example of a policy that began at the grass roots in Ireland before being endorsed by the government as official relief policy, promoted by Commissariat officers in their letters to their superiors. The Quakers ran soup kitchens from relatively early in the crisis until July 1847, with operations underway long before relief committees could get their kitchens running under the government's scheme.[45]

The soup kitchens were more pragmatic than many other relief policies—less means-tested, more universal, more directly focused on feeding the hungry. Ireland was an uneven landscape of suffering. Survivors clung to public works, storm-tossed but afloat. Others sank into the depths. Fields were abandoned. Farmers could not find workers, conacre stopped, no potatoes were planted. Without a harvest, there would be even less food, no exports, and no employment. The works had to close so that the poor could plant potatoes and other crops, but they had to be fed in the meantime.

Free food, however, was considered by political economists to threaten the smooth operation of the market, and to undermine the motivation and work ethic of the poor. Soup kitchens were a short-term compromise of the principle that relief had to be earned, rather than given without conditions, in order to make sure that potatoes and other crops were planted. As historians have shown, even opening soup kitchens was, in effect, seen as something of an experiment in political economy. Food grants, by definition, were nontransferable. Giving food directly to the hungry could be understood as an attempt by policymakers to meet the Irish where they were in the hierarchy of civilisation. If the Irish poor could no longer be trusted to spend the money they had earned on public works, they could be fed directly.[46]

On January 25, 1847, the government presented its plan to the House of Commons, a plan later enacted as the Temporary Relief of Destitute Persons (Ireland) Act. The act permitted the lord lieutenant to establish *another* set of relief committees to establish soup kitchens "so that labouring men should be allowed to work on their own plot of ground, or for the farmers, and thus tend to produce food." The act also excused half the extant debts owed by local committees for public works, provided the first half was paid. Beginning in February 1847, the act permitted Poor Law unions to offer food as outdoor relief—the first outdoor relief permitted under the Irish Poor Law. The soup kitchens were inexpensive compared with the public works. In all, they cost about £3 million to operate, about £1.6 million of which was paid by the government. Only cooked food could be distributed, and only to people who had been vetted and officially recorded as destitute.[47]

The new system required a new set of bureaucratic tools. By March 1847, more than ten thousand account books and three million tickets that could be exchanged for soup had been printed. New regulations required committees to separate the poor into four classes: the destitute and disabled or otherwise unable to help themselves, with or without access to land; the destitute and landless but able-bodied; the destitute and able-bodied with access to land; and the able-bodied employed at insufficient wages. The first three were entitled to free rations at soup kitchens, and the final category to rations at a nominal price. The worries about outdoor relief that shaped the Irish Poor Law—and the public works—remained evident in the provisions of the act. Without means testing, policymakers reckoned, outdoor relief would become nearly universal, and "the whole country will become pauperised."[48]

In January 1847, with the announcement of the Temporary Relief Act, the government indicated that it planned to shut down the public works. Financial pressure on the government made closing the works even more urgent. The government was handcuffed by its dependence on Peel's breakaway free-trade Tory followers. Under the 1844 Bank Charter Act, the Bank of England was required to hold gold reserves equal to circulating banknotes. Peelites in Parliament considered the Bank Charter Act an essential part of their leader's legacy. If the Whigs moved to repeal it, the Peelites promised a vote of no confidence. By the beginning of 1847, bankers estimated that the government had committed to spend about £13 million in Ireland. Despite a large subscription campaign, it was clear that the government would have to borrow a great deal of money to pay for famine relief. On March 1, Baring Brothers and the Rothschild banking group agreed to loan the government £8 million.[49]

The large loan put the government in what seemed to investors like an invidious position. If it was spent on Ireland, the £8 million was likely to pay for provisions and materials for soup kitchens— most of which were ordered from the United States. In theory, if American merchants held enough banknotes from the Bank of England, the bank, already low on reserves, might not have enough bullion to cover the money circulating in the UK. When the loan became public knowledge, investors panicked, beginning a bank run. It was followed by a wave of bankruptcies of major merchant houses as creditors called in their debts to protect them- selves from the possibility that the Bank of England might stop payments. The government now had to shut down the works as quickly as possible. And yet without the ability to borrow, Russell wrote, "we could have no great plan for Ireland."[50]

Unfortunately, the financial crisis and the Whigs' panicked cuts occurred at the peak of the public works. On March 20, respond- ing to the crisis, the government announced that 20 percent of the works would close immediately. The consequence was that works closed before many soup kitchens were open, "a hideous inter- regnum" when many were left without any support. A Catholic priest in County Mayo compared John Russell to Tzar Nicholas I of Russia, sardonically referring to the order to reduce the works as an *ukase*, a declaration from the tzar with the force of law. In Eyrecourt, County Galway, as many as eight hundred attacked the

Commissariat food depot. Other labourers discharged from the works rushed the workhouses; two women were trampled to death in a stampede at the Dungarvon Union workhouse in County Waterford. Several attacks on soup kitchens occurred in Clare; a crowd in Meelick smashed soup boilers and shredded the records of the relief committee, and in Kilfenora, about sixty kilometres away, a crowd hurled soup boilers into a lake. Where possible, new soup kitchens were established near police stations.[51]

As the government stumbled, reports out of Ireland caused many in the Irish diaspora, as well as other sympathetic people, to open their pockets to help. As early as January 1846, Sir John Peter Grant, the lieutenant governor of Bengal, chaired a fund-raising committee in British India that brought in nearly £15,000. The Society of Friends convened its own relief committee. In January 1847, prominent men in British politics and finance, including Thomas Baring and Lionel de Rothschild, convened an umbrella organisation, the British Association for the Relief of Extreme Distress in Ireland and the Highlands and Islands of Scotland (usually abridged as the British Association), to act as a clearinghouse for publicity and donations. On January 13, 1847, Queen Victoria published a letter urging the public to give to the British Association and declaring March 24, 1847, a day of General Fast and Humiliation in the Church of England. She also made a £2,000 donation.[52]

The queen's letter and the vivid, heartbreaking reports from Ireland taken from wire services and published around the world added to the wave of donations. The Quaker committee alone distributed more than £200,000 in relief. In total, some £171,533 was raised directly in response to the queen's letter, with the British Association's fundraising adding a further £263,000, including considerable sums from foreign donors, such as the Ottoman sultan, Abdulmejid I. Five-sixths of the donations were sent to

Ireland and one-sixth to Scotland, where the Highlands were also stricken by blight. Other major donors included the East India Company, the Bank of England, and the Corporation of the City of London. Towns across Britain formed subcommittees. In the empire, nearly every colony sent a donation, from Newfoundland to South Australia, Jamaica to India. Smaller donations became human-interest stories. The congregation of a missionary church in Basseterre, Saint Kitts, composed of formerly enslaved people and their descendants, took up a collection, as did the ordinary sailors of HMS *Hibernia*, the constables of the Metropolitan Police of London, and the labourers at Dowlais Iron Works, in south Wales. The plight of the Irish resonated with the oppressed and dispossessed, especially in the United States. Enslaved workers in Alabama, "told of the distressed condition of the Irish poor," raised $50. The Choctaw Nation donated $710, roughly $20,440 in today's money.[53]

Once again, the Great Famine, understood by many in the British establishment as the consequence of Ireland's backwardness and evidence that Ireland was asynchronous with the rest of the United Kingdom, was surprisingly modern. It was among the first international humanitarian crises to be widely publicised in newspapers worldwide and among the first to anchor a global fundraising effort. "The English people," Trevelyan reflected in 1880, "may be said to have relieved the distress caused by this mighty famine . . . through the columns of *The Times*." The centre of the fundraising effort was the British Association, technically a private organisation but one that had very close connections to the Treasury. The timing of the campaign and the impressive size and geographic diversity of donations were a boon to the government, a distraction from the failures of relief policy and a financial cushion, as Trevelyan wrote, "useful in bridging over the fearful interval between the system of relief by work and relief by food."[54]

Following the queen's letter, and amid the outpouring of donations, the government supported a publicity stunt meant to show
the world how modern and efficient a soup kitchen could be. In
February 1847, Alexis Soyer, head chef at the Reform Club, the
exclusive private club on Pall Mall in London and the semioffi-
cial headquarters of the Whigs, wrote a public letter containing
an offer to publish soup recipes for the use of relief committees.[55] Soyer was famous for his banquets at the club, including a feast in honour of the Ottoman general Ibrahim Pasha,
which featured seven main courses and more than fifty different entremets. Soyer, supported by Trevelyan and others, proposed to establish a model soup kitchen in Dublin. Trevelyan
was excited—he instructed a Liverpool ironworks to prepare for
bulk orders of custom-designed boilers and arranged for Soyer's
passage to Dublin.[56]

The chef arrived on March 1. A crew set up his kitchen on the
Croppies' Acre, parkland rumoured to be the site of a mass grave
from the 1798 rebellion, just in front of the Royal Barracks (now
renamed Collins Barracks, and the site of a branch of the National
Museum of Ireland). Soyer's rectangular kitchen measured about
two thousand square feet and was framed with wood and partly
covered in canvas. Benches and narrow tables, roughly eighteen
inches wide, were set up around the walls of the space. The benches
could seat one hundred; in front of each place was an enamelled
iron soup bowl, with a spoon attached by a chain to the rim. In the
centre was a three-hundred-gallon boiler, mounted on wheels, some
thirteen feet long and four feet wide, as well as a portable oven
able to bake one hundred pounds of bread at a time. The boiler
was surrounded by bain-marie pans, each holding a thousand gallons of water. Worktables with cutting boards were set up near the
pans. Locked safes in the corner held soup ingredients. Leading
into the space, a passage of wood and canvas was arranged in a

zigzag so that most of the people waiting in line could not see into the kitchen and dining hall. When the kitchen was in operation, a hundred people at a time filed in at the sound of a bell, picked up a bread roll at the entrance, sat down at the benches, and ate a bowl of soup each. After six minutes the bell would ring again. The diners exited from the far side of the hall, and the bowls were rinsed in specially built basins near the benches. One hundred more would file in.[57]

The boiler and steam pans Soyer designed for his soup kitchen were at the cutting edge of catering technology, and the poor who visited the kitchen sat around the boiler as spectators to Soyer's ingenuity as much as objects of relief. A visit to the kitchen became an important social occasion for wealthy Dubliners, who made a donation of five shillings to watch. Cynics complained it was a raw deal, "when the animals in the Zoological Gardens can be inspected at feeding time for *sixpence*!" The shuffling poor of Dublin were set dressing for wealthy donors and government officials, who might consider hiring the chef, or his equipment, for other projects. Soyer is fascinating—an early celebrity chef, born and trained in France and sent into self-imposed exile after the July Revolution of 1830, a relentless self-promoter and tireless inventor with a charitable streak. Soyer would later volunteer to modernise British Army catering in the Crimean War, saving many soldiers from foodborne illness. As a manufacturer of portable catering equipment, he also had a financial stake in the success of his model kitchen. Soyer walked the line between selflessness and self-interest. He was devoted to charitable work, but most especially when giving something to the poor would then help him sell something to the rich.[58]

Soyer later claimed that his Dublin kitchen served more than 1.14 million bowls of soup between March and July 1847. Soyer, alert to his real audience, claimed his soup cost about three-quarters of a penny per quart, compared with "our Irish soupmakers," whose soup cost twice as much. Before he left Dublin he was fêted at Freemasons' Hall, and then in London at a party with 150 guests, the meal served on gold and silver plates. "It was a most fitting ovation to the unbought talents of the *chef*." After returning from Ireland, Soyer published *The Poor Man's Regenerator*, an inexpensive cookbook of ostensibly simple and inexpensive recipes. The poor could buy it themselves, or middle-class reformers could buy it in bulk to give away. According to the advertising copy, a penny from every book sold was given to the poor. Many Dubliners were less enthusiastic. "Sup it up," sarcastic balladeers sang. "It will keep the hunger out, / It will cure you of the faver, an' the cholic, an' the gout." The most famous street-singer, known as Zozimus, reportedly ended his version of the song with "My curse on such imposters and bould Sawyer and his soup."[59]

Soyer saved money by stretching the vegetables and protein in the soups served on the Croppies' Acre, testing how much flavour could be squeezed from the fewest ingredients. Medical journals criticised Soyer's recipes as "soup-quackery . . . taken by the rich as a salve for their consciences." They found that every quart of soup had at most three ounces of solid food—grains, vegetables, or meat, far less than necessary for adequate nutrition. There are about four servings of soup in a quart, so if Soyer's critics were right, each bowl of soup contained about twenty-one grams of solid food (for reference, twenty-one grams of mixed vegetables provides about fourteen calories of energy). Soyer replied that "a brother *artiste*" had been unable to tell the difference between his soup and another made with more ingredients. He used gelatin to add meat flavour, increasing what he called a dish's "osmazome," or umami flavour. Soyer proved he could do more with less—an achievement appealing to any government but acutely appealing to an austerity government in a financial crisis. Still, the Irish poor needed food, not demonstrations of culinary finesse or economy. They needed *more*.[60]

Soyer's soup kitchen was the most famous in Ireland yet merely one among thousands. The kitchens might have saved or prolonged lives, but they were not remembered fondly by the people they fed. Late in 1846, inland in County Galway, a relief committee established a soup kitchen. Starving people milled around, standing in lines for bowls of stirabout that was made with maize or oatmeal, was served from boilers, and quickly congealed in the damp and cold. Gulls, rarely seen so far from shore, circled overhead. One called loudly, and the poor regarded it as another bad omen—the bird was "laughing at their misery." It landed, and someone shot it. Perhaps they ate its oily flesh in revenge.[61]

The soup kitchens began to open in substantial numbers in the spring and reached their peak in the summer of 1847. The first three months of 1847 had the highest excess deaths of the year, a trend that began to decline in April. Some historians—and some contemporaries—praised the soup kitchens for slowing the death rate by a "unique but short-lived . . . direct attack on starvation." Others argue that the kitchens opened too late to save the most vulnerable, and that they were more significant as a bridge from a centralised approach to famine relief, directed from London, into a decentralised system of Poor Law unions. Statisticians of excess mortality identify a phenomenon they call mortality displacement—or, more grimly and evocatively, the "harvesting effect." In a crisis, mortality often spikes early as vulnerable people die quickly, which front-loads excess deaths, followed by a sudden drop in the death rate because the people most at risk of death are already dead. The soup kitchens might have saved lives—or they might seem to have been effective only because of a statistical illusion.[62]

The soup kitchens kept bellies full, but the soup was not always nutritionally complete. In summer 1847, health officials recorded outbreaks of scurvy. The board of health insisted that relief committees include fresh vegetables in the soup, although the regulation was not enforced. The kitchens, along with the closing of the works, succeeded in pushing many workers back into farm labour, reassuring relief officers and the government. But the degrading experience of standing in line, watched and pitied and carefully means-tested in exchange for the cheapest possible food, was humiliating. "The feeding of dogs in a kennel was far more decent and orderly," one observer wrote. Some walked up to ten miles to get their soup during this summer of indignity and boredom. A letter to the *Times* complained, "This supply may keep our people from dying—but it certainly is not a supply for the sustenance of working men." The soup kitchens, for all that they were publicised in their time, and for all that some historians have praised them as innovative and lifesaving, had a basic similarity to the disastrous public works program. They kept people alive but not healthy; they forced people seeking relief to humiliate themselves to meet their basic needs.[63]

On my father's side of my family, it was established lore that anyone with the surname Scanlon (as opposed to Scanlan) had "taken the soup" in Ireland and ransomed their Catholic faith in exchange for thin gruel from Protestants. However, "souperism"—Catholic apostasy in exchange for food—is more folklore and folk memory than historical reality. Irish Catholics *were* among the targets of energetic Protestant evangelism in the nineteenth century. In March 1849, the Society for the Irish Church Missions to the Roman Catholics spun off from the largest Anglican missionary organisation, the Church Missionary Society, and became very active across Connaught, which was hard-hit by the last seasons of blight. There is little evidence that the mission demanded conversion in exchange for food, although the militance of the new society's leadership angered Catholic authorities. So if souperism did take place, it was rare and was most likely to have happened nearly two years after the last soup kitchens sponsored under the government's scheme had closed. But after the famine, the legend *felt* true. In one story, a Catholic bids God a friendly farewell as he gives up his faith for a meal. "Good bye, Godeen," he says, using a diminutive, "till the praties grow again." In another story, a woman takes the soup and becomes a Protestant. Then she dies, and a black moth flies to the foot of her deathbed, putting out six candles with its wingbeats.[64]

Taking the soup was a legend that expressed a deeper truth. The soup kitchens forced the poor to make humiliating and self-abasing choices to survive. The poor did not have to abandon their religion for food, but they had to lay their lives open to the scrutiny of religious and administrative officials who would measure whether their need for relief was "genuine." Generally, soup kitchens imposed not a religious test but a means test—bad enough for the starving. To receive food, at least according to the letter of the law, aid recipients needed to be on the relief committee's list of the destitute, and then have their names called out. Everyone needed to be present to receive rations. If they did not hear their names called, they went to the back of the queue, "obliged to remain until the entire parish in which they resided had been gone through, they all that time suffering cold and hunger."[65]

THE GIVING CAMPAIGN FOR IRELAND WAS AN EARLY EXAMPLE OF public generosity in response to widespread press coverage of a humanitarian crisis. It soon became an early example of how such flushes of generosity end, with the public losing patience with the cause and writing it off as an intractable crisis. Some donors,

expecting gratitude from the Irish and rapid improvement in famine conditions, wearied of terrible stories from a place that had
been the object of so much generosity. After a report from Skibbereen in the late spring of 1847 of unburied corpses on the roads,
a journalist commented, "The Government have been sending in
large supplies; private benevolence has been liberally adding con-
tributions; and yet Skibbereen will not even bury its dead." A second queen's letter, published in October 1847 to raise a second
round of funding, failed to reinvigorate the campaign. Donations
fell off.[66]

In many newspaper reports, the Irish went from pitiable objects
of charity to ingrates slapping away a helping hand. Many observers seized on an upsurge of agrarian crime in late 1847 as proof of
either the barbarity of the native Irish or the selfishness of Irish
landowners. "It was generally felt," a historian comments, that Ireland ought "to be left to the operation of 'natural causes.'" There
are more than a few books celebrating how the world gave to Ireland. But charity is provisional and temporary, a matter of marketing as much as need, and the problems in Ireland were structural.
The solution, if there was one, was more than cash donations.[67]

Just as the soup kitchens were opening, a stream of evictions
turned into a torrent. In 1847, at least 11,166 evictions were processed in Irish courts, including the Court of Queen's Bench, the
Exchequer, the Court of Common Pleas, and the quarter sessions.
Recall that an eviction of one tenant generally resulted in the
removal of more than one family, as subtenants and labourers taking conacre also lost their land, and that there were many ways to
remove a tenant other than through a court proceeding. The number of eviction proceedings continued to grow, increasing to 16,349
in 1848 and then to 16,979 in 1849. The overwhelming majority of
cases were decided in favour of landlords and their agents, leading to
tens of thousands of recorded evictions.[68]

Evictions contributed to an exodus from Ireland. Ireland had long been an important source of immigrants to Britain's colonies, but previous waves of Irish immigration had been much smaller and less desperate. Beginning in 1846, many raced to leave, in "panic and hysteria," as one historian writes. John Russell believed that emigration would be useful as a means of reducing the pressure on Irish land, but also that the government ought not interfere. He was sceptical that mass emigration would have much effect on wages. In addition, Russell argued that "to convey a million of persons at once across the ocean" at the government's expense would anger officials in the United States, who would believe that Britain had "cast our paupers on her shores, to be maintained by her." But even as other sources of donations dropped, Irish emigrants continued to send money back to Ireland, especially to assist in emigration; remittances grew from £460,000 in 1848 to £990,000 in 1851. Lord Monteagle wrote, "What had been looked upon as banishment was now regarded as release."[69]

In 1846, 129,851 Irish emigrants went to Britain; in the first three-quarters of 1847, more than 240,000 went to Canada and the United States. So many emigrants arrived in Liverpool, both to resettle in Britain and en route to North America, that the city was divided into thirteen districts, each with a relief station. In 1846–1847, as much as 3 percent of the population left Ireland. Many were desperately ill, and as many as 40,000 people—about 20 percent of all emigrants that year—died on the voyage. A deck passage to Liverpool cost about five shillings, but some steamship and sailing-ship captains offered free passage for the Irish poor, who could provide living ballast in their ships, because they were "cheaper to ship and unship . . . than . . . lime or shingle." Others went as ballast in coal ships to Newport, South Wales, where a flophouse owner claimed they would eat rotten cabbage and potato peelings from garbage heaps. Ships carrying grain to Ireland to feed the hungry returned to Britain with starving people in the holds who kept the keels level in the water.[70]

In Britain, mass immigration led to terrible overcrowding, especially in Liverpool, where in some neighbourhoods people were reputed to be living one hundred thousand to the square mile, with at least forty thousand people living in cellars. In Ireland, landlords were divided on whether emigration boded good or ill. Some complained that their tenants were taking "French leave" of them— that is, departing without paying years of back rent. Landlords complained that the "best" of the tenants were leaving, although officials in Canada and the United States complained that the Irish immigrants were sick, weak, and restive. Some American states attempted to expel the new immigrants as quickly as possible. Some Irish landlords helped their tenants emigrate, while others evicted their tenants without much thought as to where they would go. Still others pleaded with their most trusted tenants to stay. Emigration varied in intensity across Ireland. In poorer counties there were reports of roads crowded with emigrants, mostly young men but also young women and children, heading for the towns to catch a ship to Liverpool and then, if they were lucky, another to New York or Montreal or New South Wales.[71]

ONLY A FEW MONTHS INTO THE PARLIAMENTARY SESSION FOR 1847, the government was stunned by ongoing famine and spiralling financial crisis. The Whigs, who had dominated the politics of the 1830s, now depended on Tory followers of Robert Peel to pass legislation. In the pages of *Punch*, to the tune of the "College Hornpipe," John Russell was made to sing:

My accounts when I examine, I perceive, on Irish famine
I have spent about a dozen million sterling pounds or so;

For the whole of which outgoing—an amount that we are owing—
'Twill be next to nothing, I'm afraid, that we shall have to show.

THE PUBLIC WORKS HAD BEEN A DISASTER; THE SOUP KITCHENS had been a very qualified success. The Whig government, devoted to free trade and laissez-faire policy, had spent so much borrowed money that the announcement of another loan for Irish relief had almost caused the collapse of the British banking system. Lifted by a wave of public interest and sympathy, the government had shifted to a plan—soup kitchens—that attracted international praise and support but was designed to be time-limited. The Whigs needed a permanent solution. In April 1847, the government introduced the Poor Relief (Ireland) Bill, designed to make famine relief the responsibility of Poor Law unions rather than the central government. In a well-received speech, Russell had urged the Irish to act in "the spirit of self-reliance and the spirit of co-operation," to remember to "'Help yourselves, and Heaven will help you.'"[72]

In the midst of the debates, William Henry Gregory, MP for the City of Dublin, and later for County Galway, proposed an amendment to exclude anyone holding land of a quarter acre or more from eligibility for poor relief. Gregory apparently had wanted to set the floor for relief at less than a half acre but told the House that "people [in Ireland] who had more knowledge of the subject, told him half an acre was *too extensive*." The so-called Gregory Clause passed easily. The endgame of the UK's response to the famine was about to begin. The blight would return, and so would all the attendant misery. The workhouse would be open to the Irish poor, but only if they gave up their land. Sir George Grey, the home secretary, supported the clause, he declared, "because he had always understood that small holdings were the bane of Ireland."[73]

John Russell described the chaos of 1846–1847 as "a famine of the thirteenth century acting upon the population of the nineteenth." But the Great Famine was not an anachronism. Relief was a sophisticated, expensive, and bureaucratic national program that took place within a precociously modern media environment. Around the world, sympathetic people donated money and food to help the starving, taking part in one of the first coordinated international charitable campaigns. And all the horrors—the filth and blood on cabin floors, the whispers of cannibalism, the riots, the unburied bodies and abandoned children—could not have happened exactly as they did outside of capitalist modernity. To put brakes on the wheels of capital was unthinkable and impossible. It was a nineteenth-century famine, after all.[74]

6

EXPULSIONS

Their Anglo-Norman ancestors conquered the "house-less wilds" of Connemara, but by the nineteenth century the Martin family were considered good landlords. After the Union, first Richard Martin and then his son, Thomas Martin, represented Galway in the House of Commons. The elder Martin was remembered in Parliament for advocacy against cruelty to animals. "The cab horses," one writer joked, would remember "Humanity Dick . . . with tears of gratitude." When Thomas Martin came into his inheritance in 1834, he was astounded at the extent and complexity of his family's debts, some of which dated to the mid-eighteenth century. To consolidate, Thomas Martin took out a £200,000 mortgage. When the blight struck, he employed many of his tenants and arranged for the construction of a fever hospital on his estate. Like many who ministered to the sick during the famine, Thomas Martin contracted typhus. He died in April 1847. The Law Life Assurance Society, which owned the mortgage, informed Mary Letitia Martin, Thomas's only child, that she was in default and that if she did not make back payments, with interest, the society would take possession of the property. The estate was brought before the newly established Encumbered Estates Commission, convened to liquidate and sell deeply indebted and insolvent Irish estates. The commission granted the Law Life Assurance Society possession in exchange for writing off the debt. Mary Letitia, a novelist who published under the name Martin Bell, emigrated in 1850 and died ten days after she arrived in New York. In 1851, a Galway court approved a request filed by the new owners of the estate to evict more than three hundred tenants.[1]

The horrible winter of 1846–1847 did not end the Great Famine, but it did begin a new phase of the crisis. After 1847, famine conditions and epidemic disease were more localised, concentrated in Ireland's most deprived Poor Law unions. In these unions, the slaughterhouse of Black '47 never closed, and the indigent continued to die in squalor. Meanwhile, throughout Ireland, and especially in the poorest unions, a process of eviction and expulsion—driven by utter destitution among the impoverished, and by bankruptcies like the Martin family's among the rich—pushed hundreds of thousands off farmland and through the gates of union workhouses or up the gangways of emigrant ships. Ireland, again, was dismayingly modern. The returns on exploiting the labour of the Irish poor had long diminished. Now, surplus to requirements, they were expelled. Exclusion and eviction through the retrenchment of the Poor Law became the newest "natural" consequences of the alleged failure of the Irish poor to interpret the signals of the market.[2]

After the Russell government cut bait in 1847, responsibility for both famine and poor relief in Ireland devolved onto the Poor Law unions. The number of Irish unions increased from 130 to 163, and each was reorganised under the control of a board of guardians. In August 1847, Edward Twistleton, the Ceylon-born son of the Anglican archdeacon of Colombo, was appointed chief commissioner of the new system. From November 1, 1847, relief was restricted under the Gregory Clause to those labourers occupying a quarter acre of land or less. All magistrates were given the power to imprison beggars found outside their home union for up to a month's hard labour. The commissioners argued that Irish society could be protected from "a state of almost universal pauperisation" only by rigid rules.[3]

As international donations ran out, unions repeatedly raised the poor rates—taxes paid by wealthier residents in the union based on the number of people claiming workhouse relief. However, many unions did not, or could not, collect enough rates to support the poor, and Parliament was divided over how to fund these "distressed" unions. When some unions approached bankruptcy, another new law, the 1849 Rate-in-Aid Act, established an Irish national tax that could be applied in emergencies to support the poorest unions. The new system emphasised the principle adopted by the Whig government during the humanitarian and financial crisis of 1847: Irish poverty was an Irish problem, and not a problem for the wider United Kingdom. In theory, the Poor Law system was designed to impel the poor to better their station by looking for wage work, and it was up to the rich to either offer wages in exchange for labour or pay high rates to support an overflowing workhouse. However, in practice, most unions gave outdoor relief, usually in the form of food, sometimes after a stay in the workhouse, sometimes after another "test of destitution." In 1849 alone, more than 930,000 people were relieved at the workhouse, either indoors or out.[4]

The retrenchment of the Irish Poor Law accelerated and expanded an ongoing housing crisis. Evictions increased in number as more land changed hands. The poor had always been vulnerable to eviction for unpaid rent. Now they could be evicted, whether they were paid up or not, as a condition for the consolidation of their landlords' debts. Officials in Britain had noted that many Irish estates attracted little interest from potential investors since many were entangled in complex mortgages and other debts. In response, the Encumbered Estates Commission was formed to hasten the liquidation and sale of these properties. George Grey, the home secretary, argued "that a remedy for the over population of Ireland could only be found in the gradual operation of natural laws." The government had, in effect, built an eviction machine.[5]

The blight returned in 1848 and 1849 and struck hardest in the west of Ireland, where many Poor Law unions had complex, pressing needs and fragile tax bases. In late 1847, outrages became more common as the Irish poor wielded familiar weapons of last resort: murder, arson, and intimidation. In response, the Russell ministry fell back on coercion, adding to the usual powers of martial law a series of provisions to suppress a small but vocal nationalist movement. Soon, after a brief and quixotic march through the countryside of Tipperary and Kilkenny in summer 1848, the leaders of the Young Ireland movement declared open rebellion against the United Kingdom, skirmished with the Royal Irish Constabulary, were defeated, and were sent into exile. Instead of a national uprising, the grind of hunger and rent and rates and workhouse stone-breaking and lice and fever and death and leave-taking continued, and the famine years slouched to an end in 1851–1852.[6]

AFTER TWO YEARS OF FAMINE, OUTRAGES IN IRELAND INCREASED in the late summer and autumn of 1847—but one murder, of Major Denis Mahon, of Strokestown, County Roscommon, became a lightning rod. In the spring of that year, after a series of successful eviction proceedings, Mahon and his agent had arranged passage from Liverpool to Quebec for hundreds of

Mahon's former tenants. Many died on the passage or in cramped and miserable Canadian quarantine stations, and reports that Mahon had evicted his tenants and then sent them to die on "coffin ships" were repeated back on his estate. A few months later, in November, Mahon was shot and killed, and bonfires were lit across Roscommon in celebration. A Roman Catholic priest who had served on a relief committee with Mahon was suspected of having incited the murder—or even of planning it. Other attacks on landlords and their agents followed. The lord lieutenant, Lord Clarendon, requested a Coercion Bill—the usual response to rural crime in Ireland.

But at that moment, the situation was uniquely tense. The usual worries about rural unrest were augmented by rumours of organised rebellion against the United Kingdom. In the winter of 1847, the Young Ireland movement had formally split from the Repeal Association and founded a new group, the Irish Confederacy, with a charter to seek an end to the Union—by force if necessary. In early 1848, revolutions broke out over continental Europe: in Italy, Austria, France, Hungary, Sweden, Denmark, Belgium, and elsewhere. These revolutions aimed at the overthrow of monarchies and the formation of new governments based on the idea of the nation rather than the Crown. The combination of rising rural crime as the famine dragged on and revolutionary movements in Ireland and Europe made London more acutely fearful that a new, Romantic Irish nation would rise in unstoppable numbers against the United Kingdom.[7]

Irish and British newspapers reported on and evoked the 1848 revolutions in what must have felt like real time, as reports from journalists were carried quickly by steamship and sometimes by wire from Ireland and appeared in print within hours of receipt. In Britain, the Home Office worried that the People's Charter movement (or Chartism), dedicated to the reform of Parliament

through an expanded franchise, salaries for MPs, and other measures, would organise a revolt like the one in Paris that had pushed
King Louis Philippe off the French throne in February 1848. A
planned Chartist march in April 1848 was suppressed by government order, and police were on alert. In Ireland, troops camped
near towns, including a regiment in Phoenix Park in Dublin, and
"moveable columns" of infantry were activated, ready to occupy
the country if necessary.[8]

Aware of the tumult on the Continent, John Russell was sceptical that a Coercion Act would calm Ireland. Moreover, having
come to power after defeating Peel's Coercion Bill, he knew he
would seem a fool and a hypocrite if he pushed for the same measure barely two years later. Coercion, he wrote, would be "an aggra-
vation rather than a cure of the organic disorder." Instead, Russell
tried to persuade his cabinet to grant more resources to Irish Catholic clergy, protect tenants against arbitrary eviction, and extend to
all of Ireland the Ulster system of "tenant right" that offered some
compensation to tenants who improved land they rented. Lord
Lansdowne spoke for the majority in the cabinet when he dismissed Russell's plan: "You might as well propose that a landlord
should compensate the rabbits for the burrows they have made on
his land." Russell backed down, and in December 1847 the Crime
and Outrage Act came into force. But the lord lieutenant, Lord
Clarendon, wanted even more: he asked the government to suspend habeas corpus to arrest nationalist leaders. The "condition of
Ireland," Clarendon wrote to Russell, was already that of a "servile
war," a peasant or slave rebellion.[9]

The government had new legal tools with which to respond to
revolution. By law, treason—which included armed rebellion but
also advocating for the overthrow of the government in print or
in public—was punishable by death. However, the government
recognised that juries were reluctant to execute offenders for

nonviolent dissent. The Whigs did not want martyrs or humiliation at the hands of sympathetic juries willing to nullify Crown prosecutions. The 1848 Treason Felony Act reduced the penalty for treason from death to life imprisonment or transportation. In Ireland, the act was used to indict and convict John Mitchel, whose newspaper, the *United Irishman*, had called for insurrection. In May 1848, Mitchel was convicted and bundled onto HMS *Shearwater*, a steamer bound for Bermuda, whence he was transshipped to Australia. The *United Irishman* was closed and its offices raided. In June, Thomas Devin Reilly and James Fintan Lalor founded another newspaper, the *Irish Felon*. It was suppressed after only five issues, its type and printing press seized. Reilly was sentenced to transportation to Tasmania, and Lalor died in prison. To escape arrest, other prominent Young Irelanders, including William Smith O'Brien, the leader of the movement in Parliament, fled south. Large parts of counties Dublin, Cork, and Waterford, as well as the town of Drogheda, were put under martial law. On July 22, 1848, the government finally caved to Clarendon and suspended habeas corpus. In response, Young Ireland declared war.[10]

On July 29, a Manchester telegraph office received a cable relayed via Dublin and Liverpool. The south of Ireland was in open revolt. The train station in Thurles, County Tipperary, was burning, and miles of railroad track leading to and from the town had been sabotaged to slow the arrival of reinforcements. Irish soldiers in British regiments were refusing to fire and deserting in numbers. Kilkenny was under the control of the rebels. In Manchester, civic officials worried that a riot would start in the city's Irish neighbourhoods, and its Irish Confederation clubs were put under surveillance. In London, Chartists cheered "vociferously at every allusion to hostility to the Government or to physical force." A Belfast newspaper alerted "every loyal inhabitant" to make ready to fight for the Union. The London *Times* reminded readers that although the Irish countryside might be close to Britain in geography, it was distant and alien in time. The Irish poor would erupt like medieval peasants in revolt. "If, in the nineteenth century," the *Times* warned, "Ireland is to bear the pangs of internecine strife, the war will be servile also, and marked by atrocities as barbarous as the world has ever witnessed."[11]

On July 28, a crowd that some guessed was as large as five thousand people gathered in Mullinahone, in the Tipperary countryside, to hear Smith O'Brien speak. Smith O'Brien and his entourage then travelled to a coal mine near the village of Ballingarry. British Army dragoons and riflemen occupied Cork, marching from Great George's Street (now Washington Street) to the Grand Parade. Residents gathered to watch, "from motives of curiosity and wonder at this inexplicable movement."[12]

On July 29, about fifty officers of the Royal Irish Constabulary, on the march to Boulagh Common, in Ballingarry, met a group of armed rebels, led by Smith O'Brien. The size of the rebel force depends on who tells the story. Celebrations of the police claim that Smith O'Brien led five thousand men, but his followers may have been as few as four hundred. In any case, the rebels outnumbered the police. However, the rebels were mostly armed with pikes and pitchforks. The police had rifles. The constabulary retreated into a two-storey stone house near the common, surrounded by a square stone wall. According to reports, when the insurgents began piling straw and hay around the doors, to smoke out—or burn alive— the police, the officers opened fire, killing at least two. The crowd lost its nerve and melted away. "Smith O'Brien and his friends," according to one report, "then appear to have got disgusted . . . declaring that as the people would not stand by him, he would not stand by them." Smith O'Brien was arrested soon after. The rebellion was over. Many of the Irish Confederacy clubs had dissolved after Mitchel's arrest, although the *Freeman's Journal* reported that die-hard Confederates in Tipperary had holed up in a safe house, "a perfect fortress on a small and domestic scale."[13]

In the end, almost nothing had happened. Russell and his cabinet were relieved to learn that "the news . . . telegraphed from Liverpool, was totally destitute of foundation." Young Ireland failed to ignite a mass movement. Young Ireland sought an alliance among Catholics, Anglicans, and Presbyterians—a secular politics that appealed to middle- and professional-class Irish liberals but was suspicious to many others. And unlike the conservative Catholicism of Repeal, Romantic nationalism and Celtic revivalism were alien to many of the exhausted, starving rural poor. Among calls for revolution, the *Irish Felon* ran advertisements from W. J. Kelly, a Dublin engraver, who sold a range of nationalist swag, including gilded stickers to seal letters and "the celebrated Shirt Studs," made of transparent ivory, "engraved with national devices . . . a very beautiful emblem of nationality." The studs were available depicting either a harp, a shamrock, a wolfhound, a set of pikes, or a cameo of John Mitchel ("3d. per set extra for those having the likeness"). For Irish intelligentsia, the idea of an Irish *nation* was coming into focus. But for the poor, the politics of starvation were blunt, local, Catholic, and cautious.[14]

A week after the rebellion, the *Times*, which only a week earlier had warned readers of a bloody civil war, now chuckled at the "Battle of Widow McCormack's Cabbage Patch." According to the *Times* report, Smith O'Brien, "King of Munster," was found "squatted in her cabbages to avoid the fire of the little garrison." A naïve reader would have been forgiven for imagining that Ireland was a distant colony rather than a partner in the United Kingdom. The officers of the Royal Irish Constabulary were almost all Irish and many were Catholic; the victory was one of "Papists over Papists . . . of Irishmen trained in the school of loyalty and duty, over Irishmen debauched and demoralized by disaffection and rebellion." The loyal Irish troops reflected the vitality of the British Empire, while "O'Brien crawling among the cabbages" was "an emblem of the national degeneracy" of independent Ireland. There were two Irelands, the *Times* implied, on either side of a civilisational divide. One people were guided by Britain, integrated into the Union, and supplied the empire with brave and disciplined soldiers and policemen. The other rejected British rule—and were cowards, slithering in the dirt.[15]

A witness giving evidence in 1848 to a special committee of the House of Lords feared that "the only practical remedies" remaining for Irish poverty and unrest "are death or emigration." The crisis of 1846–1847 inspired pity and feelings of solidarity with the famine-stricken Irish. But after the transition to the Poor Law and the Young Ireland rebellion, British public sympathy gave way to indifference and resentment. In *Punch*, a satirical "Irish-to-English dictionary" defined "Saxon Oppression" as "Paying Irish debts out of English pockets, feeding Irish famine with English subscriptions, and supporting Irish labour out of English wages." Irish death began to appear to Britons less as a tragedy and more as a deliberate, petulant rejection of civilisation and a rebuke to British imperial prestige. The rebellion, in this context, seemed to be a final and intolerable act of ingratitude. If the Ireland that hid among the cabbages could not be reformed, it would be expelled.[16]

THE WHIGS REMAINED COMMITTED TO THE MARKET AND TO laissez-faire. But now that the Irish Poor Law unions were officially responsible for famine relief, many in government argued that there was nothing more that Parliament could or should do to intervene. "The true thing to do" in Ireland, said Charles Wood, the chancellor of the exchequer, to Lord Clarendon, is "to do nothing." As Charles Greville observed, some in government believed that the "incurable madness of the people" meant they deserved starvation. By February 1849, as Greville wrote in his journal, "the English members and constituencies have become savage and hard hearted toward the Irish." Ireland, he continued, "a few hours removed from the richest and most civilized community in the world," had fallen into "a state so savage, barbarous and destitute that we must go back to the Middle Ages or to the most inhospitable regions of the globe to look for a parallel." Ireland had not been brought into the present—if anything, it was sliding deeper into the past. "All call on the Government for a plan and a remedy," Greville wrote, "but the Government have no plan and no remedy."[17]

Instead, the bureaucracy built up around the Irish Poor Law carried the weight. It was designed with austerity and less eligibility in mind, and its officials supervised and administered layers of tests to measure hardship. The system funnelled the poor either to the workhouse or out of Ireland entirely. To qualify for relief at union workhouses, indoors or outdoors, applicants had to prove that they had no other income or work and held no parcel of land larger than a quarter acre. Tenants renting more were expected to surrender their land as proof that their poverty and need were genuine. Entering the workhouse, which some unions required as a condition of outdoor relief, was another test of destitution. Workhouses were notorious and feared. They were symbols of disease, disorder, and violence, where families were separated and housed in self-contained and usually locked wings. John Mitchel wrote that the real purpose of the Poor Laws was "uprooting the people from the land, and casting them forth to perish." The workhouses offered a bitter choice: give up land in exchange for a marginally better chance of survival.[18]

The workhouses, "of vast dimensions, tasteful in architecture, surrounded with walls, like the castle or mansion of some lord" stood out in the wide-open spaces of the countryside. Though many had impressive façades and exterior flourishes, workhouse interiors were hostile. There were heavy doors, and gates that could be barred. High walls surrounded dormitories, which were closed and locked, and segregated by age and by sex, with spaces for men, boys, women, and girls. Inmates often worked in enclosed yards. Food was limited, and workhouse officials tinkered with the inmates' diets to find the minimum calories required to preserve life and labour. Inmates usually wore uniforms. These prisonlike conditions—like the tests of destitution for admission—expressed the principle that workhouse relief should always be worse than what wages could buy outside the walls, and they reinforced the lesson that relief was only for the most desperate and that it always came at a price.[19]

The Poor Law, however, was designed to work best in a thriving economy, where the poor would have many chances to find paid work and where ratepayers would be acting in their own self-interest in offering employment rather than paying rates. Yet Ireland in 1848 and 1849 was not a normally functioning—to say nothing of thriving—economy. Although the 1847 potato harvest was good, the devastation of the previous winter meant that many farmers had planted less than usual. Families weak from hunger, fever, and grief did not return to the fields. Many relied on outdoor relief. In February 1848, the cost of outdoor relief was £72,039; by March it was £81,339. At the peak of demand during the first year of the Poor Law system, 703,762 people took outdoor relief weekly, and 140,536 were in workhouses. In addition, more than 200,000 children received cooked meals in school.[20]

During the planting season in 1848, across the poorest parts of Ireland, farmers planted more land with potatoes than in any year since the beginning of the blight: as much as three-quarters of the prefamine crop. "All the hopes and efforts of the people were directed to the re-introduction of this plant," an official noted. The consequence was a shortage of seed potatoes, which pushed many farmers to seek relief since they had planted all their food. To make up the shortfall, the Quakers distributed more than thirty-six thousand pounds of turnip seed. "The people seem aware of the benefit of turnip culture," a relief officer wrote hopefully. However, the turnip—as much as the workhouse—might have made the poor nostalgic for the world the potato had created for them in its better years. Turnips are less nutritious and vitamin-rich than potatoes, and the swollen bellies of malnourished "turnip-eaters," especially children, made many suspicious of both the crop and the people who promoted it as an alternative to the potato. The turnip began to seem like another way to starve, exclude, and evict—"a happy expedient for [a landlord's] purse."[21]

And then in autumn 1848, in the aftermath of the failed rebellion, the blight returned. In Ballinrobe, observers estimated that four out of six potatoes were dead. In the poorest Irish counties, where farmers had stretched themselves to the limit to get seed potatoes in the ground, and where infrastructure to import grain remained rudimentary, the winter of 1848–1849 was as bad as or worse than 1846–1847. In County Clare, for example, the death rate kept rising from 1847 until early 1850. By July 1849, a million people depended on workhouse relief, either indoors or out. Although this was one-third of the number who had relied on soup kitchens two years earlier, the demand for relief in 1849 was regional, concentrated in the poorest counties along the western coast and in the countryside of the southwest. Across Ireland, the cost of relief increased from £1.7 million in 1848 to £2.2 million in 1849. Although a fraction of what the UK had borrowed and spent from 1845 to 1847, this was still a very large bill—and coming due to a much less robust and creditworthy debtor. For perspective, in 2022 pounds, scaled in proportion

to the size of the economy, the Irish Poor Law unions spent
the equivalent of more than £534 million over two years. Even
in 1850, when the situation had stabilised, some unions were
still supporting one-third or more of the population in their
districts.[22]

The Poor Law unions took over relief at a perilous time. The
Irish poor were still vulnerable to famine. Many seem to have
hoped that a return to potato planting would reconstruct the
familiar, if meagre, comforts of the era before the blight. The Irish
economy was still low-capital and low-technology, and still oriented around rent and export crops. But after two years of famine, Ireland was too shattered to be rebuilt as it had been before
1845. Hundreds of thousands of people were uprooted. Families
that had once crowded into cottages were dispersed by emigration
or reduced by death. Landlords and larger farmers were poorer as
well, indebted and exposed after two years of rising poor rates,
falling rents, and abysmal yields.

And yet officially, the famine was over. The charities that had
pumped money and energy into soup kitchens and other projects in 1846–1847 closed their operations. By September 1848,
the British Association had nearly spent its capital. The association had covered a large proportion of the costs of relief after
the transfer of responsibility from the Relief Commission to the
Poor Law unions. From October 1847, the British Association
had outspent the Treasury in Irish relief at a rate of roughly five
to three. The Society of Friends also closed its soup kitchens in
order to better support the working of the Poor Law. The financial crisis had reduced its donors' finances, and the death from
disease in Ireland of "many of our best and most trusted assis-
tants" had left many Quakers demoralised. Irish property, much
reduced, would have to support Irish poverty—a poverty as raw
as ever.[23]

With the return of the blight and the withdrawal of most government and charitable support for relief, mortality spiked in
the poorest counties. From 1846 to 1850, Galway, Clare, Mayo,
Kerry, and Cork in the southwest had the highest excess death
rates—as much as 17.3 percent in Galway—while wealthier counties had excess death rates as low as 5.1 percent. Excess mortality
correlated strongly with poverty in 1848–1849, except in Ulster,
where even the poorest county, Donegal, saw a drop in excess
deaths. The potato crop in the northeast was also struck by blight,
but a good harvest of oats and financially solvent Poor Law unions
weathered the crisis. Compounding the problem, many of the
poorest unions were also among the largest. Of the 130 unions
established in 1838, more than 100 were larger than one hundred
thousand acres, and nearly a quarter were larger than two hundred
thousand acres. The Ballina Union, one of the poorest in Ireland,
was over five hundred thousand acres. As one British critic put
it, Ballina Union was so large that if it were in England it would
stretch "from London to Buckingham and Oxford, in one direction, and from London to Basingstoke in another, with a poor-
house in St. Albans."[24]

In 1848–1849 and 1849–1850, famine was regional, but little
else about it was novel. The records of the "distressed Unions" are
all too familiarly shocking. In April 1848, according to a report
in the *Galway Vindicator*, a man named John Connolly, convicted
of sheep rustling, was sentenced to three months' hard labour.
John Dopping, an officer in the Royal Marines and a magistrate,
defended Connolly. Connolly's family had been starving, Dopping explained, and Connolly's wife had resorted to eating the
body of one their children after the child had died of fever. When
the body was exhumed, "nothing but the bones remained of its
legs and feet." Thomas Carlyle, an idol to the revolutionary intellectuals of Young Ireland, visited Kildare in the summer of 1849

and wrote with characteristic disgust about "the wretchedest wild villages I ever saw . . . a harpy-swarm of clamorous mendicants—men, women, children."[25]

The shift to Poor Law unions accentuated and amplified the most ruthless elements of famine relief: a callous austerity and a procrustean faith in means testing. The new regulations, as described earlier, required that people seeking relief give up their land for outdoor relief, and their land and their freedom for workhouse relief. Political economy predicted that the poor would make the rational choice, choosing life over land, liberty, and family unity. The price of relief was designed to be high, but in the Irish countryside it may have been too high. Many were reluctant to seek relief until they or their children were near death. In one cabin, a mother and three children lay stricken with typhus. On the other side of the cabin, the father's corpse, dead for days, lay rigid and swollen. "They linger on in their miserable, unventilated hovels" before applying, a frustrated relief officer wrote, "till their cases are beyond hope." While some waited until they were nearly dead to apply for Poor Law relief, officers were sure that many others were dissembling to dodge eligibility requirements. People holding more than a quarter acre of land tried to pass their land along to relatives or collude with their landlords to keep their land and still receive relief.[26]

Before the blight, the pillars of abundant potatoes and a moral economy of generosity and collective solidarity had borne, at least to some extent, the weight of rent and land. By 1848–1849, three years of famine had demolished those supports. There were no potatoes; there could be no abundance, no sociability, no collective effort at harvest, no sharing. A cruel and ruthless world made many cruel and ruthless. Caring for the sick was dangerous. If a carer became ill, they might die—or become so ill themselves that they were forced to go to the workhouse. Either way, the family would lose food and income. Reports of children forcing their parents into the workhouse and of parents abandoning their children to workhouse care were common. As in 1846–1847, the weakest and most vulnerable were victimised. Unmarried women with children were refused shelter in many villages, "hunted from house to house in a most unfeeling and unchristian manner." Many took shelter in abandoned buildings. "Three years of famine and pestilence," argued a letter to the commissioners, "have tended to loosen all the natural ties, which formerly knit together the human family in this wretched country." Facing another season of famine and now without the limited security of soup kitchens and other universal relief, the poor had been gripped by "the fear of death . . . , which extinguish[ed] every natural feeling, save . . . a desire for self-preservation."[27]

The hardness of everyday life was created in part by the workhouse itself. The workhouse offered a cruel bargain; it embodied and stoked endless competition for resources, security, and preferment. It epitomised the notion of the market as a purifying force, a means of separating Irish workers ready for the future from those consigned to the past. Overcome with famine, some Irish people did shameful things to preserve their own lives. Others wandered the roads, begging, or went "burrowing in bogs or behind ditches," before applying to the workhouse. It is difficult to tell what to make of these anecdotes. Some people must have avoided the workhouse until it was too late, but there were also many reports of the indigent clamouring outside the walls, desperate to gain admission. Relief officials seem to have been exasperated in either case. When the poor refused to seek admission, they were deemed stupid and self-destructive. When they begged for admission, they were deemed liars or dissemblers, seeking relief to which they were not (yet) entitled. In either case, the misery and humiliation of the poor confirmed officials' belief that many of the people seeking relief in the workhouse were "scarcely human in habits and intelligence."[28]

MOST PEOPLE WHO RECEIVED RELIEF FROM FAMINE IN THE POOR Law era received outdoor relief; nevertheless, the workhouse still exemplified the logic of the system. Making industriousness second nature to the Irish remained the goal, and the Poor Law Commission and individual unions tinkered with the best way to teach Irish paupers who sought relief how to work steadily and with discipline. Recipients of both kinds of aid were expected to work for it, but the labour needed to be so tedious or difficult that other kinds of work were appealing in comparison. The commission preferred to require stone-breaking for a minimum of eight hours a day (more would have been preferable; eight was a concession to the short daylight hours in the winter in northern latitudes). Some unions, with thousands of people claiming outdoor relief, protested there were not enough rocks to go around. In Newcastle Union, the board of guardians worried that they would have to buy rocks from private quarries in order to have enough to keep five thousand or six thousand able-bodied paupers swinging sledgehammers. The commissioners' response, however, was firm: "Stone-breaking is less attractive and more capable of effectual superintendence than any other kind of out-door labour on a large scale." Still, even breaking rocks was "inferior to the workhouse as an effective test of destitution."[29]

Labour exchanged for relief at the workhouse was supposed to be strenuous but purposeless. This already austere principle became an absurdity in famine conditions as the Poor Law Commission policed the tasks assigned by unions to people seeking relief. Galway Union was scolded for putting prisoners to work farming, as it might "weaken the efficiency of the workhouse." Wages, which had been the public works plan from August 1846 to the summer of 1847, were anathema in the new system. "The strongest line," the commissioners wrote, "should . . . be drawn between relief and wages." If employers could hire workhouse labourers for next to nothing, the commission argued, it would increase unemployment outside the workhouse and drive down wages.[30]

The workhouses were funded with local poor rates. However, the poorest unions often had both the poorest labourers and the most indebted and exposed ratepayers. A long-serving workhouse doctor described the divisions within many boards of guardians supervising workhouses. "The economists," he wrote, "thought that unless expenses were controlled the Poor Law would bring ruin on the country," while others argued that "a judicious outlay was the truest economy." The principle of "less eligibility"—that conditions inside workhouses had to be worse than conditions for even the humblest workers on the outside—although a "very excellent doctrine," the doctor wrote, was no longer a deterrent to seeking relief "when most houses had little to wear and nothing to eat."[31]

This problem was compounded by the eroded, precarious tax bases in the poorest unions. The poorer the union, the smaller the rental income but the higher the rates. In these unions, funding workhouse relief became a decaying orbit, collapsing toward bankruptcy. Poor Law guardians and other ratepayers could be the people with the most to lose by raising taxes to pay for relief. Austerity had always been a principle of famine relief. Now austerity organised nearly every aspect of the workhouse. In Ballyshannon Union, it was common for crowds to form around the workhouse doors, pleading to be admitted or put on the outdoor-relief lists. Some in the crowds were naked, screaming with hunger. Some relief officers broke down and found places for people in extremis, but they knew that compassion might cost them their jobs, because most guardians "are so averse to increase the expense, that these functionaries are almost afraid to exercise a discretion."[32]

The consequence was a race to the bottom, a heedless commitment to cutting expenses in order to "preserve the existence of the inmates at the smallest possible cost." Boards of guardians were selected from among the propertied in each union. They collected rates, oversaw expenses, and hired the overseers, clerks, stewards, and matrons who staffed the workhouses. In theory, the guardians' duty was to their community. In practice, most behaved as though their duty was to their fellow ratepayers. In addition, the staff of most workhouses were often drawn from among ratepayers and their clients, generally from the families of the more precarious, larger tenant farmers and middlemen—precisely the people for whom famine meant the erosion of both rental income and opportunities for arbitrage on crops and land. Every comfort for workhouse inmates threatened the staff's security and wealthier ratepayers' solvency. Consequently, the workhouses of poorer unions were places of legendary squalor. The workhouse, one visitor wrote, was at most "a place to die" for the poor, so "they might be buried in a coffin."[33]

Virtually every workhouse operated at above capacity—more evidence that although some of the Irish poor avoided the workhouse until the brink of death, many others recognised that they had no choice but to apply. Staff often neglected the records they were expected to keep. Inspectors were shocked to find that the books of New Ross Union had not been updated for months. The inmates had been seen wandering the countryside; some even "knocked at a gentleman's door in the vicinity and demanded alms." The buildings became so crowded that dining areas and dayrooms became dormitories at night, with straw beds laid out on the floors or hammocks strung from walls. Many dormitories were unventilated, and the smell of close-packed, unwashed, ill bodies produced "a dense steam of confined air . . . almost intolerable to endure even for a moment." In one union, inmates nicknamed a dormitory the "hulk," after the decommissioned warships sitting at anchor offshore that were sometimes used as overflow for Britain's prisons.[34]

Cramming workhouse spaces with inmates under limited supervision was one way to cut costs; another way was to restrict rations or choose the cheapest possible food. Some baked bread in-house, using bran ground by the inmates mixed with maize. Many unions preferred imported maize to other grains. The American import, officials wrote, "rendered the support of human life as cheap as it was before the potato failure." Food provided as outdoor relief was usually given out cooked, or at least "steeped" in water (if not hot or fully prepared for eating), so that relief seekers could not hoard it and were less likely to be able to resell it. Meal stored in water expanded, allowing unions to give relief recipients the same overall volume of rations each day while reducing the quantity of solid food in each portion. New steam-cooking devices, in turn, saved fuel. Meanwhile, workhouse staff found ways to skim from contractors and hide other expenses. An inspector found that Listowel Union's master was ordering supplies and work without permission, "such as looking glasses, muslin for curtains, and feathers of the best kind" with which to stuff mattresses for staff. He also ordered a supply of milk for himself without permission.[35]

Full of sick and filthy people, the workhouses were ideal environments for the spread of disease, especially typhus and other louse-borne illnesses. The very ill were among the most likely to be thrown out of their homes by fearful relatives. In some unions, guardians offered people money to take in the sick outside the workhouse, but it was often refused. Their gates were often locked, but workhouses were open to circulating pathogens. The poor, sick, and well circulated in and out of confinement. Inspectors, staff, and guardians came and went. Epidemics that began inside the workhouse spread easily to the community outside, and vice-versa. In 1848, fever cases peaked in early May, when nearly one thousand people a week were dying in fever hospitals and the death rate from typhus and similar illnesses stood at nearly eight in every thousand.[36]

In December 1848, cholera appeared in Belfast, pulling Ireland—but especially Irish towns—into an epidemic that was spreading across England, Scotland, and Wales. Cholera spreads quickly in urban environments when the *Vibrio cholerae* bacillus infects the water supply. The disease causes violent, copious, and acute diarrhea and vomiting, and spreads through inadvertent ingestion of infected human feces. Between 1848 and 1850, the epidemic caused more than thirty-four thousand reported deaths in Ireland, most of them in 1849. Fear of cholera amplified the fear of contagion. Anyone with diarrhea—an extremely common affliction in famine-era Ireland—risked being thrown onto the street. One woman, already living in a cowshed, was struck with "hopeless . . . dysentery"; she was threatened with eviction from her hovel.[37]

Boredom, hunger, and brutal but uneven discipline made work-houses dangerous and unpredictable places. When opportunity appeared, staff were often attacked, inside and outside the walls. The steward of the Ballyshannon workhouse, built for five hundred but holding seven hundred, had his cowhouse burned with three cows inside. A magistrate found the smouldering ball of turf used to light the thatched roof. In another workhouse, a pet cat belonging to one of the staff hopped over the wall into the boys' yard. They chased, captured, and tortured it, breaking the animal's legs. A for-mer workhouse doctor described a riot where inmates "broke win-dows and doors, smashed forms and tables, beat the wardmasters and ward mistresses and the master if he came in their way. They screamed and yelled like maniacs and some fell into hysterical

convulsions, thus adding to the confusion." Rumours that a boy
had been beaten to death in the Ballinrobe Union workhouse
caused a Catholic priest to lead a mob in "a general attack upon
the house . . . , stones flying in every direction."[38]

However, most of the violence in workhouses was directed not
by inmates against staff, but by staff against inmates, or by stronger
inmates against weaker ones. With the doors locked and the war-
dens standing between survival and death, assault and rape were
common. One of the many reasons why parents waited to enter
the workhouse was that they would be separated from their children, exposing them to sexual violence, or "the probable contam-
ination of bad companionship," to use one official's euphemism.
Guards and stronger inmates were constant threats. Rumours circulated in many unions that members of the boards of guardians
lived their lives in "unremitted outrage upon the decencies of life."
Contraband, especially tea, tobacco, and alcohol, must have often
been exchanged for sex, and women knitted "fancy stockings" for
officers in exchange for preferment and smuggled luxuries. One
woman had "seven bastard children," inspectors wrote, with the
temerity to be "all in good health."[39]

The workhouses were dangerous, and outdoor relief scant and
uncertain. The poorest unions had to meet the greatest needs with
the fewest resources. Collecting rates was nearly as constant a
struggle as managing paupers. To collect from ratepayers, collectors could sue, or they could seize livestock, furniture, or other
property. In practice, rate collectors usually seized property from
ratepayers with more limited means, typically graziers and farmers renting larger parcels of land, and opened formal legal proceedings against wealthier ratepayers who were in arrears. Like
workhouse staff, rate collectors were drawn from the same class
of residents from whom they were most likely to seize property—
people from families tottering on the line between ratepayer and

pauper. Accounts of self-dealing filled press reports. One Galway collector seized twenty-three sheep to pay poor rates in arrears and then arranged for their sale, at far less than their value, to himself. The barrister refused to adjudicate any other bills involving the collector, and more than two hundred civil bills collecting poor rates were thrown out of court. Justice was served, but the Clifden Union board of guardians was still short of revenue.[40]

After the famine, Lord Monteagle complained that the Poor Law placed an unfair burden on taxpayers. The government might as well, he wrote, "require the proprietors of the Marine Parade at Brighton to employ or relieve all the families who hire their apartments." In Dublin, at the Northumberland Hotel, a public meeting published resolutions protesting rate increases. A local barrister gave a well-received speech at the meeting insisting that the new taxes violated the Act of Union, which specified what taxes could be collected in Ireland. The "English Parliament," he argued, was "legally incompetent" to collect the rates. Another speaker declared the rates to be "the most galling, as well as the worst-administered imposts which had ever been inflicted on a suffering people."[41]

Landowners, who were the wealthiest landlords (few ratepayers owned their land outright; many were larger tenants who collected rent from subtenants), also complained about poor rates, but were rarely at risk of being ruined by them. When collectors approached agents representing Lord Arran for £17 in rates due from "waste holdings" leased to tenants for grazing, his agent paid the bill. But as famine conditions wore on, ratepayers with lesser means became less likely to be willing or able to pay. If a ratepayer went bankrupt, it became even more difficult to collect: the bankrupt person or estate's other creditors would also expect to be made whole. The courts appointed receivers to liquidate bankrupt estates, and estates in receivership had no incentive to pay back rates. Usually, getting rates from an insolvent taxpayer required the time and expense—and uncertainty—of a lawsuit. A receiver named John Knox, Esq., paid out the £137 owed by estates he managed when the local Poor Law unions began legal proceedings. Other ratepayers died without heirs, like a Miss Palmer, who owed £19, while absentees could be impossible to contact. Some had not been in Ireland since the beginning of the blight or earlier. Charles O'Donel, "a captain in the Bengal service, now in India," owed £22 that would never be collected. Still other ratepayers were easy to find, but not worth suing for back rates—they had nothing left to pay, and had "scarcely . . . the means of supporting themselves."[42]

Collectors chased the agents of large landlords, but they risked violence at the hands of smaller and more vulnerable ratepayers. One collector in Mayo, pursuing unpaid rates, was accompanied by nine other men. A group of men and women attacked his assistant and pelted him with stones. While the assistant, Pat Mahony, bled freely from his hand, a cow that had already been seized ran away, and villagers hid the rest of their cattle. When the collectors tried to seize a small flock of sheep, a crowd gathered to follow them and "forced the sheep down a narrow road to a village, where, if we followed, our lives would be in danger." The collector took the corn of the sheep's owner, but no one would watch over it. "As I proceeded through the electoral divisions, shouts and whistling went before, and screeching after us; and in all directions, and on all sides, men, women, and children were driving and running away with their cattle."[43]

But ratepayers, even those who had slipped from genteel poverty to uncouth destitution, at least had the means to keep their homes. Among the poor, eviction proceedings—many of which were initiated by ratepayers looking to either sell or squeeze land to raise estate revenues—left many homeless. Again, faith in the market produced perverse outcomes in already market-racked

Poor Law unions. In practice, to finance famine relief, the poorest parts of Ireland were obliged to raise the most money from the least prosperous or secure ratepayers. The consequence was a centrifugal force that threw the poorest out of their homes so that ratepayers could pay the rates that would cover the cost of holding the newly homeless in the workhouses. Adding to the unwholesome folly of the process, evicted families provided a short-term boon for farmers willing to exploit them by having "labour done in exchange for food alone," instead of paying wages to working-age men and boys, "till absolute starvation brings the mother and helpless children to the workhouse; this is the history of hundreds." Tenants, an observer noted bitterly, "having thus pauperized the labouring class, get their work done for nothing, and complain of rates."[44]

The fiscal pressure that built in the poorest unions could only be relieved with infusions of cash. Through 1847–1848, unions that ran out of money were bailed out with funds from the British Association, which spent about £236,500, and from Parliament, which spent £132,000. The commissioners—using statistics that I could not find anywhere else in the records, and which were likely optimistic and self-aggrandising guesses—estimated that relief had saved two hundred thousand people from dying in the "distressed" unions in that first year of the Poor Law system of famine relief. Based on this estimate, when the blight returned before the 1848 harvest, the commissioners were confident that the Poor Laws would be "quite equal to the relief of the destitution," provided that the unions had enough money. They didn't. In 1847–1848, the pressure on the distressed unions had been intense, but not so heavy as to collapse the system utterly. Relief numbers peaked at more than 833,000 receiving outdoor relief during the week of July 15, 1848, a figure that fell during the harvest to 199,603 for the week of October 7 before rising to 264,704 for the week of November 25. Normally November would be a month of plenty, after the potatoes were taken in. Without a potato harvest, however, the pressure on the unions increased until it was overwhelming.[45]

At the beginning of 1849, the nine unions deemed distressed by the Lords of the Treasury owed £83,189 in unpaid rates. The year before, debts had been £34,844. The unions only managed to collect £74,053 in rates, and spent £232,131. In Kenmare, County Kerry, in the southwest, the workhouse was surrounded in early January 1849 by "paupers, yelling and howling for admission." But the Kenmare Union was in chaos. Officers offered relief to tenants who had land and cattle instead of to the homeless poor, and the guardians were accused of feeding their estate employees. Inspectors were appalled at "the total want of discipline of the workhouse officers, the utter confusion of the books . . . the want of food, clothing, money, or credit." The officer wondered if conditions outside the workhouse had deteriorated so much that the threat of the workhouse might no longer be useful as a tool for measuring and testing destitution.[46]

By now, the distressed unions were experiencing another spasm of the depravity and desolation that had occurred nearly nationwide in the winter of 1847. The unions could not afford to pay their everyday expenses, and their debts were growing. Poverty echoed and amplified itself until in some unions, like Ballina, "the distress which now exists among all classes has, perhaps, never been exceeded during the last three years." In Castlerea Union, the poor were selling everything they had; there were hundreds of goats in the market, as well as donkeys and emaciated cattle, selling for half of what they might normally bring. In Clonmel Union, prisoners in the county jail begged to remain imprisoned, or swore to reoffend after they were released.[47]

In Ennis Union, in the Clondegad electoral division, 37.6 percent of the 1841 population were on outdoor relief in May 1849.
Many were ill with dysentery and unable to digest maize, although
they depended on it, and thus they suffered "from actual want of
nutriment." In another union district, Clonlea, County Clare,
39.6 percent of the 1841 census population were registered for
relief. Rates could no longer be collected from some ratepayers. In
Glenties Union in 1849, inspectors reported that small occupiers
in arrears had nothing to seize and that "some of the occupiers
who are ratepayers have not tasted a drop of milk" for a year. In
Swineford Union, many applicants for relief were former landholders, now crowding the workhouse with letters and certificates aver-
ring that they had given up their land. In Scariff Union, farmers
with nothing left to eat gave up their fields, full of planted crops,
in exchange for relief. Scariff Union was broke and unable to pay
its contractors, who cut deliveries of provisions by half. A group
of women on outdoor relief in the union, upon learning that the
ration was going to be halved, chased a relief officer, throwing
rocks and threatening to stone him to death.[48]

In 1849, several unions collapsed as demand for relief increased
beyond what an eroded tax base could support. Faced with continuing parliamentary hostility toward welfare transfers from the
UK Treasury to Ireland, John Russell's government resorted in
spring 1849 to a Rate-in-Aid provision, which taxed other Irish
unions with additional rates to offset costs for the unions in
financial distress. In effect, this was a levy on ratepayers in the
north and east to assist the west. The policy angered many outside the distressed unions, and it called into question, Isaac Butt
observed, the very principle of the legislative union of 1801. Russell and Clarendon, aware of the extent of their government's failure, fell into fatalism, while others, such as Charles Wood and
Charles Trevelyan, continued to stress the palliative necessity of

enforcing "self-help" on the feckless Irish. Throughout 1848 and 1849 Edward Twistleton, the chief commissioner of the Poor Law system, continued to appeal for more support from the government for the distressed Poor Law boards. Finally, on March 10, 1849, he resigned.[49]

By that month, twenty-one unions in the west of Ireland had been declared distressed. From February to June, £114,435 was issued under the Rate-in-Aid Act to make up the shortfall. Ballina Union received the most cash, at £11,890. Twenty-three unions received aid, and some, like Scariff Union, also received hundreds of pounds' worth of biscuit. Charles Wood preferred this policy to the previous model and argued that if the cabinet was serious about the Poor Law, a Rate-in-Aid was the only option. Further grants and loans to Ireland should be forbidden, Wood insisted. Charles Greville supposed that the policy, in time, might be "the ultimate regeneration of Ireland," but until then it would cause suffering "such as never was contemplated." Some in the government suspected that Wood was in Charles Trevelyan's pocket—that Trevelyan held a "great influence" over the chancellor's mind.[50]

The Poor Law system was founded on the principle of austerity and on a faith in markets and economic incentives. The former was cruel, the latter deluded. But even if we suspend compassion and accept the ethos of the Poor Law on its face, the most poverty-stricken unions in Ireland were too unstable, too hollow, to benefit from the deterrence and discipline of the rates and the workhouse. The Poor Law was designed to test, to sift weak from strong, undeserving from deserving, industrious from lazy, useful from surplus. In the distressed unions, in addition to the fear of the workhouse and the misery of another season of blight, the Irish felt a steady pressure that pushed landlords to sell, tenants to give up their leases, and labourers to die or emigrate. The elaborate bureaucracy built to measure the eligibility of applicants for relief was, in the distressed unions, a mechanism for proving the painfully obvious—that many of the Irish poor were as vulnerable in 1849 as in 1847.

THE WHIGS AND YOUNG IRELAND AGREED, FOR DIFFERENT REA-sons, that Ireland ought to pay for its own relief—that "Irish property should support Irish poverty." Before his brief military campaign, arrest, and exile, William Smith O'Brien supported the transition from public works to the Poor Law. "The poor should be secured a livelihood in the land in which they were born," he told the House of Commons. "Ireland had no right to call on England to support her people." As the famine neared a half decade, how-ever, the poorest unions imploded. In some, there was virtually no formal work; there was little rent to collect; there was no money to pay the rates. But officially, the Great Famine was over. Critics of famine policy insisted that if only Irish property could be freed of its "encumbrances," the Poor Law would restore the natural bal-ance between poverty and property.[51]

In April 1849 *The Economist* pointed out that in the distressed unions, where hundreds of thousands depended on outdoor relief, land had been left unplanted and seemed to have passed from the bonds of the common law to anarchy. The editors wondered who really owned Irish land when the "measurings of the fields are all obliterated, so that no man—not even the actual owner—can define his own boundaries." The tangled web of Irish landhold-ing, another editorial argued, made it "practically impossible to deal with [land use] in the way which modern science has pointed out as the most profitable." In Ireland, the editors continued, a tangle of regulations, customs, and complex debts made it impos-sible to properly improve land, whether landlord and tenant were well-intentioned and hardworking or cynical and lazy. Fair con-tracts were impossible. Profit was elusive. Voiding a lease opened a landlord to assassination. Without new tools for selling land and clearing estates, the "small liberation of so much land" would be unfeasible. If the Irish would not free themselves from the land, then the land would have to be freed from them.[52]

The turn to pessimism in attitudes toward the famine, and in relief policies—to reform through expulsion—was especially visible in changing attitudes to the old eighteenth-century touchstone of "improvement," the principle that landowners had a moral obligation to increase the value and productivity of their land with scientific management. In the years before and after the Union, Ireland's bogs and impoverished masses seemed like complementary resources. Now, a pamphlet argued, the problem was too many tenants. An unproductive tenant ought to "leave the ground he is unable to improve to those who can and will." If landlords could not take back the land and cultivate it themselves, or find a better tenant, or help the existing tenant to emigrate, then the Poor Law unions, some argued, had an obligation to ensure "that the land may be well cultivated" by whatever means.[53]

Irish land was deeply embedded in the market. During the Napoleonic Wars, Irish landlords routinely used their land as collateral, borrowing freely amid frothy speculation and strong demand for Irish products. After 1815, as the rest of the UK economy sagged, this "superstructure of jointures, charges and encumbrances of every kind" began to sag and collapse too. Land was easy to entangle in leases and liens and for just that reason difficult to sell outright. In Ireland, landlords had long been permitted to "confess to judgement" when they borrowed against their land—in other words, to borrow without consolidating or paying existing debts. These debts and "confessed judgements" could be sold along with the estate, or assigned to new owners. Other legislation from the 1830s and 1840s, piecemeal solutions to the quagmire, allowed creditors to appoint their own receivers to collect debts on all land owned by the debtors, and to collect some or all of their debtor's tenants' rent. In short, buying land in Ireland required an accounting of these obligations—and required the buyer to take them on as a condition of the sale.

In 1848, to break the logjam and get the market moving more quickly, the Encumbered Estates Act created a new commission with the power to act as arbitrator between a landlord and their creditors in order to reach binding judgements that would allow owners to sell and discharge their debts. The act, one official declared, would "make land in Ireland a marketable commodity, which it is not now, or only to a very small extent." Legal encumbrances were complicated by "human encumbrances" (as the geographer David Nally puts it)—that is, tenants and dependents and their customary and legal claims. The Poor Law system had forced the poor to trade their liberty and everything they produced for the "right to live." But the Gregory Clause, one of the engines of expulsion, offered an even more perilous bargain to the Irish poor seeking workhouse relief, both within the workhouse itself and outdoors when distress was especially acute. The clause required the poor to exchange land, for generations the most important form of security for an Irish family and the object of constant labour and scheming, for access to government aid. Land, like labour, needed to be homogenised and liquified; a parcel of land needed to be as exchangeable and fungible as the people who worked it.[54]

The Poor Law, however, could potentially impede a liquid market in land. George Nicholls wrote, "Where the land has ceased to be productive . . . a poor-law will no longer be operative." In a very poor district, new owners might be deterred by the rates and by the web of old debts that could make a new landowner who was otherwise keen to employ the poor on his estate liable "to pay an increased amount of poor's rate in order to maintain the people not of his own property but of the estate of the adjacent proprietor."

Eviction seemed to solve this problem. The austerity of the workhouse, in turn, seemed to encourage the poor to leave rather than
to seek aid. The London *Daily News* sent a reporter to the Encumbered Estates Commission. He praised its work. "Ireland is in a
transition state," he wrote. By allowing—or compelling—landlords
with heavily encumbered estates to liquidate their debts, new landlords could take over, providing an "infusion of strength, capital,
and life blood . . . a new system for the people." The Poor Law, in
turn, would create a new people for the system. New investment
would clear the land both of complex debts and of the debtors
themselves. Fewer paupers and wealthier landlords in distressed
unions would, it followed, restore equilibrium in the demand for
relief and the supply of poor rates.[55]

The Encumbered Estates Commission opened in late October 1849, and within a few days at least seventeen petitions were
filed by distressed landlords or their creditors. Between October
1849 and July 1850, 1,085 estates were processed by the commission. Between 1849 and 1858, more than 10 percent of all Irish
land changed hands. The commission estimated that Irish estates
owed at least £12.5 million total—nearly the entire estimated
rental income of all Irish land combined. The *Freeman's Journal*
estimated that among the 2,416 petitions made under the act, at
least £30 million in encumbrances rested on the leases. The law
assumed that Irish landlords and tenants could be forced out of
traditional tenancy arrangements and pushed onto the open
market, "making all aspects of land tenure subject to the play of
capitalism." By 1849, evictions that had been piecemeal were considered a "clearance system," an allusion to the large-scale displacement of Highlanders from Scotland, which began after the failed
1745 Jacobite rebellion and intensified through the later eighteenth
century. Eviction had long been a familiar and feared peril for
tenants; now it seemed systematic. The papers in Tipperary, for

example, were full of accounts of eviction, "the strides of the social revolution which is hourly hastening to a crisis the destinies of this ill-fated portion of the British empire." Depopulation, by death or by eviction, seemed inevitable, "the bleak ocean of a cheerless world to swell the tide of misery."[56]

Evictions, always a feature of the Irish rural economy, became more numerous and ferocious. At least 35,416 evictions were filed in Irish courts between 1847 and 1849, but the total number of evictions was higher. First, there was no central repository of evictions until the Irish Constabulary started keeping an incomplete count in 1849. Second, as always in the Irish rent pyramid, a single eviction displaced not only the targets of the legal proceedings but also many subtenants and labourers taking conacre. A leading historian estimates that 225,000 people were evicted between 1849 and 1854. Other historians argue that the number of evictions may have been closer to 500,000, or more. In practice, legal evictions affected about 2.5 percent of all holders of land, augmented by an unknown, but significant, number of unofficial expulsions. Patterns of eviction, as the historian Christine Kinealy shows, changed after the 1847 Poor Law Amendment Act was passed. Before 1848, evictions tended to occur in wealthier counties, especially in Ulster, often as part of capital investments in farmland or plans to convert cropland to grazing land. After 1848, Ireland's poorest counties, like Clare, Galway, Limerick, Mayo, and Tipperary, experienced the most dramatic spikes in evictions and the largest overall declines in agricultural holdings, which fell by 20 percent nationally.[57]

"Unroofing" houses—pulling down cottage roofs or setting fire to the roof and walls, or both—became a routine act of terror in the era of expulsion. A clergyman wrote to the Poor Law Commission on December 17, 1847, that he had seen at Cross, in the Cong electoral division, fifteen cabins with small campfires around them and people squatting by the side of the road. A land agent named Richard O'Donnell had summoned the sheriff to unroof the homes. "I would like to know what efforts have been made by the poor-rate collectors to collect from that gentleman," the priest wrote bitterly.[58]

The number of evictions was and is hard to count, but impressions of Ireland in 1849 are replete with unroofed cottages, especially in the west. Evicted people—even with food—were vulnerable to disease and exposure. In Toomevara, County Tipperary, the homeless and landless poor, evicted from their holdings, lived in lean-tos built against the walls of the parish church, while others built their huts in the graveyard. Evictions and clearances continued, with "the certain destructiveness of the plague throughout the country." In Tipperary, the landlords had been "bitten by the mania to get rid of the poor Irish tenant, who, when the land yielded fruit, toiled like a galley slave for those who now turn upon and treat him like with the basest ingratitude."[59]

In December 1847, a woman in Erris pulled an old storage chest apart to make a coffin for her dead mother. Two months later, she was evicted. She sheltered in the ruin of her unroofed house but was chased out. In Carnboy, a village in the Belmullet division of the Ballina Union in County Mayo, almost the entire village had been unroofed, as well as nearly one-third in the entire district. A man who had been evicted from his cottage was breaking rocks in exchange for outdoor relief when he saw fire and smoke rising from a distant bog. He left his task, risking losing his place on the relief rolls, and walked toward the blaze. The bailiff had managed to find the lean-to, built out of blocks of dried turf, in which the man and his family took shelter at night, and set it on fire. Some evictions were brutal enough to prompt investigation. In County Galway, a man renting three acres, Daniel Conneely, had his house torn down around him by men with crowbars. His landlord, he explained, was "a long time wanting to get me out of it." A group of cottages at Tullymore were leveled to make room for pastureland; evicted tenants were "going from house to house, frequently sleeping in our clothes by the fire-side."[60]

In 1850, some were suspicious of reports that at least five times as much land had been planted with potatoes as in 1849. Potatoes meant conacre, one report concluded—and though the death or departure of one-fifth of the population might lower rents on conacre land, it would only invite the cycle of people and potatoes to begin again. "All judicious proprietors and others," the report concluded, "are getting rid of the population as speedily and quietly as possible, and laying down all the land to sheep and cattle pasture." The famine had not changed *enough* about Ireland to make the potato unappealing: "Cultivation will not pay here now." The Quaker reformer James Hack Tuke was appalled. Near Clogher, he found evicted Irish labourers lying by roadsides, feverish, or "squatting on the bare turf to hide their naked limbs." He argued that the physical ordeal of eviction was getting in the way of the salutary effects of a Poor Law that, in principle, demanded industriousness from the poor and prudence from the rich. If the poor were so ill from fever and exposure that they could not work, it was both a human tragedy and an obstacle to the proper operation of political economy.[61]

And yet, by the lights of political economy, mass unroofing was sound policy. The Poor Law system had raised taxes on landlords, both within distressed unions, where higher poverty rates translated into higher poor rates, and across Ireland, since the Rate-in-Aid could be used to raise rates across the country when the poorest unions were in financial peril. Eviction was an obvious, brutally straightforward solution to this problem. Struggling ratepayers could remove tenants who were in arrears, potentially lowering their tax burden. The Rate-in-Aid system meant that *all* Irish taxpayers had a financial interest in evictions anywhere in the country. Moreover, unroofing houses reduced the number of available cottages to rent. Mass death over the previous two years had lowered demand for rented land and housing. Reducing the number of available houses was a crude way to increase scarcity. Other landlords used unroofing to begin to convert their land, as in Gort Union, County Clare, to sheep walks. To either reduce taxes, raise rents, or convert tilled fields to grazing for cattle and sheep, eviction was useful.[62]

Relief could only be given in food, and as cabins were pulled down, the supply of housing decreased and the cost increased. "As cabins become fewer," a relief officer wrote, "lodgings, however miserable, become more difficult to obtain." Most of the people who left Ireland did so with their own money, on their own initiative. A small number of prominent landlords, such as Lord Monteagle, offered bonuses to tenants to emigrate, but landlord-assisted emigration accounted for at most 5 percent of all migration from Ireland in the famine era. Emigration continued to climb even after the famine, rising from ninety-three thousand in 1845 to a peak of nearly four hundred thousand in 1852—and in the next sixty years, six million more people would leave Ireland. Emigration, never centralised, and pushed along by the pressure of both famine and the Poor Law system of famine relief, was useful to British plans for Ireland. Fewer tenants simplified landholding and cut through subdivision.[63]

Mass evictions evoked conflicted, dissonant reactions to officials and landowners. On the one hand, political economy showed that evictions were necessary and inevitable. If there was a surplus of people with respect to the requirements of the market in Ireland, and if the Irish market stubbornly refused to modernise, capitalise, or expand, then the population had to shrink to make improvement and reform possible. On the other hand, many evictions were obviously cruel and violent. Providence had a strange sense of humour. In May 1848 the *Freeman's Journal* called the campaign of evictions an "agrarian war . . . [of] extermination." In July 1850, the *Times* reported sardonically on "the rights of property . . . vindicated" in the town of Loughrea, King's County, through the "assertion of the right of devastation." After tenants— many of whom had already paid rent—were evicted from their cottages, the cottages were burnt to the ground to deter squatters from taking shelter inside.[64]

John Russell considered the problem in Ireland, without the potato (as he wrote to Lord Lansdowne in November 1847), to be "the war between landlord and tenant . . . murder on one side: ejectment on the other." To his credit, Russell was appalled to find Irish landlords shirking what he considered to be their moral duty as employers of labour. The Poor Law was supposed to discipline landlords and occupiers, impelling them to virtue. Russell had built his career and his ministry on the prevailing ideology of free markets, self-help, and laissez-faire, but he squirmed to see the grim consequences of his principles for the Irish poor. Amid "the fall of thrones and the crash of armies on the Continent," a biographer put it, there was little he could do. Discomfort was a burden, but it was feather-light when weighed against an ambition to remain in office.[65]

And in any case, although Russell might have been unhappy with the pace and violence of evictions, the consequences of mass evictions were pushing Ireland toward some of the demographic changes that reformers had insisted the market could produce. By 1851, the Irish population had fallen by 20 percent, and the rural population by 25 percent. The class of cottier and conacre farmers shrank dramatically as holdings of less than an acre fell from 134,000 in 1841 to 36,000 in 1851, and the number of holdings of less than five acres fell from 440,000 to 124,000. Most emigrants were in the prime of adulthood; only 42 percent were under twenty or over fifty. The consequence, as one historian writes, was a process of "relaxing the peasant's desperate hold upon his land."[66]

Meanwhile, Irish landlords became scapegoats in the British press. One reporter urged readers to consider Ireland—an equal in the United Kingdom—as an imperial territory more akin to the kingdom of Oudh, in northern India, where generations of British officials had been slicing off and annexing territory by stages, often after British accusations of Indian mismanagement. Why not treat Irish landlords like Indian landlords, a newspaper editorial asked, and "tell them plainly that, unless they acted honestly at once, they, like the King of Oude, should lose British protection, and be left to the tender mercies of their outraged peasantry and oppressed tenants." The landlord class had once been prime movers of British colonialism in Ireland, the inheritors of Irish land taken by English and British conquerors. Now that Irish landlords as well as Irish labourers were deemed to have failed to identify with the market and with "civilisation," old landlords as well as penniless tenants were prescribed a colonial corrective.[67]

Although it seemed to many officials and critics to be a recrudescence of Ireland's stubborn, atavistic poverty and backwardness, this final phase of the Great Famine was instead a fractured glimpse at capitalism's future. Ireland had long been exploited—its land distributed to colonists and loyalists, its workers pushed into a lopsided and jerry-built export economy of low wages and high exports supported by the unusual generosity of the pre-blight potato crop. However, even before the Great Famine began, the returns on the exploitation of Irish labour were diminishing, and by the end, the expulsion of the starving poor—by death, by emigration—came to seem like the logical solution to Irish poverty. The object of the Poor Law system was not *directly* to expel the poor, but rather to create incentives that would force the poor to arrive at the "rational" decision to abandon their land. Eviction remains a potent political issue, and a powerful symbol, in contemporary Irish politics. In 2023, amid an ongoing housing crisis, the consequence of overheated real estate markets and callow neoliberal housing policy, the artist Adam Doyle, who uses the alias Spicebag, drew international attention for a piece that places twenty-first-century Irish gardaí in a nineteenth-century scene of a Great Famine–era eviction, enforcing a landlord's orders. In the twenty-first century, expulsion serves a political economy that treats real estate as a speculative asset rather than a human need. In the nineteenth century, eviction served landlords and would-be investors by "liberating" valuable land from inconvenient or unproductive tenants.[68]

The Poor Law was applied to Ireland to impose a common system across two of the partners to the United Kingdom. But events of the last years of the Great Famine—the collapse of distressed unions, the ongoing ruin and depopulation of the countryside, the pell-mell flight from Ireland, the resentment in Westminster at Irish "ingratitude" for relief, the bitter and nihilistic response to the Young Ireland rebellion—all repeated what had been true from the very beginning of the Union: Ireland was to be a part of the United Kingdom, but it was also, in many ways that counted, still colonised.

Epilogue

THE CRYSTAL PALACE

I N LONDON, ON MAY 1, 1851, THE GREAT EXHIBITION OF THE Works of Industry of All Nations opened to the public in Hyde Park. Modeled on France's successful series of national industrial exhibitions, but bigger and grander, the exposition symbolised and celebrated the commercial and industrial power of the United Kingdom and the British Empire. Before it closed in October, an estimated six million Londoners and tourists had visited the Crystal Palace, a glass and iron greenhouse three times the size of St. Paul's Cathedral, purpose-built to hold thousands of displays and exhibitors' booths from the United Kingdom, Britain's colonies, and the world. The exhibition was a watershed. Forty years later, schoolchildren memorised its opening among the principal dates of Queen Victoria's early reign.[1]

The central hall of the Crystal Palace was bright and wide, ringed by balconies supported by iron struts. The side galleries were filled with products from Britain's allies, colonies, and dependencies: crockery, cutlery, fabrics, furniture, artwork, exotic fruits under bell

jars, jewelry, metalwork, and precious stones, including the enormous Kohinoor diamond. The hall itself displayed heavy machines
and monumental works of craftsmanship and industrial design:
printing presses, locomotive engines, power looms, model ships,
and full-size boats suspended by cables from the ceiling. Trees
grew inside the structure, and a fountain, more than twenty feet
tall, flowed with Schweppes Malvern Soda Water. The exhibition,
according to the authors of one of many souvenir guides, taught a
lesson in industriousness. This emporium of products, machines,
commodities, art, and trinkets would inspire millions, especially
among the working classes, to work harder, to refine their tastes,
"to . . . rise in the scale of society."[2]

While London celebrated the bounty of the empire at the Crystal Palace, Ireland still seemed to many in Britain to be, as a report
in a medical journal commented, "the exception to almost every
rule, in religion, in politics, and in social economics." Although
the famine in Ireland was ending, late blight remained an endemic
threat to Irish potatoes, and to potato crops across the Americas
and Europe. The heroic age of the European potato—its hardiness
and yield first celebrated by Enlightenment agronomists and then
feared by political economists following Thomas Malthus—was
over. The Irish potato crop was never again as generous as in 1844.
In 1859, the total area of land in Ireland planted with potatoes was
40 percent smaller than in 1846, and the average yield per acre
had fallen by a third. The 1851 UK census also showed a shocking
decline in Ireland's population, from 8,175,124 to 6,515,794. The
population that year was lower even than the population in 1821.[3]

During the famine years, James Fintan Lalor wrote, "life lost its
form" in Ireland. But life goes on for the living, and by May 1851
Irish rural society was beginning to regain shape. Ireland remained
poor. Starvation, disease, and chaotic emigration had reduced some
of the pressure on Irish land, and poor relief had devolved onto

the Poor Law unions. The blunt logic of political economy would either relieve the Irish poor or uproot them and send them across the oceans. Those who remained in Ireland and who survived the famine years with their money in a savings bank had a chance to climb the social ladder. Some Irish emigrants remembered Ireland with nostalgia, others never mentioned it at all, and still others digested their exile into cold loathing of Britain.[4]

Collective trauma galvanised survivors on both sides of the Atlantic. In 1858, exiles in North America formed the revolutionary Fenian Brotherhood, cousin to the Irish Republican Brotherhood in Ireland. American Fenians conducted raids into Canada and coordinated with cells in Ireland, England, and Australia in the hopes of overthrowing British rule in Ireland. In the late 1870s, advocates for the rights of Irish tenants provoked an organised "Land War" of rent strikes and skirmishes with police. Bills for Home Rule—for a devolved Irish Parliament within the United Kingdom—were defeated in Parliament in 1886 and 1893. The Catholic church became more politically active, more closely associated with Irish nationalism, and more committed to suppressing folk Catholicism among the rural poor in favour of established church dogma and hierarchy. Far from offering a providential answer or resolution to the "Irish question," the blight made Irish issues even more intractable for the Union and the empire. The 1916 Easter Rising and subsequent war of independence had their own proximate causes—conflicts between republican and constitutionalist nationalists, the repeated failure of Home Rule, the tumult of the First World War—but the Great Famine was in the background, a wound that gave shape to an idea of the nation.[5]

The famine, and the steady wave of emigration it inaugurated, also made "Irishness" into a creation as much about diaspora as of Ireland itself. Although Irishness was still associated with a flair for talking, bullshitting, self-pity, and melodrama, the swaggering Irish cop, the corrupt Irish ward-heeling politician, and above all the Irish drunk replaced colonial caricatures of superstitious, lazy, and half-civilised Irish farmers in motley, filthy evening wear. The Irish drunk (you know the jokes: "What do you call an Irish seven-course meal? A potato and a six-pack," etc.) was a transnational creation—a combination of condemnations of alcohol from a temperance movement that was also very powerful in Ireland, and resentments directed at the millions of Irish immigrants crowding into already-bursting cities. Before the Great Famine, drinking culture in the United Kingdom was relatively homogeneous, and temperance activists made the same arguments to the British working classes as to the Irish poor—that drink was a waste of scarce resources, that it loosened morals. What started as sharp xenophobia directed at immigrants eroded into familiar, winking stereotypes that the Irish diaspora adopted as part of an otherwise diffuse identity.[6]

The scale and pace of emigration that began with the Great Famine made permanent changes to the texture and meaning of Irishness. The organism that caused the blight, in turn, permanently transformed Irish agriculture. *P. infestans* remains endemic in Ireland. Met Éireann, the Irish national weather service, makes regular blight forecasts based on temperature, relative humidity, and estimates of sporulation periods for the blight oomycete. Worldwide, the pathogen remains a multibillion-dollar problem. The arrival of the blight in Europe was only one of uncounted accidental introductions of new species associated with the massively expanded scale and speed of international commerce—of unpredictable and unanticipated encounters between ecologies otherwise separated by hundreds or thousands of kilometres. The world is smaller now than in 1845. Animals, plants, and micro-organisms defy borders and quarantines. Climate is even less predictable. Human beings depend for food on a homogenised agricultural biota, radically simplified and dependent on chemical pesticides, antibiotics, and sophisticated technology.

The Irish Great Famine was also only one of the first of several devastating famines to afflict the British Empire in the Victorian era. Indeed, India, not Ireland, was the epicentre of colonial famine in the nineteenth-century empire. Victoria's long reign, from 1837 to 1901—an era whose plenty, glamour, ambition, and technical and scientific achievements the Great Exhibition celebrated so effectively—began and ended with mass death from starvation in the subcontinent. The Agra famine of 1837–1838, which began with drought in the territories of the East India Company, killed an estimated 800,000 people. In 1899–1900, during the British Raj, a widespread famine in western and central India killed anywhere from 1 million to more than 4 million people, depending on the estimate. In 1865–1866, at least 1.3 million people died during a famine in Orissa, and in 1876–1878 and 1896–1902, anywhere from 12.2 million to 29.3 million people died in south and southwestern India during prolonged famines that were caused by drought and exacerbated by the demand for cotton in British and world markets.[7]

Laissez-faire remained a principle of British economic policy in India; Adam Smith's arguments against regulating the price of grain were taught at Haileybury, the East India Company's college. As in Ireland when the potatoes failed, British officials in India "convinced themselves that overly heroic exertions" against the natural laws of the economy "were worse than no effort at all." Free trade in grain pushed Indian farmers away from subsistence agriculture, and India's extensive railway network encouraged and accelerated speculation: as grain crops failed, crops that survived were whisked away for export. Also as in Ireland, the pressures of changing land use and labour in order to supply the British market with exports created conditions that turned an "act of God"—the cyclical El Niño warming of the sea surface's temperature in the southern Pacific, which affects monsoon rain patterns in India—into an unimaginably destructive and deadly famine.[8]

The great Indian famines, however, clarified the meaning of successful management of food security in Britain's colonial empire. Sir Richard Temple had overseen famine relief efforts during a shorter famine in Bengal and Bihar in 1873–1874 by arranging imports of rice and approving a massive public works campaign, measures that combined to dramatically reduce excess deaths. He was scolded for spending beyond what the Treasury had approved and for fostering dependence among Indian peasants, a reminder that the "task of saving life, irrespective of the cost, is . . . beyond our power to undertake." Temple saved his imperial career in the famine of 1876–1878 by organising austere relief works that had strict labour tests and wages set at "bare subsistence." As in Ireland, it was paramount in India that "private trade in grain should not be interfered with." "Wheat," a historian concludes, "was capital."[9]

At the Great Exhibition, there was no commemoration of the Great Famine. The exhibition was a giddy advertisement for empire and global trade, not a sober reckoning of its costs. In the Crystal Palace, Irish exhibitors presented their wares as a part of the United Kingdom's delegation, organised by industry. The turn-of-the-century dream of British capital industrialising Ireland within the United Kingdom reappeared, unscathed, in the galleries. Potatoes on display were touted for what they could become through industrial processes: farina to supplement flour for factory workers, or starches for manufacturing. Irish industrialists promoting new ways to collect and process peat set up booths alongside English and Scottish collieries and industrial chemists; an illustrated souvenir guide mentioned that the turf sellers had "attracted the attention of English capitalists." Ireland's industries, battered by British competition, were also on display. There were Irish flag-stones and slate, ore and precious metals; wool, flax, and finished linen. In a very rare mention of the famine, the official guide to the exposition noted that one manufacturer had hired unemployed women and girls to make lace after the potatoes failed.[10]

The Ordnance Survey, alongside wall hangings of other impres-sively large and detailed maps of Britain, displayed a map of Dub-lin, available for sale as a booklet of thirty-three sheets. There was also a papier-mâché model of the townlands of Kilkenny to admire, painted with topographic lines. The Irish maps were a spectacle for working-class visitors and an advertisement to the monied that Irish land was no longer a mess of rundale and townland, debt and family obligation—in short, that the knot of encumbrances had been picked. A souvenir guide praised the Irish maps as invaluable for future railway and canal projects and "as a basis for the valua-tion and registry of property and for social improvements of many kinds." The Ireland of the Great Exhibition was not mired in colo-nial legacies, caught in a gyre of increasing inequality, or battered and traumatised by one of the worst humanitarian disasters to strike western Europe in the nineteenth century. At the exhibi-tion, Ireland was a partner in an uncomplicated and unambiguous Union, and open for business.[11]

There were some three hundred Irish exhibits at the exposi-tion, almost all displaying manufacturing tools, sample materials, or artworks; but even subsumed into the collection, as one his-torian writes, Ireland was both "assimilated and distanced." The kinds of manufacturers who catered to the Irish middle class and gentry, in Ireland and Britain both, sold a romantic version of the Irish past, a Celtic Revival. The jewelers George and Samuel Waterhouse, of Dublin, displayed the outstanding Tara Brooch, a masterpiece from the late seventh or early eighth century that had been discovered on a beach near Drogheda in 1850 (and is now a highlight of the collections of the National Museum of Ireland). G. and S. Waterhouse sold replicas of the brooch and many other pieces in a similar Celtic style, some of which were selected by the Royal Commissioners of the Exhibition for inclusion in the founding collection of the museum that became the Victoria and Albert, in South Kensington, London. High-end Irish cabinetmakers showed off furniture crafted from the wood of oaks and yews recovered, preserved, from Irish bogs. The pieces were machine-tooled and then hand-engraved, many with Celtic iconography and scenes from Irish mythical history, especially the tales of the High Kings who ruled Ireland before the birth of Christ. Arthur Jones, of Dublin, displayed a "music temple," a decorative piece carved from bog yew and engraved with images of Ollamh Fodhla, a legendary lawgiver, presenting a copy of the preconquest Brehon laws to Ireland, the centre of a "chronological series commencing 700 years BC, the date of the foundation of the Irish monarchy . . . ending with the present agricultural age of Ireland, the memorable year 1851."[12]

For wealthy Irish and British consumers, exquisite Celtic jewelry and fine furniture made of bog woods reconciled the romantic past with the industrial and imperial present. The Irish poor, considered by so many political economists and imperial officials to be outside modernity and in need of the civilising power of the market and cash wages, disappeared from view. A legendary king could evoke a romantic idea of Ireland distant and abstract enough to be absorbed into British rule. The Ireland of the remote past was a fallen civilisation that could be rediscovered and remembered by imperial collectors and curators. In time, the empire might know the Irish better than they knew themselves—another reason to accept British power in the Victorian present.

THE FAMINE WAS A CRISIS OF IDEAS AS WELL AS POLICY—NOT A crisis of a lack of ideas, but of the implementation of an orthodoxy of ill-considered ideas, proven unfit for purpose in practice. In the years that followed, political economists began to revise their theories, adding nuance and exceptions to purportedly natural laws. John Stuart Mill argued that nothing could check the growth of the Irish population until Ireland's economy modernised. Britain's growing industrial cities, Mill argued, were in effect sopping up the overflow of dispossessed and deracinated agricultural workers. If the British economy shrank, or even stalled, Mill wrote, "there is no certainty that this fate may not be reserved for us." Compassion for British and Irish farmworkers was laudable, but Mill suggested what was really needed was "some application of common sense." One did not need to adopt the cruelty of many Malthusians, he argued, to recognise that Malthus was right that higher wages might affect the birth rate. Civilisation required restraint on population growth. "Want, in that age of the world," Mill concluded, "had its uses, as even slavery had." But in the civilised, emancipated world of free trade and free labour, poverty did not "make men either better workmen or more civilized beings." Nassau William Senior, however, was unpersuaded. The Irish "still depend mainly on the potato," he wrote in the 1860s. "They still depend rather on the occupation of land, than on the wages of labour. They still erect for themselves the hovels in which they dwell. They are still eager to subdivide and to sublet. They are still the tools of their priests, and the priests are still ignorant of the economical laws on which the welfare of the labouring classes depends."[13]

Anthropologists have used the term "structural violence" to describe how the choices impoverished people make can be crabbed by economic and political systems that are far beyond their control. In Ireland during the famine, the hazards of famine magnified and sharpened violent structures of rent, exploitation, and potato dependence. Some of the Irish poor risked their lives for others in the face of starvation, and others stole food, or betrayed friends, or abandoned family. Structure constrains the powerful as well as the weak, albeit at a different scale. Across the British Empire, some officials were cruel or nihilistic, vengeful or callous. But the violence of empire was carried out as much by a system as by individuals. There are wicked relief officers, landlords, and administrators in the records of the Irish famine. However, many of the people charged with the design and administration of famine relief were competent, intelligent, and moved by the suffering they saw. Still, even the most humane imperial official was limited by the economic and political realities of an era of colonialism and imperial power, and by the prevailing stereotypes, assumptions, and values that animated the empire. British imperial culture was suspicious and contemptuous of the poor everywhere, of the Irish in general, and of the Irish poor in particular. In the face of starvation, at least some relief officials—not usually rich men, but half-pay officers and assorted functionaries—risked their jobs to feed the hungry and risked their lives to treat the sick. As a leading legal historian of the British Empire writes, "Humanity and inhumanity are real dispositions." However, "even the sincerest convictions and most authentic emotional responses may be . . . subdued, or even at times reversed, by the patterns of power."[14]

History is not a parable. The history of Ireland within the British Empire, and the history of the empire itself is not a "usable past" of heroes to emulate and villains to despise. It is the history of the structures and constraints within which labourers, politicians, administrators, and priests made decisions. The new states of Great Britain, in 1707, and the United Kingdom, in 1801, were forged in an era of imperial conquest, colonial mass enslavement, commercial expansion, and military adventuring. British power was justified, however, on the basis of civilisation—on the idea that all the destruction was ultimately in the service of human flourishing, which could be measured through participation in British markets and institutions. The structures that built and justified British imperial power in Ireland meant that, in 1845, the leaders of the United Kingdom could find no other way to explain the worst subsistence crisis in the new country's short history than a definitive lack of civilisation among the Irish. The empire could conceive of no other useful tools to meet the crisis than the principles of the free market and the workhouse.

Years of famine did little to undermine the assumptions about empire, poverty, and civilisation in Ireland that shaped both British attitudes toward the Irish and the design of relief policies. In 1849, James Hewitt, the 4th Viscount Lifford, an Anglo-Irish landlord, former high sheriff of Donegal, and future Conservative peer, acutely understood the immiserating cycle of rent that forced Irish workers to take "land at an exorbitant rent" while families "lived upon the potatoes [they] produced and laboured either in England or Ireland for part of the rent" and "begged for the rest." The potato blight had forced the issue. Hewitt complained that so long as government propped up the Poor Law unions, "things will never be better. It will be as if there were an inexhaustible supply of potatoes, the rents will not be lowered, the poor will not become more industrious . . . [and] land will not be made more productive." This was no insult to the Irish, he concluded: "we are none of us industrious except some stimulus is supplied."[15]

But who was "we"? An Anglo-Irish landlord—even a good one—was not the same as a landless labourer. At the same time, neither was an Anglo-Irish landlord always the same as a British aristocrat. Imperial power was thickly layered. More important, though, Hewitt could not see his own place in the structure of power in Ireland. The forces of the economy seemed permanent, more a feature of the natural world rather than a historically specific and man-made set of relationships. The idea that markets—and not just human exchange in general, but markets on the model described, analysed, and championed by political economists and politicians in Britain—represented the natural unfolding or efflorescence of civilisation was an idea with a specific history. But in the British Empire, the history of the market was easy to erase and to replace with an idea of markets as a universal and irresistible civilising force.

THE GREAT EXHIBITION—A FANTASIA OF PRODUCTS, LUXURIES, machines, and conveniences—represented the capacity of capitalism and modernity to improve the world. The Great Famine that John Russell likened in January 1847 to a "famine of the thirteenth century" was as modern as the machinery on display in Hyde Park. Ireland was pressed into an imperial and national economic order centred on booming London; Irish farmers raised potatoes to keep up with the demands of rent and land imposed by an accelerating market; the blight arrived in a steamship after Belgian farmers ordered new potato cultivars from the Americas; the Irish starved because the idea of the free market and the industrious and individual worker was so deeply entrenched in British politics and political economy as to be effectively inviolable, even in the deepest crisis.

Between 2000 and 2011, according to experts, although many places experienced shortages and subsistence crises, there were no famines. By 2017, however, parts of eastern Nigeria, Somalia, South Sudan, and Yemen were either already experiencing famine or on the edge of famine. Now, as I write in April 2024, analysts working for the United Nations Food and Agriculture Organization and the World Food Programme warn that there are eighteen "hotspots" in twenty-two countries where people are currently enduring famine conditions or are at high risk of falling into famine. The imagery of famine can still deceive us as it deceived John Russell—skeletal limbs and swollen bellies can seem like elements of a barbaric past thrust into the civilised present. But famine in the twenty-first century, as in the nineteenth, is a disease of modernity—of war, of ecological accident, of climate change, of the vicissitudes of markets acting on the vulnerable.[16]

The idea that poor relief should cost the people who receive it something—labour or an acceptance of surveillance or a performance of gratitude to taxpayers—is still a principle of many modern welfare states, including the United Kingdom. In January 2024, Prime Minister Rishi Sunak announced plans to cut taxes and benefits, declaring that his approach to social welfare depended on "making sure that everybody who can work does work." The notion that austerity promotes industriousness, and that the moral and economic rewards of industriousness are worth the moral and material costs of petty austerity remains an article of faith for many governments. These are the same principles as the ones that animated famine relief in mid-nineteenth-century Ireland. They are even more galling in 2024, when governments have resources and technical and bureaucratic expertise far greater than the United Kingdom did in 1845.[17]

And so, the Great Famine rehearsed in Ireland many of the most destructive consequences of capitalist modernity: colonialism, exploitation, ecological disaster, sudden and panicked mass emigration, heedless destruction and exploitation giving way to expulsion—all in the name of purifying market forces. In its own time, the Great Famine showed the potential destructive power of the vigorous industrial capitalism of the Victorian United Kingdom and the British Empire. The colonial land settlement in Ireland had placed the Irish poor at a profound disadvantage within the empire's markets. After the Union, Britain's growing need for imported food increased pressure on the Irish poor and further entrenched the potato as the only anchor in a furious gale. Throughout the famine, neither Tory nor Whig governments abandoned the principle that the rigour of the market was the only way to uproot the potato and civilise Ireland—to teach the Irish, finally, the value of industry.

The Great Famine, although an event of world-historical importance, was not a singular event in world history. It wasn't even a singular event in the history of Ireland: recall that the famine of 1740–1741 killed more people by proportion of population. Other subsistence crises, wars, and ecological catastrophes in the nineteenth and twentieth centuries would also send waves of people around the world, people fleeing violence, starvation, drought, or economic collapse. But the Great Famine was a watershed in the history of Ireland and the history of the United Kingdom. It proved the hollowness of the Union, and proved that Ireland was still, in the eyes of most people making decisions, a half-civilised colony. The Great Famine also gave the British Empire a blueprint for digesting the ecological and human consequences of a burdensome and often destructive global system of agriculture and trade that benefited Britain at the expense of the empire. When the system functioned, it was civilisation. When it broke down, it was Providence.

ACKNOWLEDGMENTS

I RESEARCHED THIS BOOK IN THE GLUM DEPTHS OF THE PANdemic. I wrote the first draft as the world started to move again, splintered by the cabin fever and desocialisation of lockdown. Although history is solitary work, historians work in communities of friends and families and colleagues. For this book, especially in its early days, the ways I accessed that community were not through the same conviviality and talks and drinks and lunch on the benches outside the archives that marked anything I had ever done before. I'm grateful to the many people who helped me to write this book, in weird and enervated times.

At Robinson, thanks to Duncan Proudfoot (who has moved on to another shop), who championed my first book for a general audience and was game to take a chance on a second one, and to Emma Smith and Tamsin English, who saw the project through to publication. At Basic, Brian Distelberg and Michael Kaler provided superb guidance, editorial feedback, and notes. Kelley Blewster provided adroit copyediting, catching all kinds of embarrassing mixed metaphors and orphan quotation marks. Melissa Veronesi, Annie Chatham, and the production team at Basic did excellent work turning a manuscript into a book. Before I turned the book over to its publishers, I had the pleasure to work again with Pamela Haag, an editor with a gift for cutting through the

tics, ellipses, and clichés of academic writing. I am very grateful
to my agent, Michael Dean, of Andrew Nurnberg Associates, for
his enthusiasm, support, and guidance on this and other projects.
My research assistant at the University of Toronto, Jasmine Martin, did spectacular work, digging through digital mountains of
documents and handwritten folktales, finding patterns and chas-
ing down leads (my favourite: a parallel Jasmine noticed between
Sinéad O'Connor's 1998 song "Skibbereen" and motifs in famine
folktales).

My colleagues in the Centre for Industrial Relations and
Human Resources and in the Centre for Diaspora & Transnational Studies have been very supportive. Rafael Gomez and
Kevin Lewis O'Neill provided professional and material support,
including some timely releases from teaching. Special thanks to
my colleagues in the CIRHR for sharpening my understanding of
political economy and tolerating my suspicion of the quantitative
social sciences. I presented versions of the argument of this book
at the Princeton University Eighteenth-Century Seminar and the
Queen's University Department of History. Thanks to those audi-
ences for their questions and feedback on earlier versions of the
talk, and to David Bell, Sandra den Otter, and Amitava Chow-
dhury for invitations. Thanks, as always, to Linda Colley for her
support, mentorship, and unequalled historical insight. Thanks
also to Christopher M. Florio and Imaobong Umoren for their
generosity in reading and commenting on the whole manuscript.
Any remaining errors are mine (they were also mine to begin with,
to be fair).

My father, Lawrence Scanlan, died in 2019; my mother, Elizabeth Therrien, in 2021. They are missed, and I hope they would
have liked this book. Thanks to them, and especially to Larry for
the scraps of lore and Irish Catholic diasporic cultural patholo-
gies that, in part, prompted me to begin this project. In a decade

working on British antislavery, I had seen enough references to Irish labourers in writings on the Caribbean after emancipation to know there was a knot to unpick, but it was my father's death that pushed me to start a book on Ireland and the British Empire. Thanks also to my brother, Sean Scanlan, for giving me access to his Ancestry account; we were both struck by the same morbid curiosity about our forefathers and foremothers as our parents ailed and died. Sean's research on our family history made me think more about my own place within the history of the British Empire.

Above all, thanks to my family. To Catherine Evans, the sharpest historian under our roof, for her love, for the wonderful life we have together, and for shaping and refining this book in uncountable ways (including the title!). I started out as a historian of the eighteenth century, and Catherine has pulled me into the Victorian world—and very few people understand the neuroses of the Victorians as well as she does. Thanks finally to my children, Rafe and Moira Jane. Rafe's potato questions set me on all kinds of unexpected paths, and I treasure his effervescence, curiosity, and openheartedness. Moira, adorable, sweet, and precocious (and tyrannically two as I write this), came into our lives while this book was in the offing. The world is an uncertain place, but our house is full of love. This book is for them.

NOTES

Introduction: Irish Questions

1. *Correspondence Relating to Measures for Relief of Distress in Ireland (Commissariat Series), January–March 1847*, Command Papers 796 (London: W. Clowes and Sons, 1847), 164.

2. Cormac Ó Gráda, *Ireland: A New Economic History, 1780–1939* (Oxford, UK: Clarendon Press, 1995), 185; Joel Mokyr, *Why Ireland Starved: A Quantitative and Analytical History of the Irish Economy, 1800–1850*, new ed. (London: Routledge, 2016), 275–277.

3. Bridget Conley and Alex de Waal, "The Purposes of Starvation: Historical and Contemporary Uses," *Journal of International Criminal Justice* 17, no. 4 (September 1, 2019): 701.

4. On the spread of the potato in Europe, see William H. McNeill, "How the Potato Changed the World's History," *Social Research* 66, no. 1 (1999): 67–83; Redcliffe N. Salaman, "The Early European Potato: Its Character and Place of Origin," *Botanical Journal of the Linnean Society* 53, no. 348 (February 1, 1946): 1–27.

5. On the potato as a technical innovation in European farming, see Eric Hobsbawm, *The Age of Revolution, 1789–1848*, 1st Vintage reprint ed. (New York: Vintage, 1996), 166.

6. On Irish and British identity, and on Irish involvement in imperial administration, see R. F. Foster, *Paddy and Mr. Punch: Connections in Irish and English History* (London: Penguin, 1993); Kevin Kenny, "The Irish in the Empire," in *Ireland and the British Empire*, ed. Kevin Kenny (Oxford, UK: Oxford University Press, 2005), 90–122.

7. Joel Mokyr and Cormac Ó Gráda, "Poor and Getting Poorer? Living Standards in Ireland Before the Famine," *Economic History Review* 41, no. 2 (1988): 209–235; R. B. McDowell, "Ireland on the Eve of the

Famine," in *The Great Famine: Studies in Irish History, 1845–52*, ed. R. Dudley Edwards, T. Desmond Williams, and Cormac Ó Gráda, new ed. (Dublin: Lilliput Press, 1994), 22–30.

8. Edward Gibbon Wakefield, *An Account of Ireland, Statistical and Political: In Two Volumes* (London: Longman, Hurst, Rees, Orme, and Brown, 1812), 2:727; *Monthly Chronicle: A National Journal of Politics, Literature, Science and Art*, vol. 6 (London: Longman, Orme, Brown, Green, and Longmans, 1840), 334–335.

9. John Stuart Mill, *England and Ireland* (London: Longmans, Green, Reader, and Dyer, 1868), 3; John Wiggins, *The "Monster" Misery of Ireland: A Practical Treatise on the Relation of Landlord and Tenant, with Suggestions for Legislative Measures, and the Management of Landed Property, the Result of Above Thirty Years' Experience and Study of the Subject* (London: Richard Bentley, 1844), 283–284.

10. Nassau William Senior, *Journals, Conversations and Essays Relating to Ireland* (London: Longmans, Green, and Company, 1868), 1:19; House of Commons Debates, February 16, 1844, vol. 72, cc. 1016–1017.

11. [Douglas Jerrold], "Ireland," *Punch*, October 18, 1845, Punch Historical Archive, 1841–1992.

12. *Extracts from the Information Received by His Majesty's Commissioners as to the Administration and Operation of the Poor Laws* (London: B. Fellowes, 1834), 227; Michael Quinn, "Jeremy Bentham on the Relief of Indigence: An Exercise in Applied Philosophy," in *Jeremy Bentham*, ed. Frederick Rosen (Abingdon, UK: Routledge, 2017).

13. On the allure of the market in Europe in this era, see Christopher Clark, *Revolutionary Spring: Europe Aflame and the Fight for a New World, 1848–1849* (London: Allen Lane, 2023), chap. 1.

14. Eric Stokes, *The English Utilitarians and India* (Oxford: Clarendon Press, 1959), xiii; Karl Marx, *Capital*, vol. 1, trans. Ben Fowkes (London: Penguin, 2004), 395.

15. William Parsons, Earl of Rosse, *Letters on the State of Ireland* (London: John Hatchard and Son, 1847), 10; Edmund Burke, *Thoughts and Details on Scarcity: Originally Presented to the Right Hon. William Pitt, in the Month of November, 1795* (London: F. and C. Rivington, 1800), 32.

16. Mary Leadbeater, *Cottage Dialogues Among the Irish Peasantry, with Notes and a Preface by Maria Edgeworth*, ed. Maria Edgeworth (London: J. Johnson and Co., 1811), 270; Thomas Campbell Foster, *Letters on the Condition of the People of Ireland* (London: Chapman and Hall, 1846), 306.

17. On the tension between idealised and real markets, see Laura F. Edwards, *Only the Clothes on Her Back: Clothing and the Hidden History of Power in the Nineteenth-Century United States* (New York: Oxford University Press, 2022), 59; Hans Medick, "The Proto-Industrial Family Economy," in *Industrialization Before Industrialization*, ed. Peter Kriedte, Hans Medick, and Jurgen Schlumbohm, trans. Beate Schempp (Cambridge, UK: Cambridge University Press, 1982), 44–45; on markets and inequality, see Ellen Meiksins Wood, *Empire of Capital* (London: Verso, 2003).

18. Charles Edward Trevelyan, *The Irish Crisis* (London: Longman, Brown, Green, and Longmans, 1848), 201.

19. Mike Davis, *Late Victorian Holocausts: El Niño Famines and the Making of the Third World* (London: Verso, 2002), 35.

20. On faith in markets, see Ó Gráda, *Ireland*, 193; on laissez-faire, see Karl Polanyi, *The Great Transformation: The Political and Economic Origins of Our Time* (Boston: Beacon Press, 2001), 145.

21. Trevelyan, *Irish Crisis*, 184; *To-Day in Ireland* (London: Charles Knight, 1825), 3:163–164; Foster, *Letters on the Condition of the People of Ireland*, 622.

22. Nassau William Senior, *Journals, Conversations and Essays*, 1:178–180.

23. From *The Liberator*, March 27, 1846, Philip Foner, ed., *Life and Writings of Frederick Douglass*, vol. 1 (New York: International Publishers, 1950), 138. Thomas Carlyle's contempt for Ireland paled only in comparison with his bilious hatred of Black people, in the Caribbean and elsewhere; see Thomas Carlyle, "The Present Time," in *Latter-Day Pamphlets [1850]*, *Thomas Carlyle's Collected Works* (London: Chapman and Hall, 1870), 3–58; Thomas Carlyle, *Occasional Discourse on the Nigger Question* [Reprinted, with Additions, from *Fraser's Magazine*] (London: Thomas Bosworth, 1853), 8.

24. William Blackstone, *Commentaries on the Laws of England: In Four Books*, ed. Thomas M. Cooley, 3rd rev. ed. (Chicago: Callaghan, 1884), 1:417.

25. Charles Greville, *The Greville Memoirs: A Journal of the Reigns of King George IV and King William IV*, ed. Henry Reeve (New York: Appleton, 1885), 387–388; Trevelyan, *Irish Crisis*, 8.

26. The iconic historical analysis downplaying the impact of the Great Famine is W. E. H. Lecky, "Why Home Rule Is Undesirable," *North American Review* 152, no. 412 (1891): 361. For commentary on these arguments, see Mokyr, *Why Ireland Starved*, 289–292; K. H. Connell, "The Potato in

Ireland," *Past and Present* 23, no. 1 (1962): 65. See Trevelyan, *Irish Crisis*, 201; John Mitchel, *The Crusade of the Period and Last Conquest of Ireland (Perhaps)*, Irish-American Library 4 (New York: Lynch, Cole, and Meehan, 1878), 322–325. On hunger as a symbol in Irish revolutionary politics, see James Vernon, *Hunger: A Modern History* (Cambridge, MA: Harvard University Press, 2009), 42–43; Kevin Grant, *Last Weapons: Hunger Strikes and Fasts in the British Empire, 1890–1948*, Berkeley Series in British Studies 16 (Berkeley: University of California Press, 2019). For an overview of the academic historiography of the Great Famine, see Ó Gráda, *Ireland*, 174–176; Christine Kinealy, *This Great Calamity: The Irish Famine, 1845–52* (Dublin: Gill and Macmillan, 1994), xv–xvi; Christine Kinealy, *A Death-Dealing Famine: The Great Hunger in Ireland* (London: Pluto Press, 1997), 1–3; Mary E. Daly, "Historians and the Famine: A Beleaguered Species?," *Irish Historical Studies* 30, no. 120 (1997): 591–601; Christine Kinealy, "Beyond Revisionism: Reassessing the Great Irish Famine," *History Ireland* 3, no. 4 (1995): 28–34; Colm Tóibín, "Erasures," *London Review of Books*, July 30, 1998, www.lrb.co.uk/the-paper/v20/n15/colm-toibin /erasures.

27. On starvation and international law, see Conley and de Waal, "Purposes of Starvation."

28. Lawrence J. Taylor, "Bás InEirinn: Cultural Constructions of Death in Ireland," *Anthropological Quarterly* 62, no. 4 (1989): 175.

29. On the Irish "volcano," see Hobsbawm, *Age of Revolution*, 110; on European phenomena "nationalized in retrospect," see Clark, *Revolutionary Spring*, 2, 45.

30. On Victorian famines, see Davis, *Late Victorian Holocausts*, 7–11; see also David Lloyd, "Afterword: The Afterlife of the Untimely Dead," in *Global Legacies of the Great Irish Famine: Transnational and Interdisciplinary Perspectives*, ed. Marguérite Corporaal et al. (Oxford, UK: Peter Lang, 2014), 285–296.

31. David Lloyd, "The Political Economy of the Potato," *Nineteenth-Century Contexts* 29, no. 2–3 (June 1, 2007): 312; John Pitt Kennedy, *Instruct, Employ, Don't Hang Them: Or, Ireland Tranquilized Without Soldiers and Enriched Without English Capital* (London: Thomas and William Boone, 1835), 28–29.

32. On the Anthropocene and ecological crisis, see Simon L. Lewis and Mark A. Maslin, "Defining the Anthropocene," *Nature* 519, no. 7542 (March 2015): 171–180; Jennifer Marshman, Alison Blay-Palmer, and

Karen Landman, "Anthropocene Crisis: Climate Change, Pollinators, and Food Security," *Environments* 6, no. 2 (February 2019): 22; Ricardo Rozzi, "Biocultural Homogenization: A Wicked Problem in the Anthropocene," in *From Biocultural Homogenization to Biocultural Conservation*, ed. Ricardo Rozzi et al., Ecology and Ethics 3 (Cham, Germany: Springer International Publishing, 2018), 21–48.

33. On subsistence farming and globalisation, see B. Davis et al., "Estimating Global and Country-Level Employment in Agrifood Systems," FAO Statistics Working Paper Series (Rome: Food and Agriculture Organisation of the United Nations, February 20, 2023); June Nash, "Global Integration and Subsistence Insecurity," *American Anthropologist* 96, no. 1 (1994): 7–30.

Chapter 1: A Hungry Island

1. *Asiatic Journal and Monthly Register for British India and Its Dependencies*, vol. 16 (London: Kingsbury, Parbury, and Allen, 1823), 612–613.

2. L. De Bussche, *Letters on Ceylon: Particularly Relative to the Kingdom of Kandy* (London: J. J. Stockdale, 1817), 78–88; *Colburn's United Service Magazine and Naval and Military Journal*, vol. 1 (London: Henry Colburn, 1834), 110.

3. Thomas Bartlett, "Ireland, Empire, and Union, 1690–1801," in *Ireland and the British Empire*, ed. Kevin Kenny (Oxford, UK: Oxford University Press, 2005), 62. Greville's comments are quoted often in histories of eighteenth-century Ireland. See Thomas Bartlett, "'This Famous Island Set in a Virginian Sea': Ireland in the British Empire, 1690–1801," in *The Oxford History of the British Empire*, vol. 2, *The Eighteenth Century* (Oxford, UK: Oxford University Press, 1998), 253. On Ireland and Britain as conjoined twins, see Samuel Madden, *Reflections and Resolutions Proper for the Gentlemen of Ireland: As to Their Conduct for the Service of Their Country* (Dublin: R. Reilly, 1816), 67–70.

4. Johann Georg Kohl, *Travels in Ireland* (London: Bruce and Wyld, 1844), 164; see also Alvin Jackson, "Ireland, the Union, and the Empire, 1800–1960," in Kenny, *Ireland and the British Empire*, 133–137; David Nally, "'That Coming Storm': The Irish Poor Law, Colonial Biopolitics, and the Great Famine," *Annals of the Association of American Geographers* 98, no. 3 (September 2008): 715.

5. On Catholic dispossession, see Christine Kinealy, *A New History of Ireland*, updated ed. (Stroud, Gloucestershire: Sutton, 2004), 121.

6. David P. Nally, *Human Encumbrances: Political Violence and the Great Irish Famine* (Notre Dame, IN: University of Notre Dame Press, 2011), 30.

7. Denis Murphy, *Cromwell in Ireland: A History of Cromwell's Irish Campaign* (Dublin: M. H. Gill and Son, 1897), 44–45; Daniel O'Connell, *A Memoir on Ireland, Native and Saxon*, 2nd ed. (Dublin: James Duffy, 1844), 1:345.

8. Ebenezer Cobham Brewer, *Dictionary of Phrase and Fable: Giving the Derivation, Source, or Origin of Common Phrases, Allusions, and Words That Have a Tale to Tell* (London: Cassell, 1895), 597; Aubrey De Vere, *The Church Settlement of Ireland, or, Hibernia Pacanda* (London: Longmans, Green, Reader, and Dyer, 1866), 23. For the folktale of Cromwell and the spurting milk, see "Cromwellian Stories," Schools' Collection, National Folklore Collection, University College Dublin (hereafter Schools' Collection), vol. 0880, p. 373.

9. R. B. McDowell, "Ireland on the Eve of the Famine," in *The Great Famine: Studies in Irish History, 1845–52*, ed. R. Dudley Edwards, T. Desmond Williams, and Cormac Ó Gráda, new ed. (Dublin: Lilliput Press, 1994), 63–71. On the circuit ridden by Catholic priests, see David W. Miller, "Irish Catholicism and the Great Famine," *Journal of Social History* 9, no. 1 (1975): 88–90.

10. On steep exchange rates, see William Petty, *The Political Anatomy of Ireland with the Establishment for That Kingdom When the Late Duke of Ormond Was Lord Lieutenant* (London, 1691), 71–73. On Irish trade to the Caribbean, see Maxine Berg and Pat Hudson, *Slavery, Capitalism and the Industrial Revolution* (Cambridge, UK: Polity, 2023), 23–24.

11. Jonathan Swift, "A Modest Proposal for Preventing the Children of Poor People in Ireland, from Being a Burden on Their Parents or Country, and for Making Them Beneficial to the Publick [1729]," in *Volume IV of the Author's Works, Containing, a Collection of Tracts Relating to Ireland* (Dublin: G. Faulkner, 1735), 276–277.

12. *First Report from His Majesty's Commissioners for Inquiring into the Condition of the Poorer Classes in Ireland, with Appendix (A.) and Supplement*, Sessional Papers 369 (London: House of Commons, 1836) (hereafter *HC 1836 [369]*), 603. See also *Evidence Taken Before Her Majesty's Commissioners of Inquiry into the State of the Law and Practice in Respect to the Occupation of Land in Ireland. Part I*, Command Papers 606 (Dublin: Alexander Thom, 1845), 169–170.

13. On the patchwork of townlands, see Robert Scally, *The End of Hidden Ireland: Rebellion, Famine, and Emigration* (Oxford, UK: Oxford University Press, 1995), 13. On the complexity of rundale and other customary systems of land use, see "Ireland," *Times*, July 31, 1844, 5, The Times Digital Archive (accessed November 9, 2021); David Lloyd, "The Political Economy of the Potato," *Nineteenth-Century Contexts* 29, no. 2–3 (June 1, 2007): 311–312; Dean M. Braa, "The Great Potato Famine and the Transformation of Irish Peasant Society," *Science and Society* 61, no. 2 (1997): 200–203.

14. On Irish units of measurement, see *Correspondence Relating to Measures for Relief of Distress in Ireland (Board of Works Series), July 1846–January 1847*, Parliamentary Papers, Command Papers 764 (London: William Clowes and Sons, 1847), 4.

15. David Nally, "The Colonial Dimensions of the Great Irish Famine," in *Atlas of the Great Irish Famine, 1845–52*, ed. John Crowley, William J. Smyth, and Michael Murphy (Cork: Cork University Press, 2012), 66; John Reader, *Potato: A History of the Propitious Esculent* (New Haven, CT: Yale University Press, 2009), 147; William Maunsell, *Letters to the Right Honourable and Honourable the Dublin Society, on the Culture of the Potatoes from the Shoots* (Dublin: William Sleater, 1794), 24.

16. On peat bogs, see Hely Dutton, *Statistical Survey of the County of Clare, with Observations on the Means of Improvement* (Dublin: Graisberry and Campbell, 1808), 4; other references are from Robert Kane, *The Industrial Resources of Ireland* (Dublin: Hodges and Smith, 1844), 2–3; Arthur Young, *Arthur Young's Tour in Ireland (1776–1779)*, ed. Arthur Wollaston Hutton (London: George Bell and Sons, 1892), 1:5–6.

17. Robin Blackburn, *The Making of New World Slavery: From the Baroque to the Modern, 1492–1800*, 2nd ed. (London: Verso, 2010), 403.

18. "Tenure of Land and Landlordism in Ireland," *Our Continent*, 1882, 562; Prince Albert Victor and Prince George of Wales, *The Cruise of Her Majesty's Ship "Bacchante," 1879–1882*, vol. 1, *The West and the South* (London: Macmillan and Company, 1886), 53–54; *Papers of the New Haven Colony Historical Society*, vol. 3 (New Haven, CT: New Haven Colony Historical Society, 1882), 125–127; "A Day in Barbados," *Timehri: Being the Journal of the Royal Agricultural and Commercial Society of British Guiana*, New Series, 9 (1895): 75–76; Hermann Schomburgk, *The History of Barbados: Comprising a Geographical and Statistical Description of the Island; a Sketch of the Historical Events Since the Settlement; and an Account of Its*

Geology and Natural Productions (London: Longman, Brown, Green, and Longmans, 1848), 84.

19. On Irish emigration, see Kevin Kenny, "The Irish in the Empire," in Kenny, *Ireland and the British Empire*, 94–95. For "poor Catholicks," see Young, *Tour in Ireland*, 2:67.

20. On Irish imperial service, see Kenny, "The Irish in the Empire," 105–106; Linda Colley, *Britons: Forging the Nation, 1707–1837*, 2nd ed. (New Haven, CT: Yale University Press, 2005), 326–327. For "sinewy arms," see Dutton, *Statistical Survey of the County of Clare*, 173–174. For "Irish courage," see "Ireland," *Economist*, January 16, 1847, 67, The Economist Historical Archive (accessed October 14, 2021). On military wages, see Thomas Robert Malthus, "Newenham and Others on the State of Ireland," *Edinburgh Review* 12 (1808): 350–351; for O'Connell's praise of Irish imperial soldiers, see Henry Shaw, ed., *Shaw's Authenticated Report of the Irish State Trials, 1844* (Dublin: Henry Shaw, 1844).

21. On Irish shipping, see William J. Smyth, "The Longue Durée: Imperial Britain and Colonial Ireland," in Crowley et al., *Atlas of the Great Irish Famine, 1845–52*, 59; on Irish commodities in the Atlantic, see Blackburn, *Making of New World Slavery*, 382; Berg and Hudson, *Slavery, Capitalism and the Industrial Revolution*, 59.

22. William Thomas Thornton, *A Plea for Peasant Proprietors: With the Outlines of a Plan for Their Establishment in Ireland* (London: John Murray, 1848), 197–199.

23. William Smith, *The Substance of Mr. William Smith's Speech on the Subject of a Legislative Union Between Great Britain and Ireland: Delivered in the Irish House of Commons, on Thursday, January 24th, 1799*, 2nd ed. (Dublin: Marchbank, 1799), 2; Thomas Goold, *An Address to the People of Ireland, on the Subject of the Projected Union* (Dublin: Printed by James Moore, 1799), 87.

24. Great Britain Parliament, *The Parliamentary Register; Or, History of the Proceedings and Debates of the House of Lords and House of Commons*, vol. 7 (London: J. Debrett, 1799), 637–638; see also Bartlett, "Ireland, Empire, and Union, 1690–1801," 83–87.

25. George O'Brien, *The Economic History of Ireland from the Union to the Famine* (London: Longmans, Green and Company, 1921), 454.

26. "The Class Election," Schools' Collection, vol. 0596, p. 132; *Poor Man's Guardian*, no. 226, October 3, 1835, 688; see also Colley, *Britons*, 322–344.

27. "To Correspondents," *Times*, October 20, 1829, 2, The Times Digital Archive; "Ireland," *Times*, July 24, 1829, 2, The Times Digital Archive.

28. Mary Leadbeater, *Cottage Dialogues Among the Irish Peasantry, with Notes and a Preface by Maria Edgeworth*, ed. Maria Edgeworth (London: J. Johnson and Co., 1811), iv; Mary Leadbeater, *The Landlord's Friend, Intended as a Sequel to Cottage Dialogues* (Dublin: J. Cumming, 1813), 101–107; see also Helen O'Connell, "The Nature of Improvement in Ireland," in *Nature and the Environment in Nineteenth-Century Ireland*, ed. Matthew Kelly (Liverpool: Liverpool University Press, 2019), 18–20.

29. Daniel Defoe, *Giving Alms, No Charity, and Employing the Poor a Grievance to the Nation* (London, 1704), 5; on yields and the labour force, see Eric Hobsbawm, *The Age of Revolution, 1789–1848*, 1st Vintage reprint ed. (New York: Vintage, 1996), 150; Cornelius Walford, *The Famines of the World: Past and Present* (London: Edward Stanford, 1879), 110.

30. Sir William Petty, "The Political Anatomy of Ireland, 1672," in *Tracts; Chiefly Relating to Ireland* (Dublin: Boulter Grierson, 1769), 355–356; Young, *Tour in Ireland*, 1:463; Kohl, *Travels in Ireland*, 64–65.

31. Petty, "Political Anatomy of Ireland," 367; Edward Gibbon Wakefield, *An Account of Ireland, Statistical and Political: In Two Volumes* (London: Longman, Hurst, Rees, Orme, and Brown, 1812), 2:811–812; Martin Doyle, *Hints for the Small Farmers of Ireland*, 4th ed. (Dublin: J. Charles, 1830), 51, 12; Kane, *Industrial Resources*, 381.

32. Madden, *Reflections and Resolutions*, 23, 72–73; George Nicholls, *Poor Laws—Ireland: Three Reports by George Nicholls, Esq. to Her Majesty's Principal Secretary of State for the Home Department* (London: W. Clowes and Sons, 1838), 10–11; see also Leadbeater, *Landlord's Friend*, 109–110; O'Connell, "The Nature of Improvement in Ireland," 18–20; for a summary from the perspective of political economy, see Nassau William Senior, *Journals, Conversations and Essays Relating to Ireland* (London: Longmans, Green, and Company, 1868), 2:30–31.

33. *Poor Inquiry (Ireland): Appendix (F)—Contains Baronial Examinations Relative to Con Acre, Quarter, or Score Ground, Small Tenantry, Consolidation of Farms and Dislodged Tenantry, Emigration, Landlord and Tenant, Nature and State of Agriculture, Taxation, Roads, Observations on the Nature and State of Agriculture, and Supplement, Contains, Answers to the Questions Circulated by the Commissioners*, Command Papers 38 (London: W. Clowes and Sons, 1836), 317; see also R. D. Collison Black, *Economic Thought and*

the Irish Question, 1817–1870 (Cambridge, UK: Cambridge University Press, 1960), 246.

34. George Nicholls, *A History of the Irish Poor Law: In Connexion with the Condition of the People* (London: John Murray, 1856), 97–98; *Evidence Taken Before Her Majesty's Commissioners of Inquiry into the State of the Law and Practice in Respect to the Occupation of Land in Ireland. Part III*, Command Papers 657 (Dublin: Alexander Thom, 1845) (hereafter *HC 1845 [657]*), 454; O'Brien, *Economic History of Ireland*, 43–45; Cormac Ó Gráda, *Ireland: A New Economic History, 1780–1939* (Oxford, UK: Clarendon Press, 1995), 97.

35. Colley, *Britons*, 150; John Moseley, *The Causes and Remedies for General Distress, and the Principles of an Equitable Adjustment, Impartially Discussed in a Letter to Sir W. Parker, Bart* (Bury, Suffolk: Gedge, Son, and Barker, 1830), 5; Edward Solly, *On Free Trade, in Relation to the Present Distress* (London: James Ridgeway, 1830), 6.

36. On Irish clubs and capital flight, see O'Brien, *Economic History of Ireland*, 454–462.

37. Peter Gray, *Famine, Land, and Politics: British Government and Irish Society, 1843–1850* (Dublin: Irish Academic Press, 1999), 7.

38. Joseph Lambert, *Observations on the Rural Affairs of Ireland, or, A Practical Treatise on Farming, Planting and Gardening: Adapted to the Circumstances, Resources, Soil and Climate of the Country* (Dublin: William Curry, 1829), 112–113; on falling commodity prices, see *Poor Inquiry (Ireland): Appendix (E) Containing Baronial Examinations Relative to Food, Cottages and Cabins, Clothing and Furniture, Pawnbroking and Savings' Banks, Drinking and Supplement Containing Answers to Questions 13 to 22 Circulated by the Commissioners*, Command Papers 37 (London: William Clowes and Sons, 1836), 31; *Condition of the Labouring Poor in Ireland and Application of Funds for Their Employment: Report from the Select Committee on the Employment of the Poor, Minutes of Evidence and Appendix*, Sessional Papers 561 (London: UK House of Commons, 1823) (hereafter *HC 1823 [561]*), 115; Louis M. Cullen, *Anglo-Irish Trade, 1660–1800* (Manchester: Manchester University Press, 1968), 120; Brian Gurrin, "Population and Emigration, 1730–1845," in *The Cambridge History of Ireland*, vol. 3, *1730–1880*, ed. James Kelly (Cambridge, UK: Cambridge University Press, 2018), 204–230; Hobsbawm, *Age of Revolution*, 11; Walford, *Famines of the World*, 110; John Pitt Kennedy, *Instruct, Employ, Don't Hang Them: Or, Ireland Tranquilized Without Soldiers and Enriched Without English*

Capital (London: Thomas and William Boone, 1835), 3; P. M. Austin Bourke, "The Use of the Potato Crop in Pre-famine Ireland," *Journal of the Statistical and Social Inquiry Society of Ireland* 21 (1967–1968): 81; Kane, *Industrial Resources*, 389; Henry D. Inglis, *A Journey Throughout Ireland, During the Spring, Summer, and Autumn of 1834* (London: Whittaker and Company, 1834), 1:131.

39. Karl Marx, *Capital*, vol. 1, trans. Ben Fowkes (London: Penguin, 2004), 860; E. R. R. Green, "Agriculture," in Edwards, Williams, and Ó Gráda, *Great Famine*, 99–101; Christine Kinealy, *A New History of Ireland*, updated ed. (Stroud, Gloucestershire: Sutton, 2004), 162; Chris Otter, *Diet for a Large Planet: Industrial Britain, Food Systems, and World Ecology* (Chicago: University of Chicago Press, 2020), 6; *HC 1823 (561)*, 162–164, 183, 189.

40. Horace Green, *On the Manufacture of Pettitt's Fish Guano* (London: A. Williams, 1853), 10; *Farmer's Magazine*, vol. 21, 1850, 146–49; *HC 1823 (561)*, 25; "Why Is There a Deficient Town Population in Ireland?" *Economist*, April 18, 1846, 499, The Economist Historical Archive (accessed October 19, 2021).

41. "Why Is There a Deficient Town Population in Ireland?"; John Workman, *The Fallacy of the Late Speeches in Parliament, in Support of Corn Laws, Exposed* (Belfast: Francis D. Finlay, 1815), 2; *HC 1836 (369)*, 426, 480; Cormac Ó Gráda, *The Great Irish Famine*, New Studies in Economic and Social History (Cambridge, UK: Cambridge University Press, 1995), 20–22; William Graydon, *Reflections on the State of Ireland in the Nineteenth Century* (London: J. Ridgway, 1825), 133.

42. *Correspondence Explanatory of Measures Adopted by H.M. Government for Relief of Distress Arising from Failure of Potato Crop in Ireland*, Command Papers 735 (London: William Clowes and Son, 1846), 4–5; on the structure of Irish trade, see Gray, *Famine, Land, and Politics*; Dutton, *Statistical Survey of the County Clare*, 67–69; Wakefield, *An Account of Ireland, Statistical and Political*, 1:747.

43. Lambert, *Observations on the Rural Affairs of Ireland*, 109; *HC 1836 (369)*, 360, 198; on drill planting, see Green, "Agriculture," 96; on cattle ranching, see *Poor Inquiry (Ireland). Appendix (D.) Containing Baronial Examinations Relative to Earnings of Labourers, Cottier Tenants, Employment of Women and Children, Expenditure; and Supplement, Containing Answers to Questions 1 to 12 Circulated by the Commissioners*, Command Papers 36 (London: W. Clowes and Sons, 1836).

44. *HC 1836 (369)*, 599–601; Kohl, *Travels in Ireland*, 123; *HC 1836 (369)*, 540–541; Asenath Nicholson, *Annals of the Famine in Ireland, in 1847, 1848, and 1849* (New York: E. French, 1851), 35; Lambert, *Observations on the Rural Affairs of Ireland*, 112–113; on the rise in subsistence crises, see Wakefield, *An Account of Ireland, Statistical and Political*, 2:727.

45. Inglis, *Journey Throughout Ireland*, 2:290–291; Kohl, *Travels in Ireland*; on Ireland's coach routes and train network, see McDowell, "Ireland on the Eve of the Famine," 16–17.

46. Friedrich Engels, *The Condition of the Working Class in England in 1844, with a Preface Written in 1892*, trans. Florence Kelley Wischnewetzky, reprint ed. (London: George Allen and Unwin, 1943), 90–92; Karl Marx and Friedrich Engels, *Ireland and the Irish Question: A Collection of Writings*, ed. L. I. Golman, V. E. Kunina, and R. Dixon, trans. Angela Clifford et al. (New York: International Publishers, 1972), 74–76; "Explosion of the Emancipation Bubble," *Leeds Times*, February 14, 1835, 2; John Maxwell, *Manual Labour versus Machinery; Exemplified in a Speech on Moving for a Committee of Parliamentary Inquiry into the Condition of Half-a-Million Hand-Loom Weavers . . . with an Appendix* (London: Cochrane and McCrone, 1834), 43–44; William Cobbett, *Selections from Cobbett's Political Works: Being a Complete Abridgment of the 100 Volumes Which Comprise the Writings of "Porcupine" and the "Weekly Political Register"; with Notes, Historical and Explanatory*, ed. John M. Cobbett and James P. Cobbett (London: Anne Cobbett, 1837), 780.

47. Kohl, *Travels in Ireland*, 48–49; *HC 1823 (561)*, 38–39.

48. Lambert, *Observations on the Rural Affairs of Ireland*, 191–193; Thomas Carlyle, *Chartism: By Thomas Carlyle* (London: James Fraser, 1840); John Wiggins, *The "Monster" Misery of Ireland: A Practical Treatise on the Relation of Landlord and Tenant, with Suggestions for Legislative Measures, and the Management of Landed Property, the Result of Above Thirty Years' Experience and Study of the Subject* (London: Richard Bentley, 1844), 90–91.

49. On steamships, see Kohl, *Travels in Ireland*, 166–167; on Smithfield and Irish pork, see J. C. Platt, "Smithfield," in *London*, ed. Charles Knight, vol. 2 (London: Charles Knight and Co., 1841), 321–322; the reference to "folios of bacon" is from Kohl, *Travels in Ireland*, 164.

50. Kohl, *Travels in Ireland*, 164; Kennedy, *Instruct, Employ, Don't Hang Them*, 23; see also Gray, *Famine, Land, and Politics*, 7; Tariq Omar Ali, *A*

Local History of Global Capital: Jute and Peasant Life in the Bengal Delta (Princeton, NJ: Princeton University Press, 2018), 31.

Chapter 2: Working for the Dead Horse

1. Evelyn Philip Shirley, *Lough Fea* (London: Chiswick Press, 1859), 3–20; John Bateman, *The Great Landowners of Great Britain and Ireland: A List of All Owners of Three Thousand Acres and Upwards, Worth £3,000 a Year; Also, One Thousand Three Hundred Owners of Two Thousand Acres and Upwards, in England, Scotland, Ireland & Wales, Their Acreage, and Income from Land, Culled from the Modern Domesday Book*, 4th ed. (London: Harrison and Sons, 1883), 406; for historical conversions of the pound, see "Relative Worth Comparators and Data Sets," MeasuringWorth, accessed January 30, 2024, www.measuringworth.com/index.php; "Purchase Power of the Pound," MeasuringWorth, accessed January 30, 2024, www.measuringworth.com/calculators/ukcompare.

2. Johann Georg Kohl, *Travels in Ireland* (London: Bruce and Wyld, 1844), 89; *Evidence Taken Before Her Majesty's Commissioners of Inquiry into the State of the Law and Practice in Respect to the Occupation of Land in Ireland. Part I*, Command Papers 606 (Dublin: Alexander Thom, 1845) (hereafter *HC 1845 [606]*), 925; William Steuart Trench, *Realities of Irish Life* (London: Longmans, Green, and Company, 1868), 65–66.

3. Tariq Omar Ali, *A Local History of Global Capital: Jute and Peasant Life in the Bengal Delta* (Princeton, NJ: Princeton University Press, 2018), 2.

4. R. B. McDowell, "Ireland on the Eve of the Famine," in *The Great Famine: Studies in Irish History, 1845–52*, ed. R. Dudley Edwards, T. Desmond Williams, and Cormac Ó Gráda, new ed. (Dublin: Lilliput Press, 1994), 7–8; *Evidence Taken Before Her Majesty's Commissioners of Inquiry into the State of the Law and Practice in Respect to the Occupation of Land in Ireland. Part II*, Command Papers 616 (Dublin: Alexander Thom, 1845) (hereafter *HC 1845 [616]*), 263–264; R. D. Collison Black, *Economic Thought and the Irish Question, 1817–1870* (Cambridge, UK: Cambridge University Press, 1960), 6; "The Tenure of Land in Ireland," *Times*, February 22, 1845, The Times Digital Archive (accessed September 14, 2021); P. M. Austin Bourke, "The Extent of the Potato Crop in Ireland at the Time of the Famine," *Journal of the Statistical and Social Inquiry Society of Ireland* 20 (1960): 7–11; P. M. Austin Bourke, "The Use of the Potato Crop in Pre-Famine Ireland," *Journal of the Statistical and Social Inquiry Society of*

Ireland 21 (1967–1968): 82–86; Arthur Young, *Arthur Young's Tour in Ireland (1776–1779)*, ed. Arthur Wollaston Hutton (London: George Bell and Sons, 1892), 1:456; "The Present State of Ireland," *Freeman's Journal*, October 14, 1847, British Library Newspapers (accessed October 20, 2021); E. R. R. Green, "Agriculture," in Edwards, Williams, and Ó Gráda, *Great Famine*, 89.

5. David Cannadine, *The Decline and Fall of the British Aristocracy* (New Haven, CT: Yale University Press, 1990), 9; M. J. Daunton, "'Gentlemanly Capitalism' and British Industry, 1820–1914," *Past and Present*, no. 122 (1989): 119–158; John Wiggins, *The "Monster" Misery of Ireland: A Practical Treatise on the Relation of Landlord and Tenant, with Suggestions for Legislative Measures, and the Management of Landed Property, the Result of Above Thirty Years' Experience and Study of the Subject* (London: Richard Bentley, 1844), 54–55; Maria Edgeworth, *Castle Rackrent: An Hibernian Tale, Taken from Facts, and from the Manner of the Irish Squires Before the Year 1782* (London: R. Hunter, 1828), 23.

6. James Hack Tuke, *A Visit to Connaught in the Autumn of 1847: A Letter Addressed to the Central Relief Committee of the Society of Friends, Dublin*, 2nd ed. (London: Charles Gilpin, 1848), 6; *Correspondence Explanatory of Measures Adopted by H.M. Government for Relief of Distress Arising from Failure of Potato Crop in Ireland*, Command Papers 735 (London: William Clowes and Son, 1846), 109–110; Bourke, "The Use of the Potato Crop in Pre-Famine Ireland," 81; on wage rates, see *First Report from His Majesty's Commissioners for Inquiring into the Condition of the Poorer Classes in Ireland, with Appendix (A.) and Supplement*, Sessional Papers 369 (London: House of Commons, 1836) (hereafter *HC 1836 [369]*), 161.

7. *HC 1845 (606)*, 105–106; *Evidence Taken Before Her Majesty's Commissioners of Inquiry into the State of the Law and Practice in Respect to the Occupation of Land in Ireland. Part III*, Command Papers 657 (Dublin: Alexander Thom, 1845) (hereafter *HC 1845 [657]*), 888–889; Cormac Ó Gráda, *Ireland: A New Economic History, 1780–1939* (Oxford, UK: Clarendon Press, 1995), 31; historical conversions of value from "Relative Worth Comparators and Data Sets."

8. *HC 1845 (606)*, 384, 241–242; Thomas Campbell Foster, *Letters on the Condition of the People of Ireland* (London: Chapman and Hall, 1846), 435.

9. "Ireland," *Times*, November 14, 1829, 3, The Times Digital Archive (accessed September 8, 2021); "Ireland," *Times*, March 28, 1844, 6, The Times Digital Archive (accessed September 11, 2021).

10. *HC 1836 (369)*, 515.

11. "Ireland," *Times*, November 14, 1829, 3, The Times Digital Archive (accessed September 8, 2021); "To the Editor of The Times," *Times*, October 29, 1832, 7, The Times Digital Archive (accessed November 11, 2021); *HC 1845 (657)*, 279; *Report from the Select Committee of the House of Lords on the State of Agriculture in England and Wales; with Minutes of Evidence, Appendix and Index*, Sessional Papers 464 (London: House of Lords, 1837) (hereafter *HL 1837 [464]*), 30; *HC 1845 (606)*, 225; *Poor Inquiry (Ireland): Appendix (F)—Contains Baronial Examinations Relative to Con Acre, Quarter, or Score Ground, Small Tenantry, Consolidation of Farms and Dislodged Tenantry, Emigration, Landlord and Tenant, Nature and State of Agriculture, Taxation, Roads, Observations on the Nature and State of Agriculture, and Supplement, Contains Answers to the Questions Circulated by the Commissioners*, Command Papers 38 (London: W. Clowes and Sons, 1836) (hereafter *HC 1836 [38]*), 19.

12. *Bradford Observer*, June 22, 1843, 4, British Library Newspapers (accessed October 28, 2021); *Times*, April 25, 1842, 5, The Times Digital Archive (accessed September 14, 2021); "Ireland," *Times*, March 29, 1844, 6, The Times Digital Archive (accessed September 14, 2021); *HC 1836 (369)*, 304.

13. *HC 1845 (657)*, 780, 119, 396; "Ireland," *Morning Post*, April 23, 1841, 6, British Library Newspapers (accessed October 28, 2021). See also Cormac Ó Gráda, *The Great Irish Famine*, New Studies in Economic and Social History (Cambridge, UK: Cambridge University Press, 1995), 20; E. R. R. Green, "Agriculture," in Edwards, Williams, and Ó Gráda, *Great Famine*, 95.

14. "The Hiring-Market," Schools' Collection, National Folklore Collection, University College Dublin (hereafter Schools' Collection), vol. 0975, pp. 102–103, 135; *Poor Inquiry (Ireland). Appendix (D.) Containing Baronial Examinations Relative to Earnings of Labourers, Cottier Tenants, Employment of Women and Children, Expenditure; and Supplement, Containing Answers to Questions 1 to 12 Circulated by the Commissioners*, Command Papers 36 (London: W. Clowes and Sons, 1836) (hereafter *HC 1836 [36]*), 25; "Ireland," *Morning Post*, January 24, 1838, 5, British Library Newspapers (accessed September 23, 2021); "Ireland," *Morning Post*, January 24, 1838, 5, British Library Newspapers (accessed September 23, 2021); *Poor Inquiry (Ireland): Appendix (C)—Parts I and II—Part I: Reports on the State of the Poor, and on the Charitable Institutions in Some of the Principal Towns, with Supplement Containing Answers to Queries—Part II: Report on*

the City of Dublin, Command Papers 35 (London: House of Commons, 1836) (hereafter *HC 1836 [35]*), 35, 86; George O'Brien, *The Economic History of Ireland from the Union to the Famine* (London: Longmans, Green and Company, 1921), 387; *HC 1845 (616)*, 747.

15. *HC 1836 (35)*, 31–32; *HC 1845 (616)*, 747; *HC 1836 (35)*, Part II, 8.

16. Hely Dutton, *Statistical Survey of the County of Clare, with Observations on the Means of Improvement* (Dublin: Graisberry and Campbell, 1808), 298–299; *HC 1845 (657)*, 486; Wiggins, *"Monster" Misery of Ireland*, 21–23; see also L. M. Cullen, "Irish History Without the Potato," *Past and Present* 40, no. 1 (1968): 81.

17. Jonathan Pim, *Observations upon Certain Evils Arising Out of the Present State of the Laws of Real Property in Ireland and Suggestions for Remedying the Same* (Dublin: Alexander Thom, 1847), 20; *HC 1836 (369)*, 434; Foster, *Letters on the Condition of the People of Ireland*, 104–105; *HC 1836 (369)*, 379–380, 428–429.

18. "Buying and Selling," Schools' Collection, vol. 0638, p. 57; "Buying and Selling," Schools' Collection, vol. 0294, p. 50; *HC 1845 (616)*, 238; *HC 1845 (606)*, 340; Foster, *Letters on the Condition of the People of Ireland*, 308.

19. *HC 1845 (606)*, 345–346; *HC 1836 (369)*, 357–358; on the loan fund, see Tyler Beck Goodspeed, *Famine and Finance: Credit and the Great Famine of Ireland* (London: Palgrave Macmillan, 2018).

20. "Buying and Selling," Schools' Collection, vol. 0318, p. 179; see also "The Condition of the People of Ireland," *Times*, October 7, 1845, 6, The Times Digital Archive (accessed November 11, 2021); Foster, *Letters on the Condition of the People of Ireland*, 238, 307–308; "Money Lenders," Schools' Collection, vol. 1112, p. 415; *HC 1836 (369)*, 457, 360–361.

21. *HC 1836 (369)*, 397; *HC 1845 (606)*, 85–86; *Condition of the Labouring Poor in Ireland and Application of Funds for Their Employment: Report from the Select Committee on the Employment of the Poor, Minutes of Evidence and Appendix*, Sessional Papers 561 (London: House of Commons, 1823), 140; *HL 1837 (464)*, 360; *HC 1836 (369)*, 379–380.

22. *HC 1836 (369)*, 401; *HC 1836 (36)*, 65–66.

23. "To the Editor of The Times," *Times*, October 29, 1832, 7, The Times Digital Archive (accessed November 11, 2021).

24. Tadhg Foley, *Death by Discourse?: Political Economy and the Great Irish Famine*, Famine Folio Series (Hamden, CT: Ireland's Great Hunger Museum, Quinnipiac University, 2016).

25. Adam Smith, *An Inquiry into the Nature and Causes of the Wealth of Nations* (London: Strahan and Cadell, 1776), 1:28–29.

26. George Poulett Scrope, *Letters to the Right Hon. Lord John Russell, on the Expediency of Enlarging the Irish Poor-Law to the Full Extent of the Poor-Law of England* (London: James Ridgway, 1846), 9–10; Nassau William Senior, *Journals, Conversations and Essays Relating to Ireland* (London: Longmans, Green, and Company, 1868), 1:58; Foster, *Letters on the Condition of the People of Ireland*, 115; Henry D. Inglis, *A Journey Throughout Ireland, During the Spring, Summer, and Autumn of 1834* (London: Whittaker and Company, 1834), 1:155–156; on debt, see David Graeber, *Debt: The First 5,000 Years*, rev. ed. (London: Melville House, 2014), 34–41.

27. "The Real Grievance of Ireland," *Manchester Guardian*, February 24, 1844; William Cobbett, *Cottage Economy: Containing Information Relative to the Brewing of Beer, Making of Bread, Keeping of Cows, Pigs, Bees, Ewes, Goats, Poultry and Rabbits, and Relative to Other Matters Deemed Useful in the Conducting of the Affairs of a Labourer's Family*, 1st American ed., from the 1st London ed. (New York: Stephen Gould and Son, 1824), 37.

28. Kohl, *Travels in Ireland*, 86–88.

29. Mary Leadbeater, *Cottage Dialogues among the Irish Peasantry, with Notes and a Preface by Maria Edgeworth*, ed. Maria Edgeworth (London: J. Johnson and Co., 1811), 299; Robert Scally, *The End of Hidden Ireland: Rebellion, Famine, and Emigration* (Oxford, UK: Oxford University Press, 1995), 95; Joel Mokyr, *Why Ireland Starved: A Quantitative and Analytical History of the Irish Economy, 1800–1850*, new ed. (London: Routledge, 2016), 144; "Ireland," *Times*, January 9, 1822, 2, The Times Digital Archive (accessed November 12, 2021); "Ireland," *Lancaster Gazetter*, June 19, 1841, British Library Newspapers (accessed October 15, 2021).

30. "Ireland," *Examiner*, June 10, 1843, British Library Newspapers (accessed November 2, 2021); HC 1845 (657), 372; HC 1836 (369), 420; Senior, *Journals, Conversations and Essays*, 1:42–43; Charles Buller, *Abstract Return of Number of Persons Committed for Trial in Ireland, 1844–45; Return of Outrages Reported to Constabulary Office in Ireland, 1842–45*, Sessional Papers 217 (London: House of Commons, 1846), 1–5.

31. On rental income, see Bateman, *Great Landowners of Great Britain and Ireland*, 189.

32. Bateman, *Great Landowners of Great Britain and Ireland*, 208; *HC 1845 (616)*, Supplement, 72–73.

33. *HC 1836 (369)*, 386.

34. *Berkshire Chronicle*, September 1, 1832, 1, British Library Newspapers (accessed October 13, 2021); *Morning Chronicle*, January 21, 1833, British Library Newspapers (accessed October 13, 2021).

35. McDowell, "Ireland on the Eve of the Famine," 26–30.

36. Anthony Trollope, *The Way We Live Now* (London: Chapman and Hall, 1875), 2:85.

37. Leadbeater, *Cottage Dialogues*, 270; Foster, *Letters on the Condition of the People of Ireland*, 17–18, 306; Robert Alexander Shafto Adair, *The Winter of 1846–7 in Antrim: With Remarks on Out-Door Relief and Colonization* (London: James Ridgway, 1847), 50–51; Francis Barker and John Cheyne, *An Account of the Rise, Progress, and Decline of the Fever Lately Epidemical in Ireland* (London: Baldwin, Cradock, and Joy, 1821), 41.

38. *HC 1836 (369)*, 402–404; Cornelius Walford, *The Famines of the World: Past and Present* (London: Edward Stanford, 1879), 15–16; Jonny Geber, "Skeletal Manifestations of Stress in Child Victims of the Great Irish Famine (1845–1852): Prevalence of Enamel Hypoplasia, Harris Lines, and Growth Retardation," *American Journal of Physical Anthropology* 155, no. 1 (2014): 151.

39. Asenath Nicholson, *Annals of the Famine in Ireland, in 1847, 1848, and 1849* (New York: E. French, 1851), 35; William Butler Yeats, *Fairy and Folk Tales of the Irish Peasantry* (London: Walter Scott, 1888), 81; Leland L. Duncan, "Folklore Gleanings from County Leitrim," *Folklore* 4, no. 2 (1893): 183; William George Black, *Folk-Medicine: A Chapter in the History of Culture* (London: Folk-lore Society, 1883), 30–31; *HC 1836 (369)*, 373; see also George Nicholls, *Poor Laws—Ireland: Three Reports by George Nicholls, Esq. to Her Majesty's Principal Secretary of State for the Home Department* (London: W. Clowes and Sons, 1838), 16; O'Brien, *Economic History of Ireland*, 232; "Potatoes," Schools' Collection, vol. 0108, pp. 18–20; George Shaw-Lefevre Baron Eversley, *Peel and O'Connell: A Review of the Irish Policy of Parliament from the Act of Union to the Death of Sir Robert Peel* (London: Kegan Paul, Trench and Company, 1887), 258; *Poor Inquiry (Ireland): Appendix (E) Containing Baronial Examinations Relative to Food, Cottages and Cabins, Clothing and Furniture, Pawnbroking and Savings' Banks, Drinking and Supplement Containing Answers to*

Questions 13 to 22 Circulated by the Commissioners, Command Papers 37 (London: William Clowes and Sons, 1836), 16; William Robert Wilde, "The Food of the Irish," *Dublin University Magazine* 43, no. 254 (1854): 30–31.

40. *HC 1836 (38)*, 370; Barker and Cheyne, *An Account of the Rise, Progress, and Decline*, 35, 40–41; *HC 1836 (369)*, 161, 379, 624; William Thomas Thornton, *Over-Population, and Its Remedy: Or, An Inquiry into the Extent and Causes of the Distress Prevailing Among the Labouring Classes of the British Islands, and into the Means of Remedying It* (London: Longman, Brown, Green, and Longmans, 1846), 92–93.

41. *HC 1836 (369)*, 548–549, 676–677; Denis Charles O'Connor, *Seventeen Years' Experience of Workhouse Life* (Dublin: McGlashan and Gill, 1861), 9; *HC 1836 (369)*, 497.

42. *HC 1836 (369)*, 689, 659–660, 517.

43. *HC 1836 (369)*, 635; *Dublin Review*, vol. 29 (London: Thomas Richardson and Co., 1850), 352; Barker and Cheyne, *An Account of the Rise, Progress, and Decline*, 139; Hack Tuke, *A Visit to Connaught in the Autumn of 1847*, 6; James M. Bergquist, *Daily Life in Immigrant America, 1820–1870* (Westport, CT: Greenwood Publishing Group, 2008), 66; Wilde, "Food of the Irish," 129.

44. Nicholls, *Poor Laws—Ireland, Three Reports*, 91–92; on hiring fairs, see Thomas Walter Freeman, *Pre-Famine Ireland: A Study in Historical Geography* (Manchester, UK: Manchester University Press, 1957); for the lyrics reproduced in full, see "An Irish Wedding," *Dublin University Magazine*, September 1862.

45. Barker and Cheyne, *An Account of the Rise, Progress, and Decline*, 15, 301.

46. Barker and Cheyne, *An Account of the Rise, Progress, and Decline*, 60–64, 299–300; William Harty, *An Historic Sketch of the Causes, Progress, Extent, and Mortality of the Contagious Fever Epidemic in Ireland During the Years 1817, 1818, and 1819. With . . . Tables, Etc.* (Dublin: Hodges and McArthur, 1820), 10–21.

47. *HC 1836 (369)*, 287, 303.

48. *Correspondence and Accounts Relating to Occasions on Which Measures Were Taken for Relief of People Suffering from Scarcity in Ireland*, Command Papers 734 (London: William Clowes and Son, 1846), 5.

49. Edmund Burke, *Thoughts and Details on Scarcity: Originally Presented to the Right Hon. William Pitt, in the Month of November, 1795*

(London: F. and C. Rivington, 1800), 6; Joseph Townsend, *A Disserta-
tion on the Poor Laws*, reprint ed. (London: Ridgways, 1817), 13; see also
William Blackstone, *Commentaries on the Laws of England*, ed. William
Carey Jones (San Francisco: Bancroft-Whitney, 1915), 500; Thornton,
Over-Population, and Its Remedy, 206–208.

50. Townsend, *Dissertation on the Poor Laws*, 16; *Report from the Select
Committee on Labourers' Wages* (London: House of Commons, 1824), 4;
Harriet Martineau, *The Moral of Many Fables*, Illustrations of Political
Economy 15 (London: Charles Fox, 1834), 82–84; *Times*, September 22,
1846.

51. Thomas Robert Malthus, *Essay on the Principle of Population, as It
Affects the Future Improvement of Society with Remarks on the Speculations of
Mr. Godwin, M. Condorcet, and Other Writers* (London: J. Johnson, 1798);
Thomas Robert Malthus, "Newenham and Others on the State of Ireland,"
Edinburgh Review 12 (1808): 343; see also Ellen Meiksins Wood, *Empire of
Capital* (London: Verso, 2003), 19; Black, *Economic Thought and the Irish
Question*, 86–89.

52. Nicholls, *Poor Laws—Ireland, Three Reports*, 70–71, 5, 24–26.

53. Nicholls, *Poor Laws—Ireland, Three Reports*, 16; *Poor Inquiry (Ire-
land). Appendix (H), Part. 2. Remarks on the Evidence Taken in the Poor
Inquiry (Ireland), Contained in the Appendices (D.) (E.) (F.) by One of the
Commissioners*, Sessional Papers 42 (London: House of Commons, 1836),
5–6; see also David P. Nally, *Human Encumbrances: Political Violence
and the Great Irish Famine* (Notre Dame, IN: University of Notre Dame
Press, 2011), 109–111; Black, *Economic Thought and the Irish Question*, 33;
O'Brien, *Economic History of Ireland*, 192; Philip Harling, "Sugar Wars:
The Culture of Free Trade Versus the Culture of Anti-Slavery in Britain
and the British Caribbean, 1840–1850," in *The Cultural Construction of the
British World*, ed. Barry Crosbie and Mark Hampton (Manchester, UK:
Manchester University Press, 2015), 63; Burke, *Thoughts and Details on
Scarcity*, 32.

54. Frank M. Snowden, *Naples in the Time of Cholera, 1884–1911*
(Cambridge, UK: Cambridge University Press, 1995), 17; Mike Davis,
Planet of Slums (London: Verso, 2006), 175–183; on slums, see also June
Nash, "Global Integration and Subsistence Insecurity," *American Anthro-
pologist* 96, no. 1 (1994): 7–30; on the demography of Irish poverty, see
Cecil Woodham-Smith, *The Great Hunger: Ireland, 1845–1849*, reissue ed.
(London: Penguin, 1992), 165; on the "upper hand," see *HC 1845 (606)*.

Chapter 3: The People's Potato

1. For estimates of potato consumption in Europe and Britain, see *Report of the Committee of the Board of Agriculture, Appointed to Extract Information from the County Reports, and Other Authorities, Concerning the Culture and Use of Potatoes* (London: George Nicol, 1795), 71; John Chalmers Morton, ed., *A Cyclopedia of Agriculture, Practical and Scientific: In Which the Theory, the Art, and the Business of Farming Are Thoroughly and Practically Treated*, vol. 2 (Glasgow: Blackie and Son, 1855), 686; Timothy J. Meagher, *The Columbia Guide to Irish American History* (New York: Columbia University Press, 2005), 65–66. Among numerous examples of sources that refer to very large portions of potatoes in Ireland, see William Williams, *Tourism, Landscape, and the Irish Character: British Travel Writers in Pre-Famine Ireland* (Madison: University of Wisconsin Press, 2012), 97; James H. Murphy, *Irish Novelists and the Victorian Age* (Oxford, UK: Oxford University Press, 2011), 119; Mark Bittman, *Animal, Vegetable, Junk: A History of Food, from Sustainable to Suicidal* (New York: Houghton Mifflin Harcourt, 2021), 53; Leslie Clarkson and Margaret Crawford, *Feast and Famine: Food and Nutrition in Ireland, 1500–1920* (Oxford, UK: Oxford University Press, 2001), 93; Jean Beagle Ristaino, "Tracking Historic Migrations of the Irish Potato Famine Pathogen, Phytophthora infestans," *Microbes and Infection* 4, no. 13 (November 1, 2002): 1369; Thomas Edward Jordan, *Ireland's Children: Quality of Life, Stress, and Child Development in the Famine Era* (Westport, CT: Greenwood Press, 1998), 35; Rick Steves and Patrick O'Connor, *Rick Steves Ireland* (New York: Avalon, 2016), 361. For early versions of the twelve-to-fourteen-pounds figure, see *Poor Inquiry (Ireland): Appendix (E) Containing Baronial Examinations Relative to Food, Cottages and Cabins, Clothing and Furniture, Pawnbroking and Savings' Banks, Drinking and Supplement Containing Answers to Questions 13 to 22 Circulated by the Commissioners*, Command Papers 37 (London: William Clowes and Sons, 1836) (hereafter *HC 1836 [37]*), 31; *First Report from His Majesty's Commissioners for Inquiring into the Condition of the Poorer Classes in Ireland, with Appendix (A.) and Supplement*, Sessional Papers 369 (London: House of Commons, 1836) (hereafter *HC 1836 [369]*), 429; Isaac Weld, *Statistical Survey of the County of Roscommon, Drawn Up Under the Directions of the Royal Dublin Society* (Dublin: R. Graisberry, 1832), 429. For more plausible estimates of Irish potato consumption, see *Poor Inquiry (Ireland). Appendix (H), Part 2. Remarks on the Evidence Taken in the Poor Inquiry (Ireland), Contained in the Appendices*

(D.) (E.) (F.) by One of the Commissioners, Sessional Papers 42 (London: House of Commons, 1836) (hereafter *HC 1836 [42]*), 11; Edward Gibbon Wakefield, *An Account of Ireland, Statistical and Political: In Two Volumes* (London: Longman, Hurst, Rees, Orme, and Brown, 1812), 2:714–715; Morton, *Cyclopedia of Agriculture*, 2:2:686. For an example of the largest figures quoted as authoritative, see Wakefield, *An Account of Ireland, Statistical and Political*, 2:714–715. On speculation on potato nutrition, see *Substances Used as Food, as Exemplified in the Great Exhibition* (London: Society for Promoting Christian Knowledge, 1853), 297.

2. J. L. W. Thudichum, "The Diseases of Plants, with Special Regard to Agriculture and Forestry," *Journal of the Royal Society of Arts* 35, no. 1815 (1887): 904.

3. *Report . . . Culture and Use of Potatoes*, 71; Morton, *Cyclopedia of Agriculture*, 2:686; Meagher, *Columbia Guide to Irish American History*, 65–66. On Irish physical adaptation to the potato, see Charles Edward Trevelyan, *The Irish Crisis: Being a Narrative of the Measures for the Relief of the Distress Caused by the Great Irish Famine of 1846–7* (London: Macmillan, 1880), 143; see also Jordanna Bailkin, "The Boot and the Spleen: When Was Murder Possible in British India?," *Comparative Studies in Society and History* 48, no. 2 (April 2006): 462–493.

4. Hely Dutton, *Statistical Survey of the County of Clare, with Observations on the Means of Improvement* (Dublin: Graisberry and Campbell, 1808), 178–179; Robert Kane, *The Industrial Resources of Ireland* (Dublin: Hodges and Smith, 1844), 242; K. H. Connell, *The Population of Ireland, 1750–1845*, reprint ed. (Westport, CT: Greenwood Press, 1975), 155. The anthropologist Anna Lowenhaupt Tsing explores the phenomenon of crops both inside and outside capitalism, *The Mushroom at the End of the World: On the Possibility of Life in Capitalist Ruins* (Princeton, NJ: Princeton University Press, 2015).

5. On the history of the use of straw and rushes, see Anne O'Dowd, *Straw, Hay and Rushes in Irish Folk Tradition* (Sallins, Co. Kildare, Ireland: Irish Academic Press, 2022); on the potato as staple, see K. H. Connell, "The Potato in Ireland," *Past and Present* 23, no. 1 (1962): 63.

6. John Ramsay McCulloch, *The Principles of Political Economy: With Some Inquiries Respecting Their Application, and a Sketch of the Rise and Progress of the Science*, 4th ed. (Edinburgh: Adam and Charles Black, 1849), 403–404; James F. W. Johnston, *Notes on North America, Agricultural, Economical, and Social* (Edinburgh: William Blackwood and Sons, 1851),

1:79–80; George Pinckard, *Notes on the West Indies: Written During the Expedition Under the Command of the Late General Sir Ralph Abercromby: Including Observations on the Island of Barbadoes, and the Settlements Captured by the British Troops, Upon the Coast of Guiana; Likewise Remarks Relating to the Creoles and Slaves of the Western Colonies, and the Indians of South America: With Occasional Hints, Regarding the Seasoning, or Yellow Fever of Hot Climates*, vol. 2 (London: Longman, Hurst, Rees, and Orme, 1806), 428; *Museum of Foreign Literature and Science*, vol. 15 (Philadelphia: E. Littell and Brother, 1829), 469.

7. Rebecca Earle, *Feeding the People: The Politics of the Potato* (Cambridge, UK: Cambridge University Press, 2020), 27–52; James C. Scott, *Against the Grain: A Deep History of the Earliest States* (New Haven, CT: Yale University Press, 2017), 22.

8. Joseph Sabine, "On the Native Country of the Wild Potatoe, with an Account of Its Culture in the Garden of the Horticultural Society; and Observations on the Importance of Obtaining Improved Varieties of the Cultivated Plant, Read November 19, 1822," *Transactions of the Horticultural Society of London* 5 (1824): 257–259; Adam Smith, *The Wealth of Nations, Books 1–3*, ed. Andrew Skinner (London: Penguin Classics, 1986), 1:264–265; John E. Davies, "Giffen Goods, the Survival Imperative, and the Irish Potato Culture," *Journal of Political Economy* 102, no. 3 (1994): 547–565; William H. McNeill, "How the Potato Changed the World's History," *Social Research* 66, no. 1 (1999): 71; John Ramsay McCulloch, *A Dictionary, Practical, Theoretical, and Historical, of Commerce and Commercial Navigation: Illustrated with Maps and Plans*, new ed. (London: Longman, Orme, Brown, Green, and Longmans, 1838), 938–939.

9. *HC 1836 (37)*, 24–29; *HC 1836 (369)*, 667–668; "The Famine," Schools' Collection, National Folklore Collection, University College Dublin (hereafter Schools' Collection), vol. 0608, p. 564; Henry D. Inglis, *A Journey Throughout Ireland, During the Spring, Summer, and Autumn of 1834* (London: Whittaker and Company, 1834), 2:194–195; William Robert Wilde, "The Food of the Irish," *Dublin University Magazine* 43, no. 254 (1854): 130–131. On water with pepper, see Thomas Campbell Foster, *Letters on the Condition of the People of Ireland* (London: Chapman and Hall, 1846), 105. Cormac Ó Gráda, *Famine: A Short History* (Princeton, NJ: Princeton University Press, 2010), 77; L. M. Cullen, "Irish History Without the Potato," *Past and Present* 40, no. 1 (1968): 77; John O'Rourke, *The History of the Great Irish Famine of 1847: With Notices of Earlier Irish*

Famines (Dublin: McGlashan and Gill, 1875), 27–30; *Times*, July 25, 1840, 5, The Times Digital Archive (accessed September 14, 2021); P. M. Austin Bourke, "The Use of the Potato Crop in Pre-Famine Ireland," *Journal of the Statistical and Social Inquiry Society of Ireland* 21 (1967–1968): 78–80.

10. William Maunsell, *Letters to the Right Honourable and Honourable the Dublin Society, on the Culture of the Potatoes from the Shoots* (Dublin: William Sleater, 1794), 14–16; *The Farmer's Guide, Compiled for the Use of the Small Farmers and Cotter Tenantry of Ireland*, 2nd ed. (Dublin: Alexander Thom, 1842), 91; *An Account of the Culture of Potatoes in Ireland* (London: Shepperson and Reynolds, 1796), 28.

11. Maunsell, *Culture of Potatoes from the Shoots*, 11; for lists of early nineteenth-century potato cultivars, see *Report . . . Culture and Use of Potatoes*, 1–4; Roger J. McHugh, "The Famine in Irish Oral Tradition," in *The Great Famine: Studies in Irish History, 1845–52*, ed. R. Dudley Edwards, T. Desmond Williams, and Cormac Ó Gráda, new ed. (Dublin: Lilliput Press, 1994), 391–393.

12. *HC 1836 (42)*, 10; R. Barry O'Brien, *Thomas Drummond, Under-Secretary in Ireland, 1835–40, Life and Letters* (London: Kegan Paul, Trench and Company, 1889), 208; Warren H. R. Jackson, *An Address to the Honorable the Members of the House of Commons, on the Landlord and Tenant Question* (Cork: George Purcell and Co., 1848), 6–7; Charles Edward Trevelyan, *The Irish Crisis* (London: Longman, Brown, Green, and Longmans, 1848), 6.

13. See P. M. Austin Bourke, "The Extent of the Potato Crop in Ireland at the Time of the Famine," *Journal of the Statistical and Social Inquiry Society of Ireland* 20 (1960): 7–11; Joseph Decaisne, *Histoire de la maladie des pommes de terre en 1845* (Paris: Librarie agricole de Dusacq, 1846), 85–87; Brian J. Haas et al., "Genome Sequence and Analysis of the Irish Potato Famine Pathogen *Phytophthora Infestans*," *Nature* 461, no. 7262 (September 2009): 393–398.

14. Dutton, *Statistical Survey of the County Clare*, 43; *Poor Inquiry (Ireland): Appendix (F)—Contains Baronial Examinations Relative to Con Acre, Quarter, or Score Ground, Small Tenantry, Consolidation of Farms and Dislodged Tenantry, Emigration, Landlord and Tenant, Nature and State of Agriculture, Taxation, Roads, Observations on the Nature and State of Agriculture, and Supplement, Contains Answers to the Questions Circulated by the Commissioners*, Command Papers 38 (London: W. Clowes and Sons, 1836) (hereafter *HC 1836 [38]*), 323, 272; Robert Fraser, *Statistical Survey*

of the County of Wexford: Drawn Up for the Consideration, and by Order of the Dublin Society (Dublin: Graisberry and Campbell, 1807), 98–99; "On Raising Potatoes from Seed," *Irish Farmer's and Gardener's Magazine and Register of Rural Affairs* 1, no. 9 (July 1834): 429–430; David Ferguson, "Remarks on the Potato Plant," *Farmer's Magazine*, Old series, 39, no. 3 (September 1853): 226–228.

15. *An Account of the Culture of Potatoes in Ireland*, 26; Wilde, "Food of the Irish," 127–128; on religion and the planting calendar, see David W. Miller, "Irish Catholicism and the Great Famine," *Journal of Social History* 9, no. 1 (1975): 90–91; Redcliffe N. Salaman, *The History and Social Influence of the Potato*, ed. J. G. Hawkes, rev. ed. (Cambridge, UK: Cambridge University Press, 1985), 117.

16. *Farmer's Guide*, 91–92; *An Account of the Culture of Potatoes in Ireland*, 13–14, 17–18; "Potatoes," Schools' Collection, vol. 0108, pp. 18–20; Wakefield, *An Account of Ireland, Statistical and Political*, 1:360–363; Dutton, *Statistical Survey of the County Clare*, 36–39; on lazy-beds, see *Report . . . Culture and Use of Potatoes*, 23–39; Joseph Lambert, *Observations on the Rural Affairs of Ireland, Or, A Practical Treatise on Farming, Planting and Gardening: Adapted to the Circumstances, Resources, Soil and Climate of the Country* (Dublin: William Curry, 1829), 126–127; E. R. R. Green, "Agriculture," in Edwards, Williams, and Ó Gráda, *Great Famine*, 99–101.

17. Wakefield, *An Account of Ireland, Statistical and Political*, 1:360–363; Salaman, *History and Social Influence of the Potato*, 233; Dutton, *Statistical Survey of the County Clare*, 36–39; *HC 1836 (38)*, 401.

18. O'Rourke, *History of the Great Irish Famine of 1847*, 14–15; *An Account of the Culture of Potatoes in Ireland*, 27–28.

19. "Foods Long Ago," Schools' Collection, vol. 0278, p. 137; "How Bread was Made Long Ago," Schools' Collection, vol. 0278, p. 137; "How Bread was Made Long Ago," Schools' Collection, vol. 0022, p. 0260; Asenath Nicholson, *Ireland's Welcome to the Stranger: Or an Excursion Through Ireland, in 1844 & 1845, for the Purpose of Personally Investigating the Condition of the Poor* (London: Charles Gilpin, 1847), 218.

20. Wilde, "Food of the Irish," 127–128; McHugh, "The Famine in Irish Oral Tradition," 391–393; Kane, *Industrial Resources*, 381–382; Foster, *Letters on the Condition of the People of Ireland*, 271–272; Wakefield, *An Account of Ireland, Statistical and Political*, 2:716–717; *Report . . . Culture and Use of Potatoes*, 53–54.

21. Sabine, "On the Native Country of the Wild Potatoe," 257–259.

22. Robert Malcolmson and Stephanos Mastoris, *The English Pig: A History* (London: Hambledon Press, 1998), 45–48; *Evidence Taken Before Her Majesty's Commissioners of Inquiry into the State of the Law and Practice in Respect to the Occupation of Land in Ireland. Part I*, Command Papers 606 (Dublin: Alexander Thom, 1845), 36.

23. H. D. Richardson, *Pigs: Their Origin and Varieties, Management with a View to Profit, and General Treatment in Health and Disease* (London: William S. Orr and Company, 1847), 48; William Carleton, *Traits and Stories of the Irish Peasantry*, new ed. (London: Routledge, 1852), 409–411; William Youatt, *The Pig: A Treatise on the Breeds, Management, Feeding, and Medical Treatment of Swine; with Directions for Salting Pork, and Curing Bacon and Hams* (Philadelphia: Lea and Blanchard, 1847), 73–74; Lambert, *Observations on the Rural Affairs of Ireland*, 97; Richard Parkinson, *Treatise on the Breeding and Management of Live Stock*, vol. 2 (London: Cadell and Davies, 1810), 259.

24. Cullen, "Irish History without the Potato," 78; *Poor Inquiry (Ireland). Appendix (D.) Containing Baronial Examinations Relative to Earnings of Labourers, Cottier Tenants, Employment of Women and Children, Expenditure; and Supplement, Containing Answers to Questions 1 to 12 Circulated by the Commissioners*, Command Papers 36 (London: W. Clowes and Sons, 1836) (hereafter *HC 1836 [36]*), 84; Cormac Ó Gráda, *The Great Irish Famine*, New Studies in Economic and Social History (Cambridge, UK: Cambridge University Press, 1995), 17; Bourke, "The Use of the Potato Crop in Pre-Famine Ireland," 83–85.

25. Jamie Kreiner, *Legions of Pigs in the Early Medieval West* (New Haven, CT: Yale University Press, 2020), 31; Youatt, *The Pig*, 24; Wakefield, *An Account of Ireland, Statistical and Political*, 1:353–354; *HC 1836 (36)*, 88–89.

26. Martin Doyle, *A Cyclopædia of Practical Husbandry and Rural Affairs in General*, ed. W. Rham (London: Jeremiah How, 1844), 548; Charles Knight, *Cyclopædia of the Industry of All Nations* (London: Charles Knight, 1851), 1337; Youatt, *The Pig*, 73–74; William Charles Linnaeus Martin, *The Pig: Its General Management and Treatment* (London: George Routledge and Co., 1852), 56–61; John Gamgee, "The Prevalence and Prevention of Diseases Amongst Domestic Animals in Ireland," *Journal of the Royal Dublin Society* 4 (1866): 60.

27. Wakefield, *An Account of Ireland, Statistical and Political*, 1:353–354; Martin, *The Pig*, 20; Johann Georg Kohl, *Travels in Ireland* (London: Bruce

and Wyld, 1844), 50; Carleton, *Traits and Stories of the Irish Peasantry*, 411; Lambert, *Observations on the Rural Affairs of Ireland*, 98–99.

28. William Cobbett, *Cottage Economy: Containing Information Relative to the Brewing of Beer, Making of Bread, Keeping of Cows, Pigs, Bees, Ewes, Goats, Poultry and Rabbits, and Relative to Other Matters Deemed Useful in the Conducting of the Affairs of a Labourer's Family*, 1st American ed., from the 1st London ed. (New York: Stephen Gould and Son, 1824), 37; "Ireland," *Times*, September 27, 1845, 7, The Times Digital Archive (accessed November 12, 2021); Mary Leadbeater, *Cottage Dialogues Among the Irish Peasantry, with Notes and a Preface by Maria Edgeworth*, ed. Maria Edgeworth (London: J. Johnson and Co., 1811), 310–311.

29. Brett Mizelle, *Pig* (London: Reaktion Books, 2012), 116–119; for a version of the Dolocher ghost story, see Leitch Ritchie, *Ireland Picturesque and Romantic* (London: Longman, Rees, Orme, Brown, Green, and Longman, 1837).

30. Ireland Census Office, *Report of the Commissioners Appointed to Take the Census of Ireland, for the Year 1841* (Dublin: Alexander Thom, 1843), 539.

31. Gamgee, "Diseases Amongst Domestic Animals," 58–59; Chris Otter, *Diet for a Large Planet: Industrial Britain, Food Systems, and World Ecology* (Chicago: University of Chicago Press, 2020), 111.

32. B. Daniel, "Parasitical Diseases as Influenced by Cooking," *The Lancet* 70, no. 1782 (October 24, 1857): 415–416; Great Britain Parliament House of Commons, *Public Health Act: Report of the Medical Officer of the Privy Council for 1862*, Sessional Papers 161 (London: House of Commons, 1863) (hereafter *HC 1862 [161]*), 232; Gamgee, "Diseases Amongst Domestic Animals," 58–59.

33. Doyle, *A Cyclopædia of Practical Husbandry and Rural Affairs*, 549; *HC 1862 (161)*, 232; George Armatage, *Every Man His Own Cattle Doctor: With Copious Notes, Recipes, Etc. and Upwards of Three Hundred and Fifty Practical Illustrations, Showing Forms of Disease and Treatment* (New York: Orange Judd, 1882), 748–751; "A Few Words on Our Meat," *Once a Week*, October 16, 1863, 425–426.

34. Lorenzo Gitto et al., "Death Caused by a Domestic Pig Attack," *Forensic Science, Medicine and Pathology* 17, no. 3 (September 1, 2021): 469–474; Kreiner, *Legions of Pigs*, 43; Youatt, *The Pig*, 117; Martin, *The Pig*, 23.

35. Leadbeater, *Cottage Dialogues*, 2–3; Frederick Douglass, "The Liberator," March 27, 1846, Philip Foner, ed., *Life and Writings of Frederick Douglass*, vol. 1 (New York: International Publishers, 1950), 138.

36. Robert Jameson, ed., *Edinburgh New Philosophical Journal* (Edinburgh: Adam Black, 1831), 116–117; John Bateman, *The Great Landowners of Great Britain and Ireland: A List of All Owners of Three Thousand Acres and Upwards, Worth £3,000 a Year; Also, One Thousand Three Hundred Owners of Two Thousand Acres and Upwards, in England, Scotland, Ireland & Wales, Their Acreage, and Income from Land, Culled from the Modern Domesday Book*, 4th ed. (London: Harrison and Sons, 1883), 192.

37. On peatlands and folklore, see William Butler Yeats, *Fairy and Folk Tales of the Irish Peasantry* (London: Walter Scott, 1888), 81; John Feehan et al., *The Bogs of Ireland: An Introduction to the Natural, Cultural and Industrial Heritage of Irish Peatlands* (Dublin: University College Dublin, Environmental Institute, 1996), 169–170. On peat and the carbon cycle, see J. Leifeld and L. Menichetti, "The Underappreciated Potential of Peatlands in Global Climate Change Mitigation Strategies," *Nature Communications* 9, no. 1 (March 14, 2018): 1071; Andrea Hinwood and Clemencia Rodriguez, "Potential Health Impacts Associated with Peat Smoke: A Review," *Journal of the Royal Society of Western Australia* 88 (January 1, 2005): 133–138; David L. A. Gaveau et al., "Major Atmospheric Emissions from Peat Fires in Southeast Asia During Non-Drought Years: Evidence from the 2013 Sumatran Fires," *Scientific Reports* 4, no. 1 (August 19, 2014): 6112.

38. Caoimhín Ó Danachair, "Traditional Forms of the Dwelling House in Ireland," *Journal of the Royal Society of Antiquaries of Ireland* 102, no. 1 (1972): 77–96; Feehan et al., *Bogs of Ireland*, 7–17; Weld, *Statistical Survey of the County of Roscommon*, 316–18; Martin Doyle, *Hints for the Small Farmers of Ireland*, 4th ed. (Dublin: J. Charles, 1830), 16.

39. On peat-powered steamships, see Feehan et al., *Bogs of Ireland*, 76–77; on regional peat shortages, see Feehan et al., *Bogs of Ireland*, 7–8; Muiris O'Sullivan and Liam Downey, "Turf-Harvesting," *Archaeology Ireland* 30, no. 1 (2016): 31; Liam Kennedy, "'The People's Fuel': Turf in Ireland in the Nineteenth and Twentieth Centuries," *RCC Perspectives*, no. 2 (2013): 26–27.

40. Kohl, *Travels in Ireland*, 37; Feehan et al., *Bogs of Ireland*, 2; Kevin O'Neill, *Family and Farm in Pre-Famine Ireland: The Parish of Killashandra* (Madison: University of Wisconsin Press, 2003), 117.

41. On ancient pollen and particulate matter preserved in boglands, see Chunshui Lin et al., "Characterization of Primary Organic Aerosol from Domestic Wood, Peat, and Coal Burning in Ireland," *Environmental Science and Technology* 51, no. 18 (September 19, 2017): 10624–10632; Martin Novak et al., "A Comparison of Lead Pollution Record in Sphagnum Peat with Known Historical Pb Emission Rates in the British Isles and the Czech Republic," *Atmospheric Environment* 40, no. 42 (2008): 8997–9006; T. M. Mighall et al., "An Atmospheric Pollution History for Lead-Zinc Mining from the Ystwyth Valley, Dyfed, Mid-Wales, UK, as Recorded by an Upland Blanket Peat," *Geochemistry: Exploration, Environment, Analysis* 2, no. 2 (May 1, 2002): 175–184; on "bog people" found in Ireland, see Raghnall Ó Floinn, "Irish Bog Bodies," *Archaeology Ireland* 2, no. 3 (1988): 95; Feehan et al., *Bogs of Ireland*, 470–471.

42. Arthur Young, *Arthur Young's Tour in Ireland (1776–1779)*, ed. Arthur Wollaston Hutton (London: George Bell and Sons, 1892), 36.

43. James Fintan Lalor, *The Writings of James Fintan Lalor: With an Introduction Embodying Personal Recollections*, ed. John O'Leary (Dublin: T. G. O'Donoghue and Francis Nugent, 1895), 14; Nassau William Senior, *Journals, Conversations and Essays Relating to Ireland* (London: Longmans, Green, and Company, 1868), 1:18; see also David P. Nally, *Human Encumbrances: Political Violence and the Great Irish Famine* (Notre Dame, IN: University of Notre Dame Press, 2011), 86.

44. On folkloric accounts of plenty, see McHugh, "The Famine in Irish Oral Tradition," 395.

45. Robin Wall Kimmerer, "The Serviceberry: An Economy of Abundance," *Emergence Magazine*, October 26, 2022, https://emergencemagazine.org/essay/the-serviceberry/; on moral economies, see E. P. Thompson, "The Moral Economy of the English Crowd in the Eighteenth Century," *Past and Present*, no. 50 (1971): 131.

46. *HC 1836 (37)*, 24–29; *HC 1836 (369)*, 667–668; "The Famine," Schools' Collection, vol. 0608, p. 564; Inglis, *Journey Throughout Ireland*, 2:194–195; Wilde, "Food of the Irish," 130–131.

47. *HC 1836 (42)*, 11; *HC 1836 (369)*, 493; on gifts and the value of a "good name," see Robert Scally, *The End of Hidden Ireland: Rebellion, Famine, and Emigration* (Oxford, UK: Oxford University Press, 1995), 31.

48. Young, *Tour in Ireland*, 1:59–60; *HC 1836 (369)*, 393–394.

49. *HC 1836 (42)*, 5–6; Inglis, *Journey Throughout Ireland*, 1:129; Miller, "Irish Catholicism and the Great Famine," 86–87.

50. Robert Allan, *The Sportsman in Ireland, with His Summer Route Through the Highlands of Scotland* (London: Henry Colburn, 1840), 71; Young, *Tour in Ireland*, 2:120.

51. Foster, *Letters on the Condition of the People of Ireland*, 369; "Band-Begging or Straw Men," Schools' Collection, vol. 0229, p. 206; Young, *Tour in Ireland*, 1:446–447; Leadbeater, *Cottage Dialogues*, 277; "Wakes," Schools' Collection, vol. 0788, pp. 47–48; "The Origin of Tobacco at Wakes," Schools' Collection, vol. 0122, p. 329; Martin Doyle, *Irish Cottagers* (Dublin: William Curry Jr. and Co., 1830), 19.

52. Dutton, *Statistical Survey of the County Clare*, 179–180; *Farmer's Guide*, 169–170; on the circulation of clothing, see William Graydon, *Reflections on the State of Ireland in the Nineteenth Century* (London: J. Ridgway, 1825), 78; William E. Devlin, "Shrewd Irishmen: Irish Entrepreneurs and Artisans in New York's Clothing Industry, 1830–1880," in *The New York Irish*, ed. Ronald H. Bayor and Timothy Meagher, paperback ed. (Baltimore, MD: Johns Hopkins University Press, 1997), 170–172.

53 Quoted in Salaman, *History and Social Influence of the Potato*, 291; Tadhg Foley, *Death by Discourse?: Political Economy and the Great Irish Famine*, Famine Folio Series (Hamden, CT: Ireland's Great Hunger Museum, Quinnipiac University, 2016), 19.

54. *Farmer's Guide*, 95; *HC 1836 (38)*, 313; see also Salaman, *History and Social Influence of the Potato*, 288.

55. *Times*, September 22, 1846, The Times Digital Archive (accessed June 20, 2024); Asenath Nicholson, *Annals of the Famine in Ireland, in 1847, 1848, and 1849* (New York: E. French, 1851), 56.

56. Trevelyan, *The Irish Crisis* (1848 ed.), 2–9.

Chapter 4: Peel's Brimstone

1. *Correspondence Explanatory of Measures Adopted by H.M. Government for Relief of Distress Arising from Failure of Potato Crop in Ireland*, Command Papers 735 (London: William Clowes and Son, 1846) (hereafter *HC 1846 [735]*), 245; "Famine Times," Schools' Collection, National Folklore Collection, University College Dublin (hereafter Schools' Collection), vol. 0151, p. 374; William Robert Wilde, "The Food of the Irish," *Dublin University Magazine* 43, no. 254 (1854): 134.

2. M. Bergman, "The Potato Blight in the Netherlands and Its Social Consequences (1845–1847)," *International Review of Social History* 12, no. 3 (December 1967): 390–431; Esther Beeckaert Vanhaute Eric, "Whose

Famine?: Regional Differences in Vulnerability and Resilience During the 1840s Potato Famine in Belgium," in *An Economic History of Famine Resilience* (Abingdon, UK: Routledge, 2019).

3. V. K. Agarwal and James B. Sinclair, *Principles of Seed Pathology* (Boca Raton, FL: CRC Press, 1996), 467; Andrew F. Smith, *Potato: A Global History* (London: Reaktion Books, 2011), 51–52.

4. On the reproductive cycle of the blight mould, see William E. Fry and Stephen B. Goodwin, "Resurgence of the Irish Potato Famine Fungus," *BioScience* 47, no. 6 (1997): 363–371; on ecological invasions, see C. Dutech et al., "Multiple Introductions of Divergent Genetic Lineages in an Invasive Fungal Pathogen, *Cryphonectria parasitica*, in France," *Heredity* 105, no. 2 (August 2010): 220–228; Marie-Laure Desprez-Loustau et al., "The Fungal Dimension of Biological Invasions," *Trends in Ecology and Evolution* 22, no. 9 (September 1, 2007): 472–480; on the theory of a single lineage for the European pandemic, see S. B. Goodwin, B. A. Cohen, and W. E. Fry, "Panglobal Distribution of a Single Clonal Lineage of the Irish Potato Famine Fungus," *Proceedings of the National Academy of Sciences* 91, no. 24 (November 22, 1994): 11591–11595; Kentaro Yoshida et al., "The Rise and Fall of the *Phytophthora infestans* Lineage That Triggered the Irish Potato Famine," ed. David Baulcombe, *eLife* 2 (May 28, 2013): e00731; D. Andrivon, "The Origin of *Phytophthora infestans* Populations Present in Europe in the 1840s: A Critical Review of Historical and Scientific Evidence," *Plant Pathology* 45, no. 6 (1996): 1027–1035; Jean Beagle Ristaino, "Tracking Historic Migrations of the Irish Potato Famine Pathogen, Phytophthora infestans," *Microbes and Infection* 4, no. 13 (November 1, 2002): 1369–1377.

5. Ristaino, "Tracking Historic Migrations of the Irish Potato Famine Pathogen," 1371–1372; "Famine Times," Schools' Collection, vol. 0051, p. 231; John O'Rourke, *The History of the Great Irish Famine of 1847: With Notices of Earlier Irish Famines* (Dublin: McGlashan and Gill, 1875), 48.

6. See Edward D. Melillo, "The First Green Revolution: Debt Peonage and the Making of the Nitrogen Fertilizer Trade, 1840–1930," *American Historical Review* 117, no. 4 (October 1, 2012): 1028–1060; E. C. Large, *The Advance of the Fungi* (London: Jonathan Cape, 1946), 25–26; P. M. Austin Bourke, "The Extent of the Potato Crop in Ireland at the Time of the Famine," *Journal of the Statistical and Social Inquiry Society of Ireland* 20 (1960): 7–11; Joseph Decaisne, *Histoire de la maladie des pommes de terre en 1845* (Paris: Librarie agricole de Dusacq, 1846), 85–87; Brian J. Haas

et al., "Genome Sequence and Analysis of the Irish Potato Famine Pathogen *Phytophthora infestans*," *Nature* 461, no. 7262 (September 2009): 393–398; Dieter Bruneel, Hanne Cottyn, and Esther Beeckaert, "Potato Late Blight Follows Crowding and Impoverishment," in *Feral Atlas: The More-than-Human Anthropocene* (Redwood City, CA: Stanford University Press, 2020), http://hdl.handle.net/1854/LU-8680488.

7. *Rapport fait au conseil de Salubrité publique sur la maladie des Pommes de Terre* (Brussels: Delevingne et Callewaert, 1845), 3; Smith, *Potato*, 36–38; John Kelly, *The Graves Are Walking: The Great Famine and the Saga of the Irish People*, reprint ed. (London: Picador, 2013); Large, *Advance of the Fungi*, 20.

8. George Phillips, "On the Nature and Cause of the Potato Disease," *Journal of the Royal Agricultural Society of England* 7 (1846): 313.

9. Jacob Bell, ed., "The Potato Disease," *Pharmaceutical Journal: A Weekly Record of Pharmacy and Allied Sciences* 5 (1846): 262–263; O'Rourke, *History of the Great Irish Famine of 1847*, 63–64; "Potatoes" in *Family Herald: A Domestic Magazine of Useful Information and Amusement for the Million*, vol. 3 (London: George Biggs, 1845), 333.

10. Phillips, "On the Nature and Cause of the Potato Disease," 301; *Gardeners' Chronicle*, August 23, 1845; Large, *Advance of the Fungi*, 15–16.

11. For estimates of crop loss, see *Potatoes (Ireland): Copy of a Report of Dr. Playfair and Mr. Lindley on the Present State of the Irish Potato Crop, and on the Prospect of Approaching Scarcity*, Sessional Papers 28 (London: House of Commons, 1846); Robert Peel, *Memoirs by the Right Honourable Sir Robert Peel, Part II: The New Government, 1834–5 and Part III: Repeal of the Corn Laws, 1845–6* (London: John Murray, 1857), 172.

12. Bell, "Potato Disease," 265–268; [Douglas Jerrold], "Tremendous Potato Discovery," *Punch*, September 19, 1846, Punch Historical Archive, 1841–1992 (accessed June 20, 2024).

13. O'Rourke, *History of the Great Irish Famine of 1847*, 51–52.

14. William Cooke Taylor, *Life and Times of Sir Robert Peel* (London: Peter Jackson, Late Fisher, Son and Co., 1851), 3:450; *An Insight into the Political Character of Sir Robert Peel, Bart., in a Letter to the Electors of Great Britain* (London: James Ridgway, 1837), 12; Sir Lawrence Peel, *A Sketch of the Life and Character of Sir Robert Peel* (London: Longman, Green, Longman, and Roberts, 1860), 12.

15. Spencer Walpole, *The Life of Lord John Russell* (London: Longmans, Green, and Company, 1889), 1:384–400.

16. On O'Connell's politics within a wider European context, see Eric Hobsbawm, *The Age of Revolution, 1789–1848*, 1st Vintage reprint ed. (New York: Vintage, 1996), 138.

17. *Times*, August 17, 1843, 6, The Times Digital Archive (accessed June 15, 2023); *Times*, August 18, 1843, 4, The Times Digital Archive (accessed June 15, 2023).

18. Thomas Doubleday, *The Political Life of Sir Robert Peel: An Analytical Biography* (London: Smith, Elder, 1856), 2:365; "Suppression of the Repeal Agitation," *Times*, October 9, 1843, The Times Digital Archive (accessed June 15, 2023).

19. Charles Greville, *The Greville Memoirs: A Journal of the Reigns of King George IV and King William IV*, ed. Henry Reeve (New York: Appleton and Co., 1885), 81–82; Taylor, *Life and Times of Sir Robert Peel*, 3:200–201; on the timeline of Peel's change of heart, see Christine Kinealy, *A Death-Dealing Famine: The Great Hunger in Ireland* (London: Pluto Press, 1997), 59.

20. *Correspondence and Accounts Relating to Occasions on Which Measures Were Taken for Relief of People Suffering from Scarcity in Ireland*, Command Papers 734 (London: William Clowes and Son, 1846), 8–9; Thomas P. O'Neill, "The Organisation and Administration of Relief in Ireland," in *The Great Famine: Studies in Irish History, 1845–52*, ed. R. Dudley Edwards, T. Desmond Williams, and Cormac Ó Gráda, new ed. (Dublin: Lilliput Press, 1994), 212–213; Christine Kinealy, *This Great Calamity: The Irish Famine, 1845–52* (Dublin: Gill and Macmillan, 1994), 37–38.

21. Cecil Woodham-Smith, *The Great Hunger: Ireland, 1845–1849*, reissue ed. (London: Penguin, 1992), 48–49; Christine Kinealy, *A New History of Ireland*, updated ed. (Stroud, Gloucestershire: Sutton, 2004), 164–165; O'Rourke, *History of the Great Irish Famine of 1847*, 54; John Mitchel, *The Crusade of the Period and Last Conquest of Ireland (Perhaps)*, Irish-American Library 4 (New York: Lynch, Cole, and Meehan, 1878), 199; George Shaw-Lefevre Baron Eversley, *Peel and O'Connell: A Review of the Irish Policy of Parliament from the Act of Union to the Death of Sir Robert Peel* (London: Kegan Paul, Trench and Company, 1887), 267; [William Newman], "The Real Potato Blight of Ireland (From a Sketch Taken in Conciliation Hall)," *Punch*, December 13, 1845, Punch Historical Archive, 1841–1992 (accessed June 20, 2024).

22. Louis J. Jennings, ed., *The Croker Papers: The Correspondence and Diaries of John Wilson Croker* (London: John Murray, 1885), 3:68.

23. Kinealy, *This Great Calamity*, 50; *Relief in Ireland—A Statement of the Total Expenditure for the Purposes of Relief in Ireland Since November 1845, Distinguishing Final Payments from Sums Which Have Been or Are to Be Repaid*, Sessional Papers 615 (London: House of Commons, 1846).

24. [Douglas Jerrold], "A Prophecy from the Potato," *Punch*, February 28, 1846, Punch Historical Archive, 1841–1992 (accessed June 20, 2024).

25. Peel, *Memoirs*, 113–114; Greville, *Greville Memoirs*, 99–100.

26. John Sherren Bartlett, *Maize, or Indian Corn: Its Advantages as a Cheap and Nutritious Article of Food for the Poor and Labouring Classes of Great Britain and Ireland, with Directions for Its Use* (New York, 1845), 4, 12; N. B. Cloud, ed., *The American Cotton Planter: A Monthly Journal Devoted to Improved Plantation Economy*, vol. 3 (Montgomery, AL: N. B. Cloud, 1855), 346; Thomas J. Sumner, "Suggestions as to the Successive Cultivation of Cotton and Indian Corn," ed. J. S. Skinner, *The Plough, the Loom, and the Anvil* 1, no. 2 (1848): 111–113; Benjamin Thompson, *Count Rumford's Essay on Food, and Particularly on Feeding the Poor, Published in the Year 1795 and Now Reprinted for the Friends of the Poor* (Youghal, Co. Cork, 1846), 33–34.

27. O'Rourke, *History of the Great Irish Famine of 1847*, 72–73; Jennings, *Croker Papers*, 3:42–43, 341–343.

28. *Times*, December 4, 1845, 4, The Times Digital Archive (accessed June 15, 2023).

29. O'Rourke, *History of the Great Irish Famine of 1847*, 104.

30. Greville, *Greville Memoirs*, 99–100; Jennings, *Croker Papers*, 3:142–143; "Cotton Twist," *The Free Trader. Plenty to Do, High Profits, Good Wages, and Cheap Bread. Letters to the Right Hon. Sir Robert Peel, Bart. By Cotton Twist* (London, 1842), 45.

31. Eversley, *Peel and O'Connell*, 269–270; Greville, *Greville Memoirs*, 106; Peel, *Memoirs*, 289–293; House of Commons Debates, April 3, 1846, vol. 85, cc. 506; Benjamin Disraeli, *Lord George Bentinck: A Political Biography*, 3rd ed. (London: Colburn and Co., 1852), 159–161.

32. Greville, *Greville Memoirs*, 117–118; House of Commons Debates, June 25, 1846, vol. 87, cc. 990–991; see also O'Neill, "Organisation and Administration of Relief," 209.

33. For an easily accessible version of the Philalethes letter, see "Repeal Agitation in Ireland," *Southern Australian* (Adelaide), April 5, 1846, 4, accessed June 22, 2023, http://nla.gov.au/nla.news-article71628757.

34. G. Kitson Clark, "'Statesmen in Disguise': Reflexions on the History of the Neutrality of the Civil Service," *Historical Journal* 2, no. 1 (1959): 30–31.

35. "To the Citizens of Kilkenny," *Freeman's Journal*, October 19, 1843, British Library Newspapers (accessed June 21, 2023).

36. Woodham-Smith, *Great Hunger*, 105; Mike Davis, *Late Victorian Holocausts: El Niño Famines and the Making of the Third World* (London: Verso, 2002), 37; Tim Pat Coogan, *The Famine Plot: England's Role in Ireland's Greatest Tragedy* (New York: Palgrave Macmillan, 2012), 61–64; Peter Gray, "National Humiliation and the Great Hunger: Fast and Famine in 1847," *Irish Historical Studies* 32, no. 126 (2000): 194; Charles Read, "Laissez-Faire, the Irish Famine, and British Financial Crisis," *Economic History Review* 69, no. 2 (2016): 411–434.

37. Sir George Otto Trevelyan, ed., *The Life and Letters of Lord Macaulay* (New York: Harper and Brothers, 1880), 1:339–341.

38. Christine Kinealy and Gerard Moran, eds., *The History of the Irish Famine* (London: Routledge, 2020), 371.

39. David P. Nally, *Human Encumbrances: Political Violence and the Great Irish Famine* (Notre Dame, IN: University of Notre Dame Press, 2011), 59.

40. Charles Edward Trevelyan, *The Irish Crisis* (London: Longman, Brown, Green, and Longmans, 1848), 190, 201.

41. Edmund Burke, *Thoughts and Details on Scarcity: Originally Presented to the Right Hon. William Pitt, in the Month of November, 1795* (London: F. and C. Rivington, 1800), 1–2, 10; *HC 1846 (735)*, 113.

42. Charles Gavan Duffy, *Young Ireland: A Fragment of Irish History, 1840–1845* (London: T. Fisher Unwin, 1896), 1:173; "The Commissariat and the Treasury, with Personal Sketches and Anecdotes," *Colburn's United Service Magazine*, 1850, 40–47; Robert Phipps Dod, *The Peerage, Baronetage, and Knightage of Great Britain and Ireland* (London: Whittaker and Co., 1848), 146.

43. *Correspondence Relating to Measures for Relief of Distress in Ireland (Board of Works Series), July 1846–January 1847*, Parliamentary Papers, Command Papers 764 (London: William Clowes and Sons, 1847), 15–16; *Weekly Reports of Scarcity Commission Showing Progress of Disease in Potatoes, Complaints and Applications for Relief, March 1846*, Sessional Papers 201 (London: House of Commons, 1846), 1–2.

44. *HC 1846 (735)*, 219–223; *Correspondence Relating to Measures for Relief of Distress in Ireland (Commissariat Series), July 1846–January 1847*, Command Papers 761 (London: W. Clowes and Sons, 1847), 2.

45. *HC 1846 (735)*, 4, 152–153.

46. *HC 1846 (735)*, 15–17.

47. *HC 1846 (735)*, 178, 95–96; National Archives of Ireland, Relief Commission Papers: Numerical Sub-Series, Cork, RLFC3/1/3174.

48. *HC 1846 (735)*, 33.

49. *HC 1846 (735)*, 166; Asenath Nicholson, *Annals of the Famine in Ireland, in 1847, 1848, and 1849* (New York: E. French, 1851), 30–33.

50. *HC 1846 (735)*, 158, 174–175.

51. *HC 1846 (735)*, 36; Kinealy, *This Great Calamity*, 42.

52. "Famine Times," Schools' Collection, vol. 0012, p. 241; "Famine Times," Schools' Collection, vol. 0277, pp. 109–110.

53. *Times*, April 21, 1846, 7, The Times Digital Archive (accessed September 27, 2021); RLFC 3/1/3174; *HC 1846 (735)*, 131–132.

54. *Times*, April 21, 1846, 7, The Times Digital Archive (accessed September 27, 2021).

55. *HC 1846 (735)*, 122–123.

56. *HC 1846 (735)*, 197–198, 99–100, 279, 124–125.

57. *HC 1846 (735)*, 295.

58. *HC 1846 (735)*, 293, 318, 107–109.

59. George Nicholls, *A History of the Irish Poor Law: In Connexion with the Condition of the People* (London: John Murray, 1856), 312–313; *HC 1846 (735)*, 351–353.

60. *HC 1846 (735)*, 293, 351–353; Kinealy, *This Great Calamity*, 58–59.

61. *HC 1846 (735)*, 274–275.

62. *HC 1846 (735)*, 351–353, 341–343.

63. *HC 1846 (735)*, 109–110; "Ireland," *Daily News*, April 11, 1846, British Library Newspapers (accessed October 6, 2021).

64. National Archives of Ireland, Relief Commission Papers: Numerical Sub-Series, Galway, RLFC3/1/4693.

65. *Disease (Ireland)—Abstracts of the Most Serious Representations Made by the Several Medical Superintendents of Public Institutions (Fever Hospitals, Infirmaries, Dispensaries, &c.) in the Provinces of Ulster, Munster, Leinster and Connaught*, Sessional Papers 120 (London: House of Commons, 1846), 1–9.

66. Cormac Ó Gráda, *The Great Irish Famine*, New Studies in Economic and Social History (Cambridge, UK: Cambridge University Press, 1995), 34; *HC 1846 (735)*, 223–226.

67. "Shall England Furnish Ireland with Food," *Newcastle Guardian and Tyne Mercury*, September 19, 1846, 3.

68. *HC 1846 (735)*, 149, 201.

69. John McPhee, *The Control of Nature* (New York: Farrar, Straus and Giroux, 1990), 143; Michael J. Watts, *Silent Violence: Food, Famine, and Peasantry in Northern Nigeria* (Athens: University of Georgia Press, 2013), 463; Davis, *Late Victorian Holocausts*, 288.

70. National Archives of Ireland, Relief Commission Papers: Numerical Sub-Series, Cork, RLFC3/1/3712; *HC 1846 (735)*, 128.

Chapter 5: The End of the World

1. William Carleton, *The Black Prophet: A Tale of Irish Famine* (London: Simms and McIntyre, 1847), 20, vii; *Correspondence Relating to Measures for Relief of Distress in Ireland (Commissariat Series), July 1846–January 1847*, Command Papers 761 (London: W. Clowes and Sons, 1847) (hereafter *HC 1847 [761]*), 4–5, 10.

2. Andrew F. Smith, *Potato: A Global History* (London: Reaktion Books, 2011), 46–48.

3. Christine Kinealy, *This Great Calamity: The Irish Famine, 1845–52* (Dublin: Gill and Macmillan, 1994), 71; Thomas P. O'Neill, "The Organisation and Administration of Relief in Ireland," in *The Great Famine: Studies in Irish History, 1845–52*, ed. R. Dudley Edwards, T. Desmond Williams, and Cormac Ó Gráda, new ed. (Dublin: Lilliput Press, 1994), 222; Isaac Butt, *The Famine in the Land: What Has Been Done and What Is to Be Done*, A Voice for Ireland (Dublin: James McGlashan, 1847), 6–7.

4. Asenath Nicholson, *Annals of the Famine in Ireland, in 1847, 1848, and 1849* (New York: E. French, 1851), 83.

5. Karl Marx, "Lord Russell [1855]," in *Marx/Engels Collected Works* (London: Lawrence and Wishart, 1977), 14:371.

6. "Measures for Ireland," *The Economist* 4, no. 156 (August 22, 1846), 1082–1083; House of Commons Debates, March 22, 1847, vol. 91, c. 310; House of Commons Debates, August 17, 1846, vol. 88, c. 778; *Correspondence Relating to Measures for Relief of Distress in Ireland (Board of Works Series), July 1846–January 1847*, Parliamentary Papers, Command Papers 764 (London: William Clowes and Sons, 1847) (hereafter *HC 1847 [764]*),

144–145; Peter Gray, *Famine, Land, and Politics: British Government and Irish Society, 1843–1850* (Dublin: Irish Academic Press, 1999), 337; Peter Gray, "National Humiliation and the Great Hunger: Fast and Famine in 1847," *Irish Historical Studies* 32, no. 126 (2000): 194.

7. Charles Read, "Laissez-Faire, the Irish Famine, and British Financial Crisis," *Economic History Review* 69, no. 2 (2016): 412–413.

8. Charles Edward Trevelyan, *The Irish Crisis* (London: Longman, Brown, Green, and Longmans, 1848), 31; John O'Rourke, *The History of the Great Irish Famine of 1847: With Notices of Earlier Irish Famines* (Dublin: McGlashan and Gill, 1875), 376–377; Cecil Woodham-Smith, *The Great Hunger: Ireland, 1845–1849*, reissue ed. (London: Penguin, 1992), 119–120; "Ireland," *Manchester Times*, March 5, 1847, British Library Newspapers (accessed September 21, 2021); *HC 1847 (761)*, 479–492; Thomas Power O'Connor, *The Parnell Movement with a Sketch of Irish Parties from 1843* (London: Kegan Paul, Trench and Co., 1886), 46–47; *Times*, January 13, 1847, 5, The Times Digital Archive (accessed September 28, 2021); Trevelyan, *The Irish Crisis* (1848 ed.), 71; O'Neill, "Administration of Relief," 225–226.

9. *HC 1847 (761)*, 96–97, 361–362; *Correspondence Relating to Measures for Relief of Distress in Ireland (Commissariat Series), January–March 1847*, Command Papers 796 (London: W. Clowes and Sons, 1847) (hereafter *HC 1847 [796]*), 15–16.

10. Charles Edward Trevelyan, *The Irish Crisis: Being a Narrative of the Measures for the Relief of the Distress Caused by the Great Irish Famine of 1846–7* (London: Macmillan, 1880), 54.

11. *HC 1847 (761)*, 199, 381–382; Kinealy, *This Great Calamity*, 76–77.

12. "Ireland," *Manchester Courier and Lancashire General Advertiser*, January 16, 1847, 34, British Library Newspapers (accessed October 28, 2021); *HC 1847 (761)*, 16–17.

13. Christine Kinealy, *A Death-Dealing Famine: The Great Hunger in Ireland* (London: Pluto Press, 1997), 77; P. M. Austin Bourke, "The Extent of the Potato Crop in Ireland at the Time of the Famine," *Journal of the Statistical and Social Inquiry Society of Ireland* 20 (1960): 12; Smith, *Potato*, 44–45.

14. Kinealy, *Death-Dealing Famine*, 77; *Times*, February 26, 1847, 3, The Times Digital Archive (accessed September 28, 2021); Cormac Ó Gráda, *Black '47 and Beyond: The Great Irish Famine in History, Economy, and Memory* (Princeton, NJ: Princeton University Press, 2000), 123;

Thomas Francis Meagher, *Meagher of the Sword: Speeches of Thomas Francis Meagher in Ireland, 1846–1848, His Narrative of Events in Ireland in July 1848, Personal Reminiscences of Waterford, Galway, and His Schooldays* (Dublin: M. H. Gill and Son, 1916), 57.

15. *An Account of All Cattle, Sheep, and Swine Imported into Great Britain from Ireland, from 5 July 1846 to 5 January 1847*, Sessional Papers 133 (London: House of Commons, 1847); *HC 1847 (761)*, 333–334; H. D. Richardson, *Pigs: Their Origin and Varieties, Management with a View to Profit, and General Treatment in Health and Disease* (London: William S. Orr and Company, 1847), 49.

16. House of Commons Debates, January 25, 1847, vol. 89, cc. 459–460; David P. Nally, *Human Encumbrances: Political Violence and the Great Irish Famine* (Notre Dame, IN: University of Notre Dame Press, 2011), 142–143.

17. Anti-Slavery Society, *Negro Apprenticeship in the British Colonies* (London: Anti-Slavery Society and Hatchard and Son, 1838), 51; Padraic X. Scanlan, *Slave Empire: How Slavery Built Modern Britain*, 1st paperback ed. (London: Robinson, 2022), chap. 8; Spencer Walpole, *The Life of Lord John Russell* (London: Longmans, Green, and Company, 1889), 1:439.

18. George O'Brien, *The Economic History of Ireland from the Union to the Famine* (London: Longmans, Green and Company, 1921), 253; *HC 1847 (764)*, 14–15.

19. "Famine Times," Schools' Collection, National Folklore Collection, University College Dublin (hereafter Schools' Collection), vol. 0151, p. 374; Butt, *Famine in the Land*, 14; O'Rourke, *History of the Great Irish Famine of 1847*, 173–174, 194; see also Gray, *Famine, Land, and Politics*, 133.

20. *HC 1847 (764)*, 81–82, 423–425; see also S. H. Cousens, "The Regional Variation in Mortality During the Great Irish Famine," *Proceedings of the Royal Irish Academy. Section C: Archaeology, Celtic Studies, History, Linguistics, Literature* 63 (1962): 132.

21. Nassau William Senior, *Journals, Conversations and Essays Relating to Ireland* (London: Longmans, Green, and Company, 1868), 1:287–291; O'Rourke, *History of the Great Irish Famine of 1847*, 229–232.

22. *HC 1847 (761)*, 363–366, 128; Thomas Carlyle, *Reminiscences of My Irish Journey in 1849*, ed. James Anthony Froude (New York: Harper and Brothers, 1882), 192–193.

23. *Correspondence Relating to Measures for Relief of Distress in Ireland (Board of Works Series), January–March 1847*, Command Papers 797

(London: W. Clowes and Sons, 1847) (hereafter *HC 1847 [797]*), 13–15; *HC 1847 (761)*, 331; O'Rourke, *History of the Great Irish Famine of 1847*, 214–215.

24. *HC 1847 (764)*, 273–275, 189, 195–199, 252, 271–272; *HC 1847 (797)*, 23; see also Kinealy, *Death-Dealing Famine*; George Nicholls, *A History of the Irish Poor Law: In Connexion with the Condition of the People* (London: John Murray, 1856), 314.

25. *HC 1847 (761)*, 399–400.

26. *Times*, December 21, 1847, 4, The Times Digital Archive (accessed September 16, 2021); "To the Editor of the Times," *Times*, October 5, 1847, 5, The Times Digital Archive (accessed September 17, 2021); *HC 1847 (761)*, 399–400; *HC 1847 (764)*, 143–144.

27. Senior, *Journals, Conversations and Essays*, 1:191–192.

28. *Evidence Taken Before Her Majesty's Commissioners of Inquiry into the State of the Law and Practice in Respect to the Occupation of Land in Ireland. Part I*, Command Papers 606 (Dublin: Alexander Thom, 1845), 84–85; *HC 1847 (764)*, 167–168, 94–96, 115, 93, 309–311.

29. *HC 1847 (797)*, 271; *HC 1847 (764)*, 162–163, 172, 159, 161; Trevelyan, *The Irish Crisis* (1848 ed.), n. 59.

30. O'Rourke, *History of the Great Irish Famine of 1847*, 301–302; *HC 1847 (764)*, 27; O'Neill, "Administration of Relief," 231; "England and Ireland," *Bristol Mercury*, February 20, 1847, British Library Newspapers (accessed September 22, 2021).

31. For historical currency conversions, see "Relative Worth Comparators and Data Sets," MeasuringWorth, accessed January 30, 2024, www .measuringworth.com/index.php; for lists and census data, see Kinealy, *This Great Calamity*; *HC 1847 (796)*, 179–180.

32. *HC 1847 (764)*, 326–327, 344–345; Trevelyan, *The Irish Crisis* (1848 ed.), 151.

33. Zohar Lederman and Teck Chuan Voo, "The Minnesota Starvation Experiment and Force Feeding of Prisoners: Relying on Unethical Research to Justify the Unjustifiable," *Journal of Bioethical Inquiry* 18, no. 3 (2021): 408; see also Kevin Grant, *Last Weapons: Hunger Strikes and Fasts in the British Empire, 1890–1948*, Berkeley Series in British Studies 16 (Berkeley: University of California Press, 2019), 23–26.

34. Manfred James Müller et al., "Metabolic Adaptation to Caloric Restriction and Subsequent Refeeding: The Minnesota Starvation Experiment Revisited 12," *American Journal of Clinical Nutrition* 102, no. 4

(October 1, 2015): 807–819; Harold Steere Guetzkow and Paul Hoover Bowman, *Men and Hunger: A Psychological Manual for Relief Workers* (Elgin, IL: Brethren Publishing House, 1946), 21–24; see also David Grann, *The Wager: A Tale of Shipwreck, Mutiny and Murder* (New York: Doubleday, 2023), 113–122.

35. James Fintan Lalor, *The Writings of James Fintan Lalor: With an Introduction Embodying Personal Recollections*, ed. John O'Leary (Dublin: T. G. O'Donoghue and Francis Nugent, 1895), 14; Robert Scally, *The End of Hidden Ireland: Rebellion, Famine, and Emigration* (Oxford, UK: Oxford University Press, 1995), 112–113.

36. O'Rourke, *History of the Great Irish Famine of 1847*, 234–235; *HC 1847 (796)*, 162–164; "Ireland," *Times*, December 31, 1846, 8, The Times Digital Archive (accessed September 15, 2021); "Ireland," *Times*, February 4, 1847, 4, The Times Digital Archive (accessed September 11, 2021); John Bateman, *The Great Landowners of Great Britain and Ireland: A List of All Owners of Three Thousand Acres and Upwards, Worth £3,000 a Year; Also, One Thousand Three Hundred Owners of Two Thousand Acres and Upwards, in England, Scotland, Ireland & Wales, Their Acreage, and Income from Land, Culled from The Modern Domesday Book*, 4th ed. (London: Harrison and Sons, 1883), 363; *Poor Inquiry (Ireland). Appendix (D.) Containing Baronial Examinations Relative to Earnings of Labourers, Cottier Tenants, Employment of Women and Children, Expenditure; and Supplement, Containing Answers to Questions 1 to 12 Circulated by the Commissioners*, Command Papers 36 (London: W. Clowes and Sons, 1836); *HC 1847 (797)*, 158–159; Cormac Ó Gráda, *Ireland: A New Economic History, 1780–1939* (Oxford, UK: Clarendon Press, 1995), 202–203; *HC 1847 (764)*, 286.

37. The letter was widely quoted. It appeared in the *Times* and many other publications and in histories of the Great Famine throughout the nineteenth century and afterward—for example, in William Patrick O'Brien, *The Great Famine in Ireland: And a Retrospect of the Fifty Years 1845–95; with a Sketch of the Present Condition and Future Prospects of the Congested Districts* (London: Downey and Co., 1896), 79–80; *HC 1847 (761)*, 459–460; "The Famine of 1847," Schools' Collection, vol. 0298, p. 68.

38. Guetzkow and Bowman, *Men and Hunger*, 26–27; National Archives of Ireland, Relief Commission Papers: Baronial Sub-Series, Mayo, RLFC3/2/21/16; "The Famine in This District," Schools' Collection,

vol. 0393, p. 026; "The Famine," Schools' Collection, vol. 0288, pp. 20–22; "The Famine of 1847," Schools' Collection, vol. 0021, p. 260; "Famine Stories IV," Schools' Collection, vol. 0096, pp. 498–499; "Famine Times," Schools' Collection, vol. 0016, pp. 341–342; "The Famine," Schools' Collection, vol. 0406, p. 469; "Famine Times," Schools' Collection, vol. 0401, pp. 080–081.

39. Quoted in Denis Murphy, *Cromwell in Ireland: A History of Cromwell's Irish Campaign* (Dublin: M. H. Gill and Son, 1897), 44–45; *Times*, September 22, 1846, The Times Digital Archive (accessed June 20, 2024).

40. *HC 1847 (797)*, 112; Cormac Ó Gráda, *Eating People Is Wrong, and Other Essays on Famine, Its Past, and Its Future* (Princeton, NJ: Princeton University Press, 2015), 14, 31–37; "Penal Times and Famine Times," Schools' Collection, vol. 0282, p. 427.

41. National Archives of Ireland, Relief Commission Papers: Baronial Sub-Series, Mayo, RLFC3/2/21/16; *HC 1847 (796)*, 194–195; Mary Leadbeater, *Cottage Dialogues Among the Irish Peasantry, with Notes and a Preface by Maria Edgeworth*, ed. Maria Edgeworth (London: J. Johnson and Co., 1811), 254; Laurence Geary, "Epidemic Diseases of the Great Famine," *History Ireland* 4, no. 1 (1996): 28–30; Nicholls, *History of the Irish Poor Law*, 326; Joel Mokyr and Cormac Ó Gráda, "What Do People Die of During Famines: The Great Irish Famine in Comparative Perspective," *European Review of Economic History* 6, no. 3 (December 2002): 40–52.

42. Geary, "Epidemic Diseases of the Great Famine," 32; William P. MacArthur, "Medical History of the Famine," in Edwards, Williams, and Gráda, *Great Famine*, 265–306; Mokyr and Ó Gráda, "What Do People Die of During Famines," 341–343; Woodham-Smith, *Great Hunger*, 193; *HC 1847 (797)*, 180–181; O'Rourke, *History of the Great Irish Famine of 1847*, 390–402.

43. Phelim P. Boyle and Cormac Ó Gráda, "Fertility Trends, Excess Mortality, and the Great Irish Famine," *Demography* 23, no. 4 (1986): 553–555; Jonny Geber, "Reconstructing Realities: Exploring the Human Experience of the Great Famine Through Archaeology," in *Global Legacies of the Great Irish Famine: Transnational and Interdisciplinary Perspectives*, ed. Marguerite Corporaal et al. (Oxford, UK: Peter Lang, 2014), 142–148; "Wakes," Schools' Collection, vol. 0788, pp. 47–48; "Ancient Customs," Schools' Collection, vol. 0118, p. 58; "Horrors of the Famine," Schools' Collection, vol. 0288, pp. 061–062.

44. *Times*, March 8, 1847, 4, The Times Digital Archive (accessed September 15, 2021); *Times*, December 19, 1846, 4, The Times Digital Archive (accessed September 17, 2021); James Hack Tuke, *A Visit to Connaught in the Autumn of 1847: A Letter Addressed to the Central Relief Committee of the Society of Friends, Dublin*, 2nd ed. (London: Charles Gilpin, 1848), 26–27; O'Rourke, *History of the Great Irish Famine of 1847*, 163–165.

45. *HC 1847 (796)*, 14; *Transactions of the Central Relief Committee of the Society of Friends During the Famine in Ireland, in 1846 and 1847* (Dublin: Hodges and Smith, 1852), 54.

46. *HC 1847 (761)*, 333; Ó Gráda, *Ireland*, 197.

47. Woodham-Smith, *Great Hunger*, 172; O'Brien, *Economic History of Ireland*, 254–257.

48. Woodham-Smith, *Great Hunger*, 172; O'Rourke, *History of the Great Irish Famine of 1847*, 428; *HC 1847 (796)*, 105–109.

49. Charles Read, *The Great Famine in Ireland and Britain's Financial Crisis* (Woodbridge, UK: Boydell & Brewer, 2022), 120; David Morier Evans, *The Commercial Crisis, 1847–1848* (London: Letts, Son, and Steer, 1848), 55–56; Charles Read, *Calming the Storms: The Carry Trade, the Banking School and British Financial Crises Since 1825* (London: Palgrave Macmillan, 2023), 137–138.

50. Read, *Calming the Storms*, 148–151.

51. O'Neill, "Administration of Relief," 232; O'Connor, *The Parnell Movement with a Sketch of Irish Parties from 1843*, 63; House of Commons Debates, March 25, 1847, vol. 91, cc. 375–376; *Exeter and Plymouth Gazette*, May 15, 1847, 2, British Library Newspapers (accessed September 22, 2021); *Bristol Mercury*, March 27, 1847, British Library Newspapers (accessed September 22, 2021); *HC 1847 (797)*, 251.

52. Trevelyan, *The Irish Crisis* (1880 ed.), 85–86.

53. *Transactions of the Central Relief Committee*, 44–50; Gray, "National Humiliation and the Great Hunger," 209; Trevelyan, *The Irish Crisis* (1848 ed.), 126–132; Henry Barnard, ed., *American Journal of Education*, vol. 1 (Hartford, CT: F. C. Brownell, 1856), 635–636; Christine Kinealy, *Charity and the Great Hunger in Ireland: The Kindness of Strangers* (London: Bloomsbury Academic, 2013); Padraig Kirwan, "Recognition, Resilience, and Relief: The Meaning of Gift," in *Famine Pots: The Choctaw-Irish Gift Exchange, 1847–Present*, ed. LeAnne Howe and Padraig Kirwan (East Lansing: Michigan State University Press, 2020), 3–38.

54. This comment is from the foreword to a later edition of the book, published as the movement for Irish Home Rule became a more organised force in Irish and British politics: Trevelyan, *The Irish Crisis* (1880 ed.), v; Trevelyan, *The Irish Crisis* (1848 ed.), 125.

55. Alexis Soyer, *Memoirs of Alexis Soyer: With Unpublished Receipts and Odds and Ends of Gastronomy*, ed. F. Volant, J. R. Warren, and J. G. Lomax (London: W. Kent and Company, 1859), 100.

56. Soyer, *Memoirs*, 88–100; *HC 1847 (796)*, 148–149, 156.

57. Alexis Soyer, *Soyer's Charitable Cookery: Or the Poor Man's Regenerator* (London: Simpkin, Marshall and Co., 1848), 39–42, 107–108; Woodham-Smith, *Great Hunger*, 178–179.

58. O'Rourke, *History of the Great Irish Famine of 1847*, 435–436; Nicholson, *Annals*, 231–235; William Robert Wilde, "The Food of the Irish," *Dublin University Magazine* 43, no. 254 (1854): 139–140.

59. Soyer, *Memoirs*, 109–111; *HC 1847 (796)*, 195; Soyer, *Charitable Cookery*, vi; Mrs. White, "Man Versus Metal: The Hated Weight of Poverty," ed. William Harrison Ainsworth, *Ainsworth's Magazine: A Miscellany of Romance, General Literature and Art* 16 (1849): 312; Wilde, "Food of the Irish," 140.

60. Soyer, *Charitable Cookery*, 14; "The Proposed Relief of Irish Famine by M. Soyer's Soup-Quackery," *The Lancet: A Journal of British and Foreign Medicine, Surgery, Obstetrics, Physiology, Chemistry, Pharmacology, Public Health and News* 1, no. 9 (1847): 232–233; Henry Marsh, *On the Preparation of Food for the Labourer: In Letter to Joshua Harvey, M.D.* (Dublin: James McGlashan, 1847), 6–8; O'Rourke, *History of the Great Irish Famine of 1847*, 428–429.

61. J. Wesley Van der Voort, *The Natural History of the Ocean: A Graphic Account of the Mighty Deep: Its Laws and Phenomena, Its Products and Inhabitants, Its Currents, Tides and Trade Winds, Pearls, Shells and Sponges* (New York: Union Publishing House, 1890), 327–328.

62. Kinealy, *Death-Dealing Famine*, 98–99; Cormac Ó Gráda, *The Great Irish Famine*, New Studies in Economic and Social History (Cambridge, UK: Cambridge University Press, 1995), 37–39; Mohamed Salah Harzallah, "Accountability and Administrative Efficiency: The Administration of the Soup Kitchen Act in Ireland (1847)," *The Historian* 8, no. 2 (2010): 99; Christine Kinealy, "Beyond Revisionism: Reassessing the Great Irish Famine," *History Ireland* 3, no. 4 (1995): 32; Gray, *Famine, Land, and Politics*, 266–267; Liam Kennedy and Donald M. MacRaild,

"Perspectives on the Great Irish Famine," QUCEH Working Paper Series (Belfast: Queen's University Centre for Economic History, 2022), 17–20, www.econstor.eu/handle/10419/252318; Steven Roberts and Paul Switzer, "Mortality Displacement and Distributed Lag Models," *Inhalation Toxicology* 16, no. 14 (January 1, 2004): 879–888; Shakoor Hajat et al., "Mortality Displacement of Heat-Related Deaths: A Comparison of Delhi, São Paulo, and London," *Epidemiology* 16, no. 5 (2005): 613–620.

63. Harzallah, "Accountability and Administrative Efficiency," 103; Alexander Martin Sullivan, *New Ireland* (Philadelphia: J. B. Lippincott, 1878), 88–90; Mohamed Salah Harzallah, "The Construction of Famine Memory in the Irish Oral Tradition," *Nordic Irish Studies* 6 (2007): 47; *Times*, March 23, 1847, 7, The Times Digital Archive (accessed September 29, 2021).

64. Irene Whelan, "The Stigma of Souperism," in *The Great Irish Famine*, ed. Cathal Póirtéir (Cork: Mercier Press, 1995), 135–154; Kinealy, *This Great Calamity*, 142; Harzallah, "Accountability and Administrative Efficiency," 119; "Famine Times," Schools' Collection, vol. 0029, p. 0326.

65. *Times,* April 20, 1847, 7, The Times Digital Archive (accessed September 17, 2021).

66. Norbert Götz, "Lionel de Rothschild and the Great Irish Famine: The Origins of the British Relief Association," *History Ireland* 30, no. 5 (2022): 24; *Times*, March 15, 1847, 6, The Times Digital Archive (accessed September 29, 2021); Harzallah, "Accountability and Administrative Efficiency," 117.

67. Gray, "National Humiliation and the Great Hunger," 213–214.

68. "Ireland: Ejectments by Irish Landlords," *The Observer*, February 1, 1847; *Times*, April 14, 1851, 7, The Times Digital Archive (accessed September 11, 2021).

69. Oliver MacDonagh, "Irish Emigration to the United States of America and the British Colonies During the Famine," in Edwards, Williams, and Ó Gráda, *Great Famine*, 320–321; House of Commons Debates, January 25, 1847, vol. 89, cc. 448–449; O'Brien, *Economic History of Ireland*, 242.

70. Trevelyan, *The Irish Crisis* (1880 ed.), 100–101; MacDonagh, "Irish Emigration," 322; Woodham-Smith, *Great Hunger*, 270.

71. Woodham-Smith, *Great Hunger*, 272; HC 1847 (797), 144–145; on Irish immigrants and North American authorities, see Trevelyan, *The Irish Crisis* (1848 ed.), 132–133; Hidetaka Hirota, *Expelling the Poor: Atlantic*

Seaboard States and the Nineteenth-Century Origins of American Immigration Policy (New York: Oxford University Press, 2017).

72. [Percival Leigh], "The Mishaps of Ministers; A Song for the Premier," *Punch*, July 24, 1847, Punch Historical Archive, 1841–1992 (accessed June 20, 2024); Walpole, *Life of Lord John Russell*, 1:439.

73. Quoted in O'Rourke, *History of the Great Irish Famine of 1847*, 331–332; see also O'Neill, "Administration of Relief," 240.

74. House of Commons Debates, January 25, 1847, vol. 89, 429–430; *HC 1847 (797)*, 3, 150–151; O'Neill, "Administration of Relief," 230; Nicholson, *Annals*, 83.

Chapter 6: Expulsions

1. Richard Lalor Sheil, *Sketches of the Irish Bar* (New York: Redfield, 1854), 1:166; *The Encumbered Estates of Ireland* (London: Bradbury and Evans, 1850), 81–82; *Morning Chronicle*, July 5, 1851, British Library Newspapers (accessed October 27, 2021).

2. This chapter draws on work in political theory and sociology analysing the relationship between the development of capitalism and processes of eviction and expulsion. See especially Saskia Sassen, *Expulsions: Brutality and Complexity in the Global Economy* (Cambridge, MA: Belknap Press, 2014); Matthew Desmond, *Evicted: Poverty and Profit in the American City* (New York: Crown, 2016).

3. Cecil Woodham-Smith, *The Great Hunger: Ireland, 1845–1849*, reissue ed. (London: Penguin, 1992), 134–135.

4. Thomas P. O'Neill, "The Organisation and Administration of Relief in Ireland," in *The Great Famine: Studies in Irish History, 1845–52*, ed. R. Dudley Edwards, T. Desmond Williams, and Cormac Ó Gráda, new ed. (Dublin: Lilliput Press, 1994), 246–249.

5. Spencer Walpole, *The Life of Lord John Russell* (London: Longmans, Green, and Company, 1889), 70–76.

6. Peter Gray, "Famine and Land, 1845–80," in *The Oxford Handbook of Modern Irish History*, ed. Alvin Jackson (Oxford, UK: Oxford University Press, 2014), 552.

7. Sir Charles Gavan Duffy, *Four Years of Irish History, 1845–1849* (London: Cassell, Petter, Galpin and Co, 1883), 84.

8. Woodham-Smith, *Great Hunger*, 348.

9. Woodham-Smith, *Great Hunger*, 329; Walpole, *Life of Lord John Russell*, 2:462–464.

10. *Irish Felon* 1, no. 1 (June 24, 1848); Walpole, *Life of Lord John Russell*, 2:67–68; "The Irish Insurrection," *Leeds Times*, July 22, 1848, 4, British Library Newspapers (accessed September 22, 2021).

11. "Cutlasses Ready in Alarm over Ireland," *Manchester Guardian*, July 29, 1848; "The Anticipated Outbreak," *Times*, July 29, 1848, 8, The Times Digital Archive (accessed September 19, 2023).

12. "The Insurrectionary Movement," *Times*, July 31, 1848, 8, The Times Digital Archive (accessed September 19, 2023).

13. *Times*, August 1, 1848, 8, The Times Digital Archive; "Encounter with the Rebels," *Manchester Courier and Lancashire General Advertiser*, August 2, 1848, 3, British Library Newspapers (accessed September 19, 2023).

14. Walpole, *Life of Lord John Russell*, 2:73; David W. Miller, "Irish Catholicism and the Great Famine," *Journal of Social History* 9, no. 1 (1975): 81–98; John Newsinger, "Revolution and Catholicism in Ireland, 1848–1923," *European Studies Review* 9, no. 4 (October 1, 1979): 457–480; *Irish Felon* 1, no. 4 (July 15, 1848); on peasant conservatism, see Joseph Henrich and Richard McElreath, "Are Peasants Risk-Averse Decision Makers?," *Current Anthropology* 43, no. 1 (February 2002): 172–181; George M. Foster, "Peasant Society and the Image of Limited Good," *American Anthropologist* 67, no. 2 (1965): 293–315; George Dalton, "How Exactly Are Peasants 'Exploited'?," *American Anthropologist* 76, no. 3 (1974): 553–561.

15. "Battle of Boulagh," *Melbourne Argus*, November 28, 1848, http://nla.gov.au/nla.news-article4766099.

16. [Tom Taylor], "English Definitions, for an Irish Dictionary," *Punch*, May 20, 1848, Punch Historical Archive, 1841–1992; *Select Committee on Poor Laws (Ireland): Seventh Report with Minutes of Evidence*, Sessional Papers 237 (London: House of Commons, 1849), 27; Walpole, *Life of Lord John Russell*, 2:79–81.

17. Walpole, *Life of Lord John Russell*, 70–76; Woodham-Smith, *Great Hunger*, 375; Charles Greville, *The Greville Memoirs: A Journal of the Reigns of King George IV and King William IV*, ed. Henry Reeve (New York: Appleton and Co., 1885), 334–335, 387–388.

18. John Mitchel, *The Crusade of the Period and Last Conquest of Ireland (Perhaps)*, Irish-American Library 4 (New York: Lynch, Cole, and Meehan, 1878), 315.

19. Asenath Nicholson, *Annals of the Famine in Ireland, in 1847, 1848, and 1849* (New York: E. French, 1851), 166–171.

20. R. D. Collison Black, *Economic Thought and the Irish Question, 1817–1870* (Cambridge, UK: Cambridge University Press, 1960), 120–121; John O'Rourke, *The History of the Great Irish Famine of 1847: With Notices of Earlier Irish Famines* (Dublin: McGlashan and Gill, 1875), 505.

21. *Papers Relating to Proceedings for Relief of Distress, and State of Unions and Workhouses in Ireland (Fifth Series)*, Sessional Papers 919 (London: William Clowes and Son, 1848) (hereafter *HC 1848 [919]*), 25–27; *Papers Relating to Aid to Distressed Unions in the West of Ireland*, Sessional Papers 1010 (London: William Clowes and Sons, 1849) (hereafter *HC 1849 [1010]*), 24; *Transactions of the Central Relief Committee of the Society of Friends During the Famine in Ireland, in 1846 and 1847* (Dublin: Hodges and Smith, 1852), 76–77; *Papers Relating to Proceedings for Relief of Distress, and State of Unions and Workhouses in Ireland (Sixth Series)*, Sessional Papers 955 (London: William Clowes and Son, 1848) (hereafter *HC 1848 [955]*), 17–18; Nicholson, *Annals*, 172–174.

22. *HC 1848 (919)*, 21; S. H. Cousens, "The Regional Variation in Mortality During the Great Irish Famine," *Proceedings of the Royal Irish Academy. Section C: Archaeology, Celtic Studies, History, Linguistics, Literature* 63 (1962): 3; Christine Kinealy, *This Great Calamity: The Irish Famine, 1845–52* (Dublin: Gill and Macmillan, 1994), 269–270; currency conversions based on data from "Relative Worth Comparators and Data Sets," MeasuringWorth, accessed January 30, 2024, www.measuringworth.com /index.php.

23. Kinealy, *This Great Calamity*, 208–209; *Transactions of the Central Relief Committee*, 67–68.

24. Cousens, "Regional Variation in Mortality," 135–146; Kinealy, *This Great Calamity*, 233; Woodham-Smith, *Great Hunger*, 310.

25. "Ireland," *Manchester Guardian*, April 8, 1848; Thomas Carlyle, *Reminiscences of My Irish Journey in 1849*, ed. James Anthony Froude (New York: Harper and Brothers, 1882), 64–65.

26. *HC 1848 (919)*, 393–394, 430–432.

27. *HC 1848 (919)*, 393–394; *Further Papers Relating to the Aid Afforded to the Distressed Unions in the West of Ireland*, Sessional Papers 1019 (London: William Clowes and Son, 1849) (hereafter *HC 1849 [1019]*), 28–29; *Further Papers Relating to the Aid Afforded to the Distressed Unions in the West of Ireland (in Continuation of Papers Presented 8th February 1849)*,

Sessional Papers 1023 (London: William Clowes and Son, 1849) (hereafter *HC 1849 [1023]*), 36–37.

28. *HC 1849 (1023)*, 16–17; *HC 1848 (955)*, 816–820.

29. *HC 1848 (919)*, 219–222, 354.

30. *HC 1848 (955)*, 143; *HC 1848 (919)*, 71.

31. Denis Charles O'Connor, *Seventeen Years' Experience of Workhouse Life* (Dublin: McGlashan and Gill, 1861), 14–15.

32. *HC 1848 (919)*, 44–46.

33. O'Connor, *Seventeen Years' Experience*, 50; Nicholson, *Annals*, 172–174.

34. *HC 1848 (955)*, 701–704, 312–315; O'Connor, *Seventeen Years' Experience*, 29.

35. *HC 1848 (955)*, 597–598, 13.

36. *HC 1848 (955)*, 185–186; *HC 1849 (1010)*, 9.

37. William P. MacArthur, "Medical History of the Famine," in Edwards, Williams, and Ó Gráda, *Great Famine*, 306–307; *HC 1849 (1019)*, 28–29.

38. *HC 1848 (919)*, 43; O'Connor, *Seventeen Years' Experience*, 19–20; *Papers Relating to Proceedings for Relief of Distress, and State of Unions and Workhouses in Ireland (Seventh Series)*, Sessional Papers 999 (London: William Clowes and Son, 1848), 146–147.

39. *HC 1848 (955)*, 906–908; Thomas Power O'Connor, *The Parnell Movement with a Sketch of Irish Parties from 1843* (London: Kegan Paul, Trench and Co., 1886), 19–20; *HC 1848 (955)*, 312–315.

40. *Morning Chronicle*, July 5, 1851, British Library Newspapers (accessed October 27, 2021).

41. Nassau William Senior, *Journals, Conversations and Essays Relating to Ireland* (London: Longmans, Green, and Company, 1868), 1:293–294; *Irish Felon* 1, no. 5 (July 22, 1848).

42. *HC 1848 (955)*, 205–207; *HC 1849 (1010)*, 14–15.

43. *HC 1848 (955)*, 43–44.

44. *HC 1848 (955)*, 816–820.

45. *HC 1849 (1010)*, 4–9.

46. *HC 1849 (1019)*, 4–5; *HC 1849 (1010)*, 47–48.

47. *HC 1849 (1023)*, 31–33.

48. *HC 1849 (1023)*, 33, 34–35.

49. Gray, "Famine and Land," 554.

50. Cousens, "Regional Variation in Mortality," 143; *HC 1849 (1023)*, 49; Greville, *Greville Memoirs*, 387–388.

51. House of Commons Debates, March 15, 1847, vol. 90, cc. 1398–1399; see also William Smith O'Brien, *Plan for the Relief of the Poor in Ireland: With Observations on the English and Scotch Poor Laws, Addressed to the Landed Proprietors of Ireland* (London: J. M. Richardson, 1830), 11–12; John George Hodges, *Report of the Trial of W. S. O'Brien for High Treason, with the Judgment of the Court of Queen's Bench, Ireland, and of the House of Lords, on the Writs of Error* (Dublin: Alexander Thom, 1849), 542.

52. "Ireland," *Economist*, April 28, 1849, 470, The Economist Historical Archive (accessed October 19, 2021); "The Question Still Is—What Is to Be Done with Ireland?" *Economist*, October 20, 1849, 1157ff, The Economist Historical Archive (accessed October 18, 2021).

53. Robert Alexander Shafto Adair, *The Winter of 1846–7 in Antrim: With Remarks on Out-Door Relief and Colonization* (London: James Ridgway, 1847), 55–56.

54. W. L. Burn, "Free Trade in Land: An Aspect of the Irish Question," *Transactions of the Royal Historical Society* 31 (1949): 69; David P. Nally, *Human Encumbrances: Political Violence and the Great Irish Famine* (Notre Dame, IN: University of Notre Dame Press, 2011), 150–151.

55. George Nicholls, *A History of the Irish Poor Law: In Connexion with the Condition of the People* (London: John Murray, 1856), 309; *Encumbered Estates of Ireland*, 1–9.

56. *Encumbered Estates of Ireland*, 2–3; *Times*, September 8, 1852, 8, The Times Digital Archive (accessed September 14, 2021); Oliver MacDonagh, *Ireland: The Union and Its Aftermath* (London: George Allen and Unwin, 1977), 44–45; *Times*, June 11, 1849, 5, The Times Digital Archive (accessed September 14, 2021); David Nally, "'That Coming Storm': The Irish Poor Law, Colonial Biopolitics, and the Great Famine," *Annals of the Association of American Geographers* 98, no. 3 (September 2008): 731; see also Karl Polanyi, *The Great Transformation: The Political and Economic Origins of Our Time* (Boston: Beacon Press, 2001).

57. Nally, *Human Encumbrances*, 158–159; George O'Brien, *The Economic History of Ireland from the Union to the Famine* (London: Longmans, Green and Company, 1921), 59; Kinealy, *This Great Calamity*, 216–219.

58. *HC 1848 (919)*, 365–367; *Manchester Times*, June 20, 1849, British Library Newspapers (accessed October 27, 2021).

59. *HC 1848 (919)*, 365–367; *Manchester Times*, June 20, 1849, British Library Newspapers (accessed October 27, 2021).

60. James Hack Tuke, *A Visit to Connaught in the Autumn of 1847: A Letter Addressed to the Central Relief Committee of the Society of Friends, Dublin*, 2nd ed. (London: Charles Gilpin, 1848), 63–64; *HC 1848 (955)*, 193; *HC 1849 (1023)*, 16–17; *HC 1848 (919)*, 466–470.

61. "Agricultural Intelligence," *Newcastle Guardian and Tyne Mercury*, May 18, 1850, 2, British Library Newspapers (accessed October 22, 2021); Hack Tuke, *A Visit to Connaught*, 65–66.

62. *HC 1848 (955)*, 184–185.

63. *HC 1849 (1023)*, 16–17; Kinealy, *This Great Calamity*, 314; on emigration, see Auguste J. Thébault, *The Irish Race in the Past and Present* (New York: Peter F. Collier, 1879); Kinealy, *This Great Calamity*, 297; Oliver MacDonagh, "Irish Emigration to the United States of America and the British Colonies During the Famine," in Edwards, Williams, and Ó Gráda, *Great Famine*, 324.

64. *Leicestershire Mercury*, May 20, 1848, 1, British Library Newspapers (accessed November 2, 2021); *Times*, July 26, 1850, 5, The Times Digital Archive (accessed September 13, 2021).

65. Walpole, *Life of Lord John Russell*, 1:467, 2:28.

66. MacDonagh, "Irish Emigration," 328–331.

67. "Ireland," *Norfolk News*, November 13, 1847, 1, British Library Newspapers (accessed October 26, 2021).

68. Megan Specia, "'The Social Contract Has Been Completely Ruptured': Ireland's Housing Crisis," *New York Times*, January 15, 2024, www.nytimes.com/2024/01/15/world/europe/ireland-housing-crisis.html; on the political economy of the Irish housing market, see Rory Hearne, *Gaffs: Why No One Can Get a House, and What We Can Do About It*, rev. ed. (Dublin: HarperCollins, 2023).

Epilogue: The Crystal Palace

1. Jeffrey A. Auerbach, *The Great Exhibition of 1851: A Nation on Display* (New Haven, CT: Yale University Press, 1999); Osmund Airy, *Text-Book of English History from the Earliest Times for Colleges and Schools* (London: Longmans, Green, and Company, 1891), 499.

2. *The Crystal Palace and Its Contents: Being an Illustrated Cyclopaedia of the Great Exhibition of the Industry of All Nations, 1851, Embellished with Upwards of Five Hundred Engravings* (London: W. M. Clark, 1852), 1.

3. "The Census for Ireland, 1841–1851," *Medical Times and Gazette*, July 12, 1851; P. M. Austin Bourke, "The Extent of the Potato Crop in Ireland at the Time of the Famine," *Journal of the Statistical and Social Inquiry Society of Ireland* 20 (1960): 62–63; Cormac Ó Gráda, *The Great Irish Famine*, New Studies in Economic and Social History (Cambridge, UK: Cambridge University Press, 1995), 62–63.

4. James Fintan Lalor, *The Writings of James Fintan Lalor: With an Introduction Embodying Personal Recollections*, ed. John O'Leary (Dublin: T. G. O'Donoghue and Francis Nugent, 1895), 11–12; Colm Tóibín, "Erasures," *London Review of Books*, July 30, 1998, www.lrb.co.uk/the-paper/v20/n15/colm-toibin/erasures.

5. Spencer Walpole, *The Life of Lord John Russell* (London: Longmans, Green, and Company 1889), 1:451.

6. Richard Stivers, "Historical Meanings of Irish-American Drinking," in *The American Experience with Alcohol: Contrasting Cultural Perspectives*, ed. Linda A. Bennett and Genevieve M. Ames (Boston, MA: Springer US, 1985), 109–129; Colm Kerrigan, "The Social Impact of the Irish Temperance Movement, 1839–1845," *Irish Economic and Social History* 14 (1987): 20–38; James Kelly, "The Consumption and Sociable Use of Alcohol in Eighteenth-Century Ireland," *Proceedings of the Royal Irish Academy: Archaeology, Culture, History, Literature* 115C (2015): 219–255.

7. Jill Bender, "The Imperial Politics of Famine: The 1873–74 Bengal Famine and Irish Parliamentary Nationalism," *Éire-Ireland* 42, no. 1 (2007): 135.

8. Mike Davis, *Late Victorian Holocausts: El Niño Famines and the Making of the Third World* (London: Verso, 2002), 27–32.

9. *Allen's Indian Mail and Official Gazette*, vol. 35 (London: William H. Allen and Co., 1877), 250; Davis, *Late Victorian Holocausts*, 36–37; Chris Otter, *Diet for a Large Planet: Industrial Britain, Food Systems, and World Ecology* (Chicago: University of Chicago Press, 2020), 71.

10. Robert Kane, *The Industrial Resources of Ireland* (Dublin: Hodges and Smith, 1844), 407; Robert Hunt, ed., *Hunt's Hand-Book to the Official Catalogues: An Explanatory Guide to the Natural Productions and Manufactures of the Great Exhibition of the Industry of All Nations, 1851* (London: Spicer Brothers, and W. Clowes and Sons, 1851), 1:44–45; *The Illustrated Exhibitor, a Tribute to the World's Industrial Jubilee: Comprising Sketches,*

by Pen and Pencil, of the Principal Objects in the Great Exhibition of the Industry of All Nations, 1851 (London: John Cassell, 1851), 178; *Official Descriptive and Illustrated Catalogue of the Great Exhibition of the Works of Industry of All Nations: 1851* (London: Spicer Brothers, and W. Clowes and Sons, 1851), 2:568; William Gaspey, *The Great Exhibition of the World's Industry Held in London in 1851: Described and Illustrated by Engravings, from Daguerrotypes by Beard, Mayall, Etc* (London: J. Tallis and Co., 1852), 4:165.

11. *Official Catalogue of the Great Exhibition*, 1:341; Hunt, *Hunt's Hand-Book*, 1:449.

12. Louise Purbrick, "Defining Nation: Ireland at the Great Exhibition of 1851," in *Britain, the Empire, and the World at the Great Exhibition of 1851*, ed. Jeffrey A. Auerbach and Peter H. Hoffenberg (London: Routledge, 2016), 47–76; *Official Catalogue of the Great Exhibition*, 2:675; *Connemara and the Irish Highlands: A Pocket Guide* (Dublin: Hodges and Smith, 1852), front matter; Gaspey, *Great Exhibition*, 143–144; *Illustrated Exhibitor*, 165; Hunt, *Hunt's Hand-Book*, 1:172; *Guide-Book to the Industrial Exhibition, with Facts, Figures and Observations on the Manufactures and Produce Exhibited* (London: Partridge and Oakey, 1851), 130–131.

13. John Stuart Mill, *Principles of Political Economy, with Some of Their Applications to Social Philosophy*, 4th ed., vol. 1 (London: John W. Parker and Son, 1857), 426–428; Nassau William Senior, *Journals, Conversations and Essays Relating to Ireland* (London: Longmans, Green, and Company, 1868), 1:viii–ix.

14. Paul Farmer, "An Anthropology of Structural Violence," *Current Anthropology* 45, no. 3 (2004): 307; Douglas Hay, "Property, Authority and the Criminal Law," in *Albion's Fatal Tree: Crime and Society in Eighteenth-Century England*, 2nd ed. (London: Verso, 2011), 54.

15. James Hewitt, *Thoughts on the Present State of Ireland* (London: John Murray, 1849), 21.

16. Bridget Conley and Alex de Waal, "The Purposes of Starvation: Historical and Contemporary Uses," *Journal of International Criminal Justice* 17, no. 4 (September 1, 2019): 721–722; *Hunger Hotspots: FAO–WFP Early Warnings on Acute Food Insecurity: November 2023 to April 2024 Outlook* (Rome: United Nations, 2023); Alex de Waal, "Starvation as a Method of Warfare," *LRB Blog*, January 11, 2024, www.lrb.co.uk/blog/2024/january/starvation-as-a-method-of-warfare.

17. Kiran Stacey, "Sunak Says He Wants to Reduce Workers' Taxes This Year and May Cut Benefits," *Guardian*, January 7, 2024, www.theguardian.com/politics/2024/jan/07/rishi-sunak-says-he-wants-to-cut-workers-taxes-this-year-and-may-reduce-benefits; Xander Elliards, "Rishi Sunak Pledges to Cut Welfare and Benefits to Fund Tax Cuts," *Yahoo News*, January 7, 2024, https://uk.news.yahoo.com/rishi-sunak-pledges-cut-welfare-124654127.html.

INDEX

Credit: Audrey Cooper

Padraic X. Scanlan is an associate professor at the Centre for Industrial Relations and Human Resources and the Centre for Diaspora & Transnational Studies at the University of Toronto. His writing has appeared in the *Washington Post, Guardian, Times Literary Supplement*, and *New Inquiry*. The author of two previous books, he lives in Toronto.